IMAGES
of America

TAMPA'S HYDE PARK

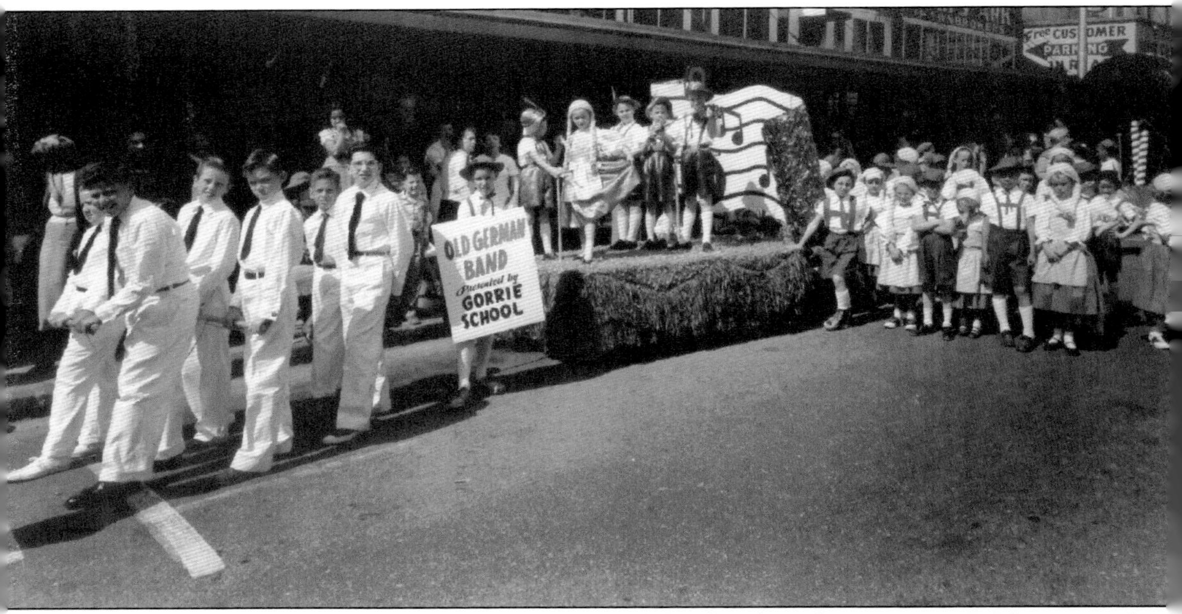

Children, tradition, pride, festivals, and fun have defined Hyde Park since Henry B. Plant opened the Tampa Bay Hotel. This early-1950s photograph shows the John B. Gorrie Elementary School entry in the annual Gasparilla festivities. The float was powered by the school's safety patrols. Younger students were assigned to ride on the float, while the remaining students walked to the music of local school bands. Most area schools participated in the parade. Hyde Park's Bayshore Boulevard provides the route for the present-day Children's Gasparilla Parade. (Gorrie School Archives.)

On the Cover: Helen Hill School was a regular entrant in the annual Children's Gasparilla Parade. The school's founders were early advocates of student participation in the visual and performing arts as well as community activities and festivals. The elaborate costumes worn by the students often represented a favorite person from history or a contemporary hero. Teachers had students write stories or present small plays about their characters. (Tampa Bay History Center.)

IMAGES
of America

TAMPA'S HYDE PARK

Delphin Acosta

ARCADIA
PUBLISHING

Copyright © 2012 by Delphin Acosta
ISBN 978-0-7385-9117-9

Published by Arcadia Publishing
Charleston, South Carolina

Printed in the United States of America

Library of Congress Control Number: 2011934871

For all general information, please contact Arcadia Publishing:
Telephone 843-853-2070
Fax 843-853-0044
E-mail sales@arcadiapublishing.com
For customer service and orders:
Toll-Free 1-888-313-2665

Visit us on the Internet at www.arcadiapublishing.com

To Irene

Contents

Acknowledgments

This book was envisioned over the course of 15 years and draws upon a career spent as an urban planner-designer, architectural historian, and educator. I have incurred much indebtedness to longtime friends, librarians throughout Florida, my wonderful Hyde Park neighbors, and the new friends acquired while researching historical facts and obtaining photographs.

The inspiration for *Tampa's Hyde Park* came when my friend Saburo Horikawa visited Tampa during his tenure as a visiting scholar from Japan at Harvard University. Exploring Hyde Park on foot with Professor Horikawa reinforced my commitment to the community as an architectural and cultural resource. I soon began to see Hyde Park as not simply contributing to local history, but having an influential impact on bungalow communities throughout the United States.

As I was researching this book, I maintained a careful log of all the people who provided photographs and historical facts with the intent of individual recognition in this book. Now, as I attempt to acknowledge everyone, I humbly realize that there are too many people to recognize, and I am fearful that I would omit someone. Yet, I feel obligated to thank several people who contributed to this book from the inception of my initial book outline to the final days of writing before the book was submitted to the publisher.

I owe special thanks to David Parsons, Jennifer Dietz, and Margaret Rials, of the Tampa-Hillsborough County Public Library System, who never tired of my many requests, offering help at every stage. They were always available to provide access to the remarkable Burgert Brothers Photography collection that became the main source of photographs for this book. Also included are Cynthia Gandee and Susan Carter, of the Henry B. Plant Museum, for their continuous research assistance and support irrespective of my many requests for materials.

To Jim Sykes, a genuine gratitude for all the technical assistance and photographs that complete the story. Finally, my deepest gratitude goes to Ann Altman, book editor and project coordinator for this book. Ann's uncompromising determination, fact-based knowledge, and dedication to Hyde Park infused this book with logical coherence.

Unless otherwise noted, all images appear courtesy of the Tampa-Hillsborough County Public Library System.

Introduction

The oldest home in Tampa's Hyde Park neighborhood dates back to the early 1870s, but the area's history stretches much further back into the past. The Hyde Park section of Tampa, located south and west of the Hillsborough River, was settled hundreds of years earlier.

Despite the area being the first site of European colonization, most early North American settlers paid little attention to the Florida peninsula. When control of the territory transferred from Spain to England in 1763, Florida was divided into East and West Florida, which became the 14th and 15th British colonies. It was during this era that Hillsborough Bay and the Hillsborough River were named in honor of Lord Hillsborough, secretary of state of the British colonies under King George III. These southernmost colonies remained loyal to the crown during the American Revolution, and at the end of the conflict in 1783, Spain resumed ownership.

The Second Spanish Period (1783–1821) was marked by the growing conflict between the Seminoles and the US citizens living on either side of Florida's northern border. Spain was powerless to stop the aggressors on either side. National and international attention shifted to Florida when, in 1817, Gen. Andrew Jackson made an illegal foray into Spanish territory to aid Americans living on the Florida/Georgia border in fighting the Seminoles. Jackson's action also provided Americans with an opportunity to capture runaway slaves.

Because of early fighting between the Seminoles and white settlers, the American government established a series of forts throughout Florida. One of these, Fort Brooke, was situated on the east bank of the Hillsborough River at the head of Hillsborough Bay, in the southern portion of today's downtown Tampa. Established in 1824 by Col. George Mercer Brooke and Col. James Gadsden, Fort Brooke served as the US Army's southern headquarters. Future US president Zachary Taylor, who fought in the second Seminole War, served at Fort Brooke.

By the early 1800s, things were beginning to happen on the west side of the Hillsborough River. Around the start of the 19th century, a small settlement known as Spanishtown formed on the shores of Hillsborough Bay, becoming home to Cuban fishermen and women. Spanishtown Creek, which bisected the settlement, emptied into the bay near the present-day intersection of Swann Avenue and Bayshore Boulevard.

Massachusetts-born Levi Collar (and his family) also established a settlement on the west bank of the Hillsborough River during this era, becoming the first Anglo residents of what would eventually be the Hyde Park area. One of Collar's daughters, Nancy, married Robert Jackson, and their homestead sat along the west bank, at the mouth of the river, at a place known as Jackson Point.

Within a few years of Fort Brooke's founding, a small village sprang from its northern boundary. The first post office (established in 1831) officially named the village of Tampa Bay, but the name was soon shortened to Tampa. The meaning and origin of the name has been debated for years—with no consensus—but a strong theory claims it was the name of a native village (sometimes spelled Tanpa) on Tampa Bay.

The Civil War came on the heels of the Third Seminole War (1855–1858), but unlike the final conflict with the Florida natives, the Civil War was anything but a boon to the state. While the state was far from the main battlefields, economic and personal disasters plagued Floridians during and after the war.

Florida, and Tampa, remained destitute for almost two decades after the Civil War; finally, in 1881, relief was on the (northern) horizon. Henry Bradley Plant was bringing his new railroad south, and he picked Tampa as the railhead. The railroad, known as the Plant System of Railways, arrived in 1884. The following year, construction began on Tampa's first two cigar factories—Sanchez y Haya and V.M. Ybor and Co.—in a new suburb called Ybor City. The railroad and cigars shaped Tampa like nothing else. Plant improved the fledgling port at the southwestern tip of the Interbay Peninsula, and Port Tampa was soon shipping goods and passengers throughout ports along the Gulf of Mexico.

In 1886, the same year that Ybor and Haya opened their cigar factories, pebble phosphate was discovered in the Peace River in Polk County, Florida. Phosphate was later discovered in the Hillsborough River and in the largely undeveloped southern portion of Hillsborough County. Though not mentioned as often as the cigar industry and the railroad, the phosphate industry outlasted both. Today, trains carrying loads of phosphate to the docks at Port Tampa still traverse the tracks through downtown Tampa, just as they have since 1889.

Once the phosphate trains crossed the river to head south, they rumbled past another new Tampa suburb founded in the mid-1880s—Hyde Park. O.H. Platt moved to Tampa in 1886, purchased land, subdivided it, and named the development after his hometown of Hyde Park, Illinois.

Platt received some unexpected assistance in 1888 when plans were revealed for Plant's Tampa Bay Hotel. One of the conditions for construction of Plant's palace was that the city and country build a bridge over the Hillsborough River; this became the first modern bridge to span the waterway. The bridge was built at Lafayette Street (Kennedy Boulevard), displacing the outdated ferry, and Plant constructed his hotel.

Around the hotel, growth soon followed, but the city's affluent first chose to live in Tampa Heights rather than across the river in Hyde Park. It would take other developers—notably William Morrison, Alfredo Swann, and Eugene Holtsinger—to draw Tampa's elite to the west side of the Hillsborough River.

After the end of the 1800s, Hyde Park also became home to Tampa's growing middle class. Bungalows began to outnumber the larger, Victorian-style homes, and the neighborhood's population blossomed.

Tampa's upper- and middle-class white residents were not the only people who found a home in Hyde Park—many of Tampa's black residents lived in the Dobyville section of the neighborhood. Dobyville, named for longtime resident and philanthropist Richard Doby, was located on the northwestern side of Hyde Park, bounded roughly by Grand Central (Kennedy Boulevard) on the north, Swann Avenue on the south, Newport Avenue on the east, and Albany Avenue on the west.

The building boom in Hyde Park in the 1910s and 1920s fizzled out by the early 1930s. The Great Depression had a profound effect on Florida, and Tampa's Hyde Park was not immune. Many of the neighborhood's grand homes were converted to boardinghouses. World War II continued this trend, and many returning servicemen used their GI Bill money to buy a home in the "newer" suburbs rather than the "old" neighborhood of Hyde Park.

Decline continued in the 1950s and 1960s, furthered by the construction of the Crosstown Expressway (now known as the Lee Roy Selmon Expressway), which cut through the center of Hyde Park—and took dozens of Victorian-period homes with it. When the City of Tampa, following the lead of the federal government, recognized Hyde Park as a local historic district in 1985, life began a renewal in the old suburb. Preservation guidelines were established to ensure that the original architecture would be preserved and that new construction would conform to the old styles. Though these guidelines are sometimes ignored or appealed, they have worked in most cases, and both Hyde Park and Tampa have benefited.

—Rodney Kite-Powell,
Saunders Foundation Curator of History at the Tampa Bay History Center

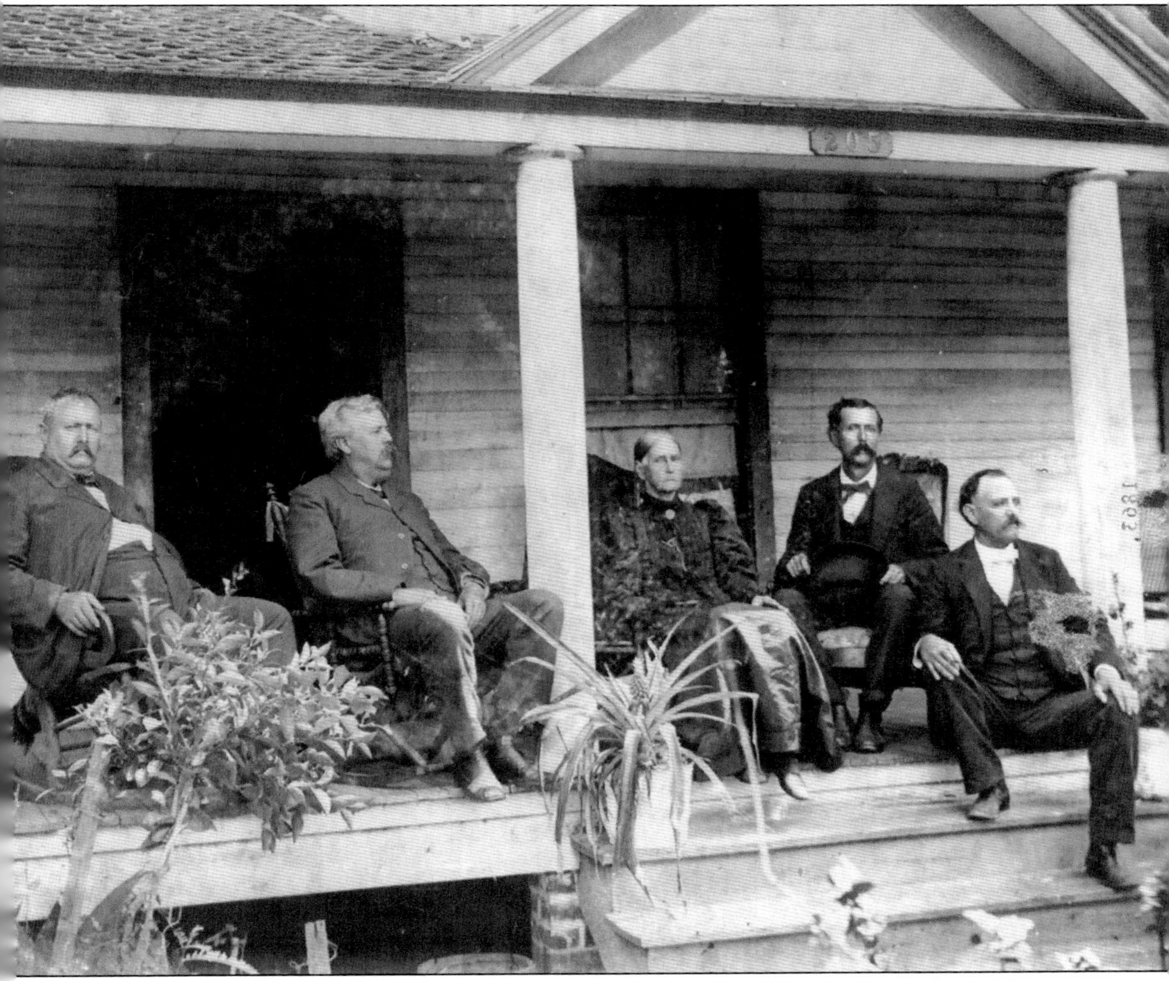

This c. 1893 photograph includes the following people: Capt. Bill Jackson, Oscar Jackson, Nancy Jackson, Robert A. Jackson (then sheriff of Hillsborough County), and John B. Jackson. The photograph was taken at the home of Nancy Jackson at 205 Platt Street. The home was demolished in the late 1960s. (Tampa Bay History Center.)

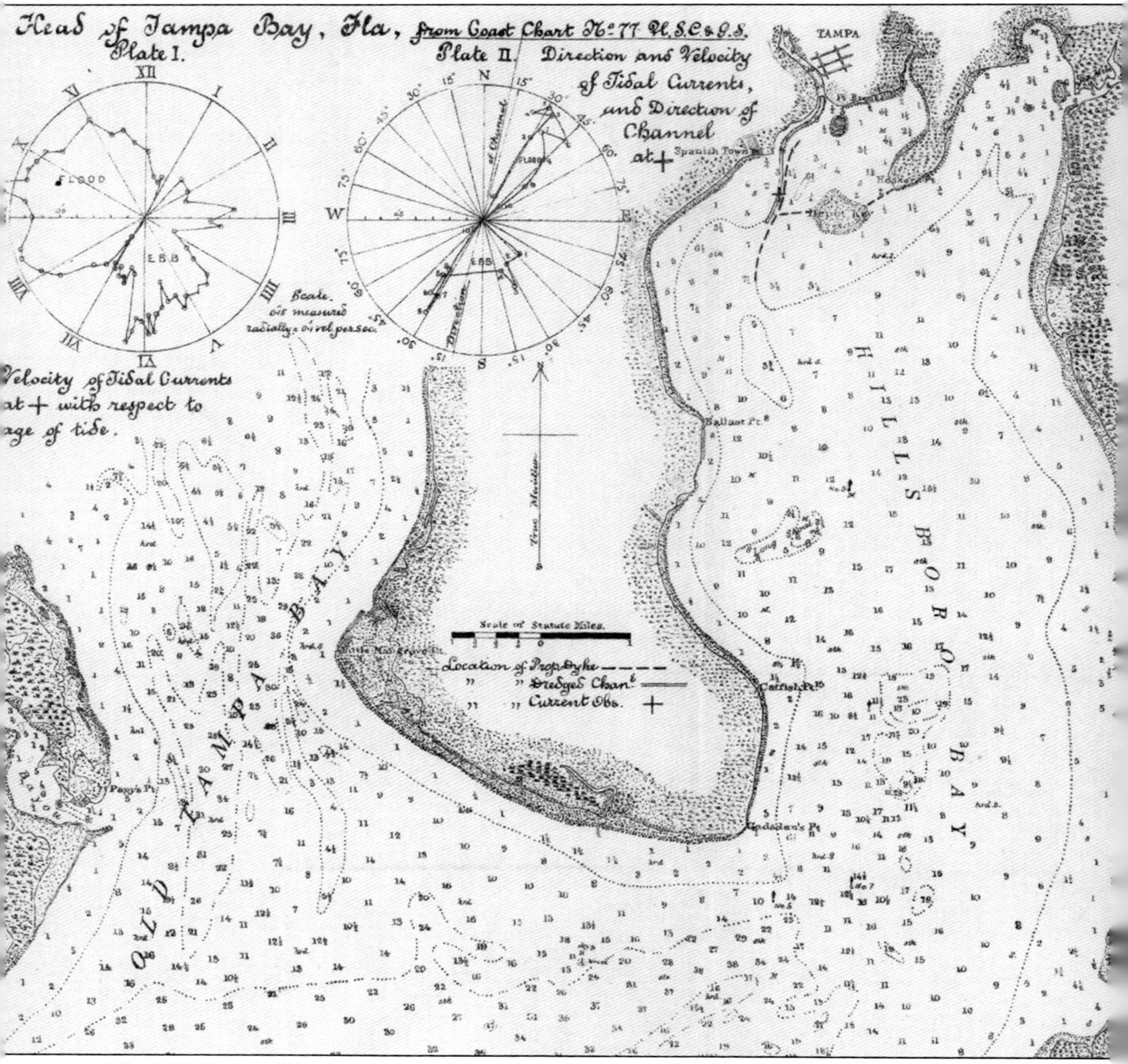

The US Corps of Engineers completed this navigational chart of the head of Tampa Bay in 1887. Within a decade after the chart's completion, the Port of Tampa would become one of the busiest ports along the Gulf of Mexico, exporting phosphate, cattle, oranges, and other agricultural commodities. Products imported into the port included tobacco, building materials, and machinery. Tiny, but now growing, downtown Tampa is delineated at the top middle of the chart. Spanish Town Creek, later absorbed by the development of Hyde Park, is below and west of downtown Tampa. The railroad crossing the peninsula was under construction when this chart was completed. The railroad would eventually travel to the area identified on the map as Little Mangrove Point, where Tampa's first deep water port was developed. (Tampa Bay History Center.)

One

The Early Years of Hyde Park

Between 1870 and 1880, Tampa's population dropped from 796 to 720 residents who lived in small settlements along both sides of the Hillsborough River at Hillsborough Bay. They had little contact with the rest of Florida's early pioneers or other parts of the United States. Cattle were shipped to Cuba from Tampa's small, natural harbor, and ships from Cuba arrived in Hillsborough Bay carrying basic supplies for the remote community.

Tampa's residents existed on the abundant seafood and game that was readily available and their ability to harvest food practically year-round. But an unexpected event was about to bring significant change to Tampa—the arrival of the railroad.

On Florida's eastern coast, Henry Morrison Flagler had achieved success with the development of hotels along his railroad line, the Florida East Coast Railway. Henry B. Plant was determined to create an unmatched resort of his own, and a railhead in Tampa, on Florida's west coast. The 1884 arrival of Plant's railroad brought unexpected opportunities to the area from throughout the United States, Cuba, and distant ports. Tampa quickly began to reverse its downward population trend and, by the beginning of the 20th century, became the fastest growing city in the United States.

One of the area's early arrivals was O.H. Platt, who, in 1886, purchased land across the river from downtown Tampa and began developing what he called Hyde Park, named after his hometown of Hyde Park, Illinois. Ideally located, in terms of its natural amenities, Hyde Park was perfectly positioned for the upcoming explosive growth. The construction of Plant's extraordinary Tampa Bay Hotel, one of the jewels of America's Gilded Age, assured the success of recently subdivided Hyde Park. The hotel provided a variety of cultural and recreational activities for the residents of Hyde Park as well as hotel guests.

The first residential buildings in Hyde Park reflected various Victorian architectural styles. Peter O. Knight and Thomas C. Taliaferro were among the young entrepreneurs who arrived in Tampa in the late 1880s. They were responsible for some of the first important homes built in Hyde Park. Soon, other families began building homes in the community along beautiful Hillsborough Bay.

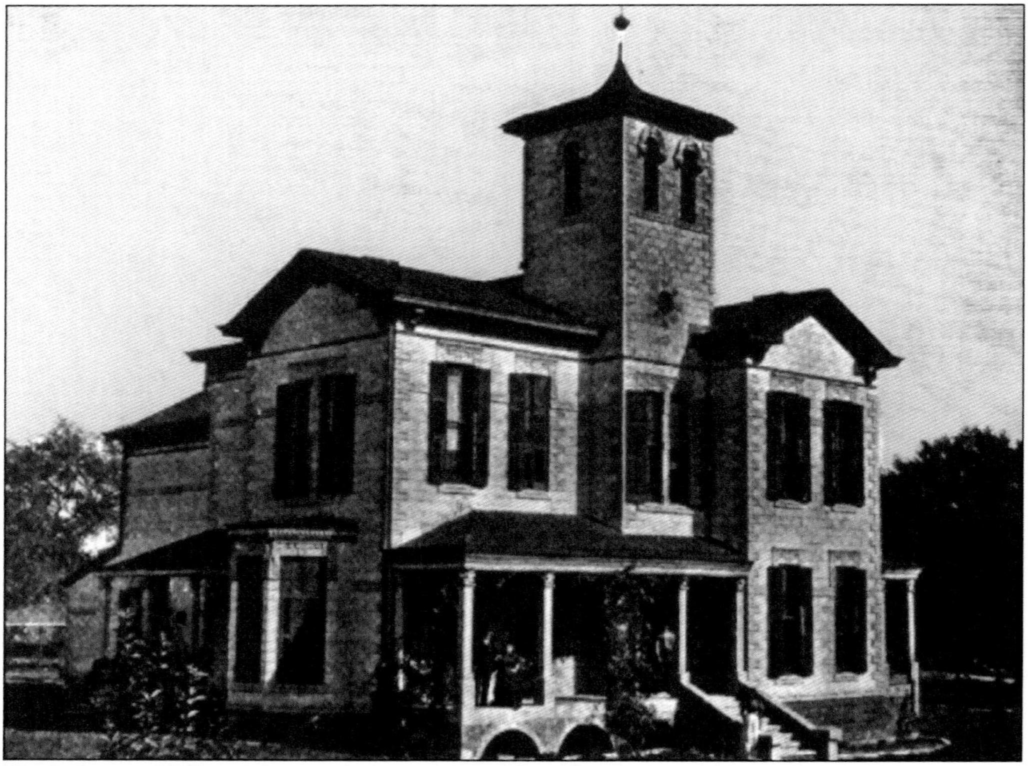

The Italianate William Morrison house is among the oldest surviving homes in Tampa. Constructed between 1879 and 1881, the building plans and components were selected from a book of home-style patterns. Upon completion of the house, Morrison planted his 60-acre site with citrus trees. (Tampa Bay History Center.)

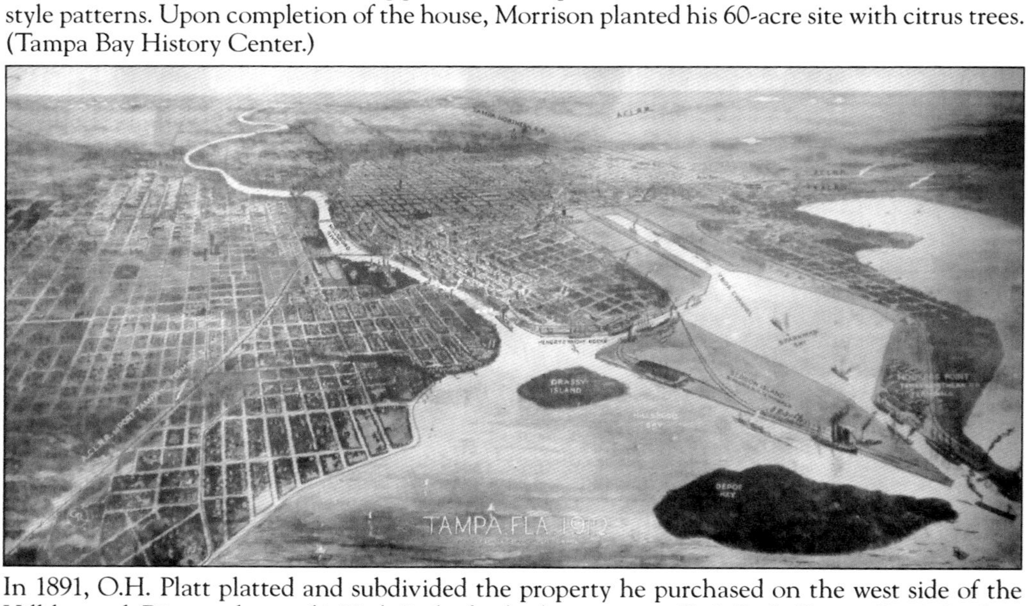

In 1891, O.H. Platt platted and subdivided the property he purchased on the west side of the Hillsborough River and named it Hyde Park after his hometown—Hyde Park, Illinois. By 1918, when the lithograph shown above was prepared, almost all of the property adjacent to the west side of the Hillsborough River was subdivided into a residential community. (Tampa Bay History Center.)

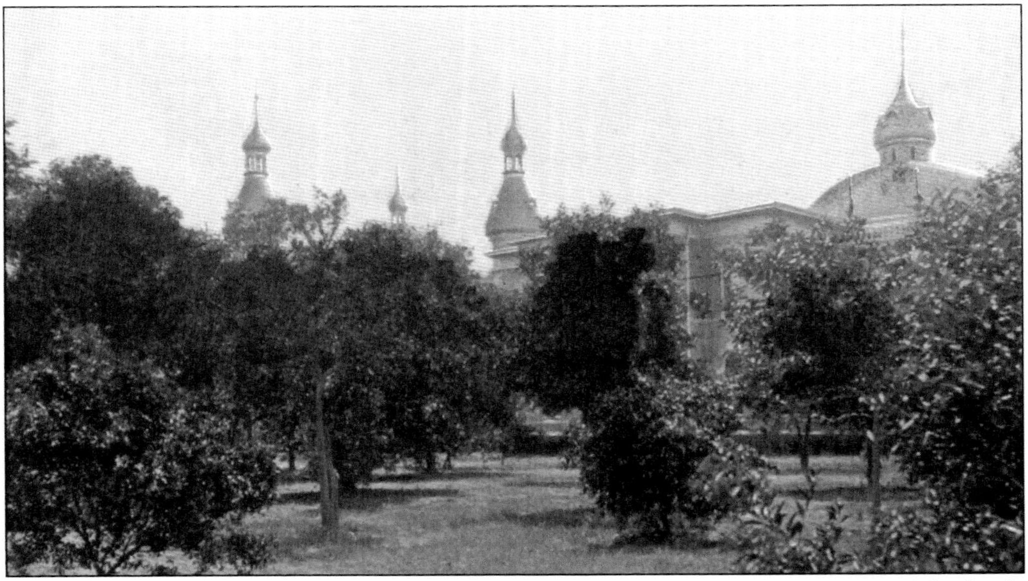

Citrus was the most important export crop planted in Hyde Park in the 1880s. Most of the fertile acreage was planted with oranges, grapefruits, or tangerines. Packinghouses were located along the railroad line through Hyde Park, enabling shipment to markets across the United States by rail, or to Cuba, Jamaica, or Nova Scotia by water. This photograph, taken on the grounds of the Tampa Bay Hotel, demonstrates how guests could see a productive orange grove without traveling through the wilderness. (Henry B. Plant Museum Archives, Tampa, Florida.)

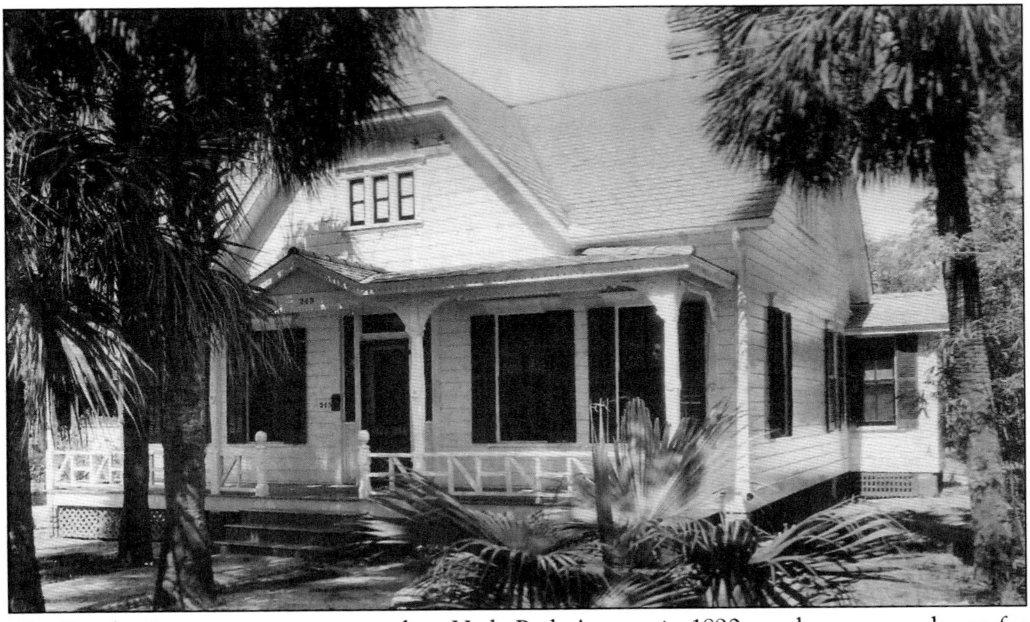

The Knight Cottage was constructed on Hyde Park Avenue in 1890 as a honeymoon home for the newly married Peter O. Knight and Lillie Frierson. Knight was a young attorney who had been living in Fort Myers, Florida; he rapidly became a civic leader. This cottage was built as an intermediary residence until the couple's mansion was constructed on property located two blocks south. (Tampa Historical Society.)

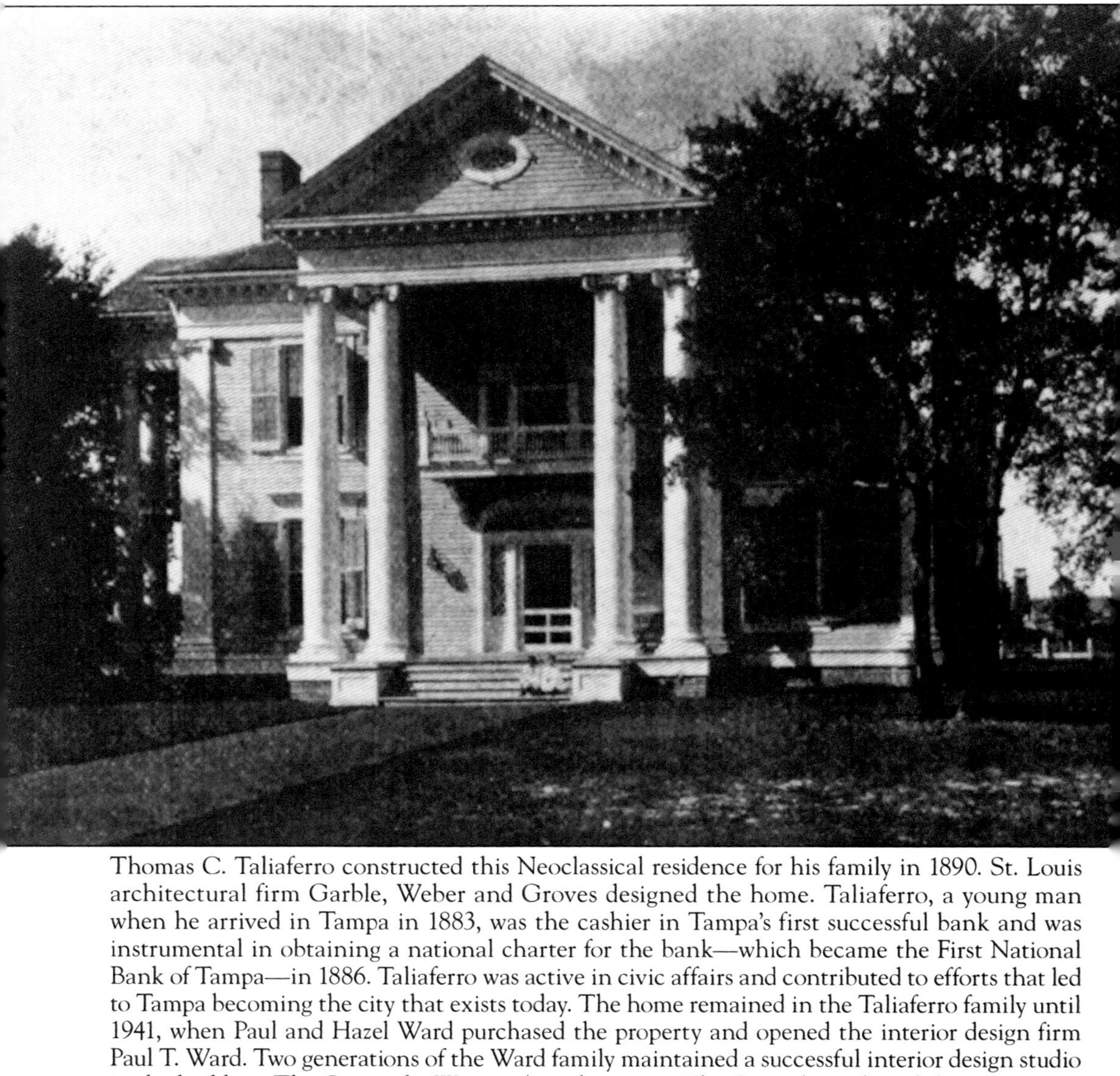

Thomas C. Taliaferro constructed this Neoclassical residence for his family in 1890. St. Louis architectural firm Garble, Weber and Groves designed the home. Taliaferro, a young man when he arrived in Tampa in 1883, was the cashier in Tampa's first successful bank and was instrumental in obtaining a national charter for the bank—which became the First National Bank of Tampa—in 1886. Taliaferro was active in civic affairs and contributed to efforts that led to Tampa becoming the city that exists today. The home remained in the Taliaferro family until 1941, when Paul and Hazel Ward purchased the property and opened the interior design firm Paul T. Ward. Two generations of the Ward family maintained a successful interior design studio in the building. The Centre for Women (now known as The Centre) purchased the property in 1979. The building, still operated by The Centre, continues to command an imposing presence on Hyde Park Avenue. (Tampa Bay History Center.)

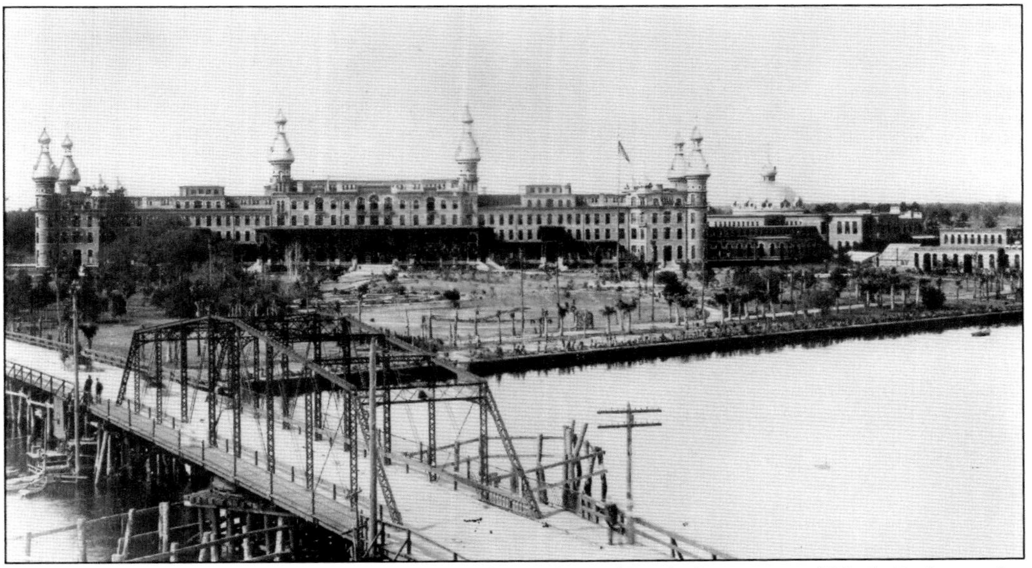

The Lafayette Street Bridge (now the Kennedy Boulevard Bridge) connected Hyde Park, on the west side of the Hillsborough River, with downtown Tampa. One of the conditions for construction of the Tampa Bay Hotel, seen under construction in the background of this 1889 photograph, was that the city and county build a bridge over the Hillsborough River. The Lafayette Street Bridge, the first to span the waterway, replaced the outdated ferry that shuttled people from Hyde Park to Tampa.

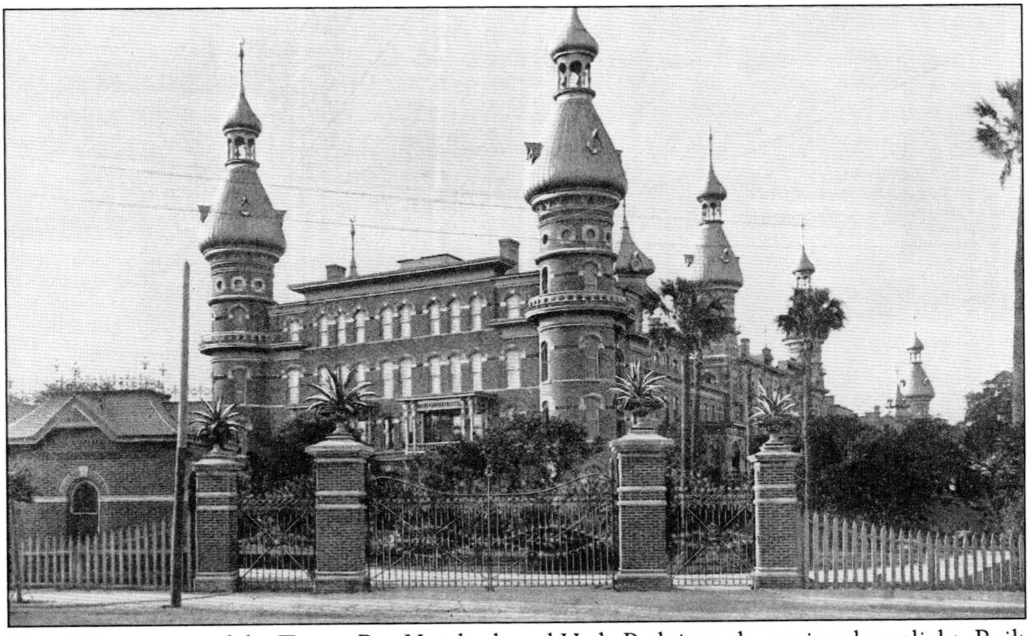

The 1891 opening of the Tampa Bay Hotel ushered Hyde Park into the national spotlight. Built by railroad magnate Henry B. Plant, the 511-room hotel became the cultural and social center of Tampa. The main entrance was located north of O.H. Platt's original Hyde Park subdivision. The opulent hotel was designed by New York City architect J.A. Wood to convey the sumptuousness of a palace. (Henry B. Plant Museum Archives, Tampa, Florida.)

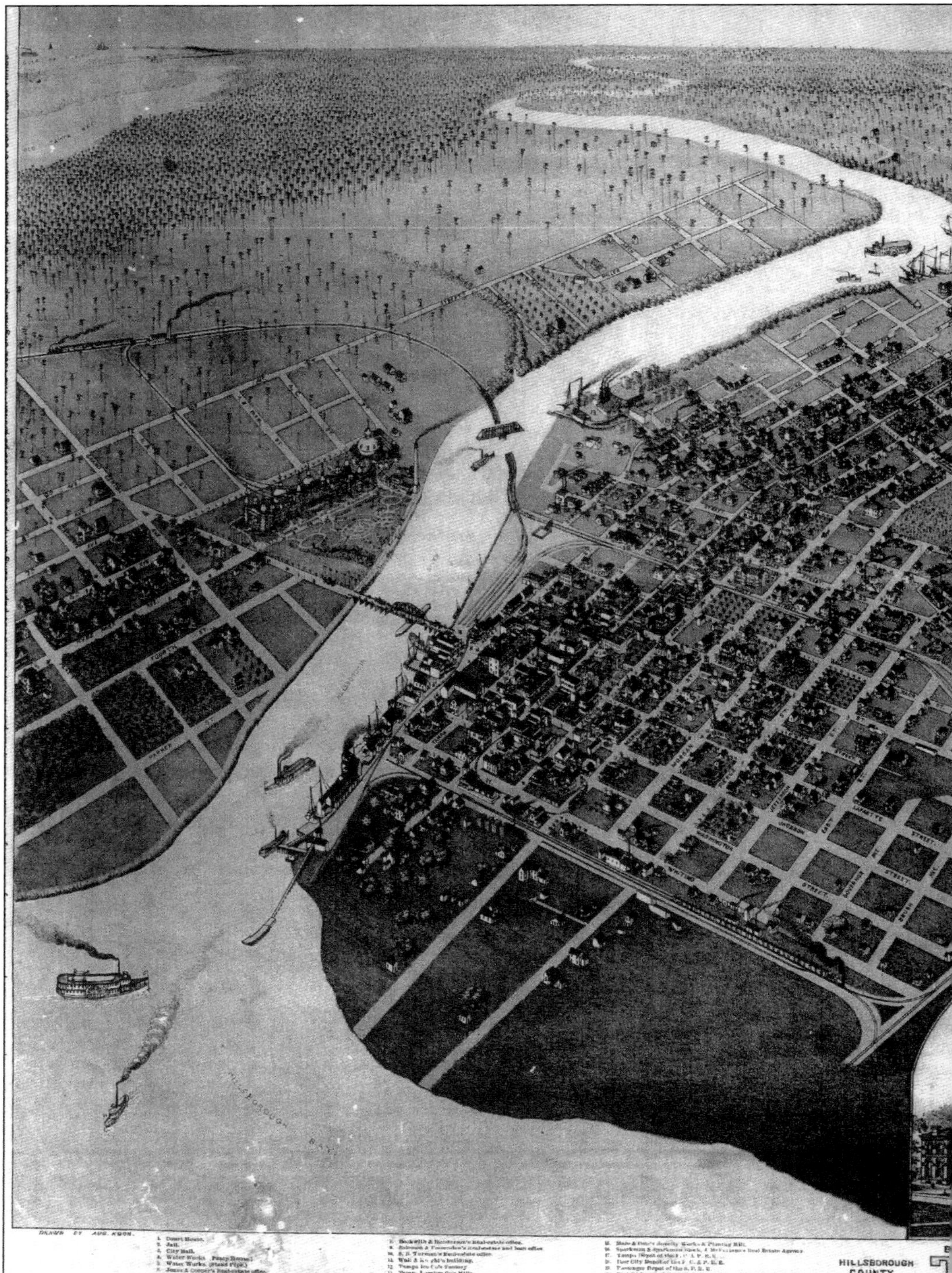

Tampa had a growing population of over 5,600 people when this bird's-eye image of the city was drawn in 1892. Completion of the Lafayette Street Bridge connected Hyde Park and the Tampa Bay Hotel, with downtown Tampa on the east side of the Hillsborough River. Within three

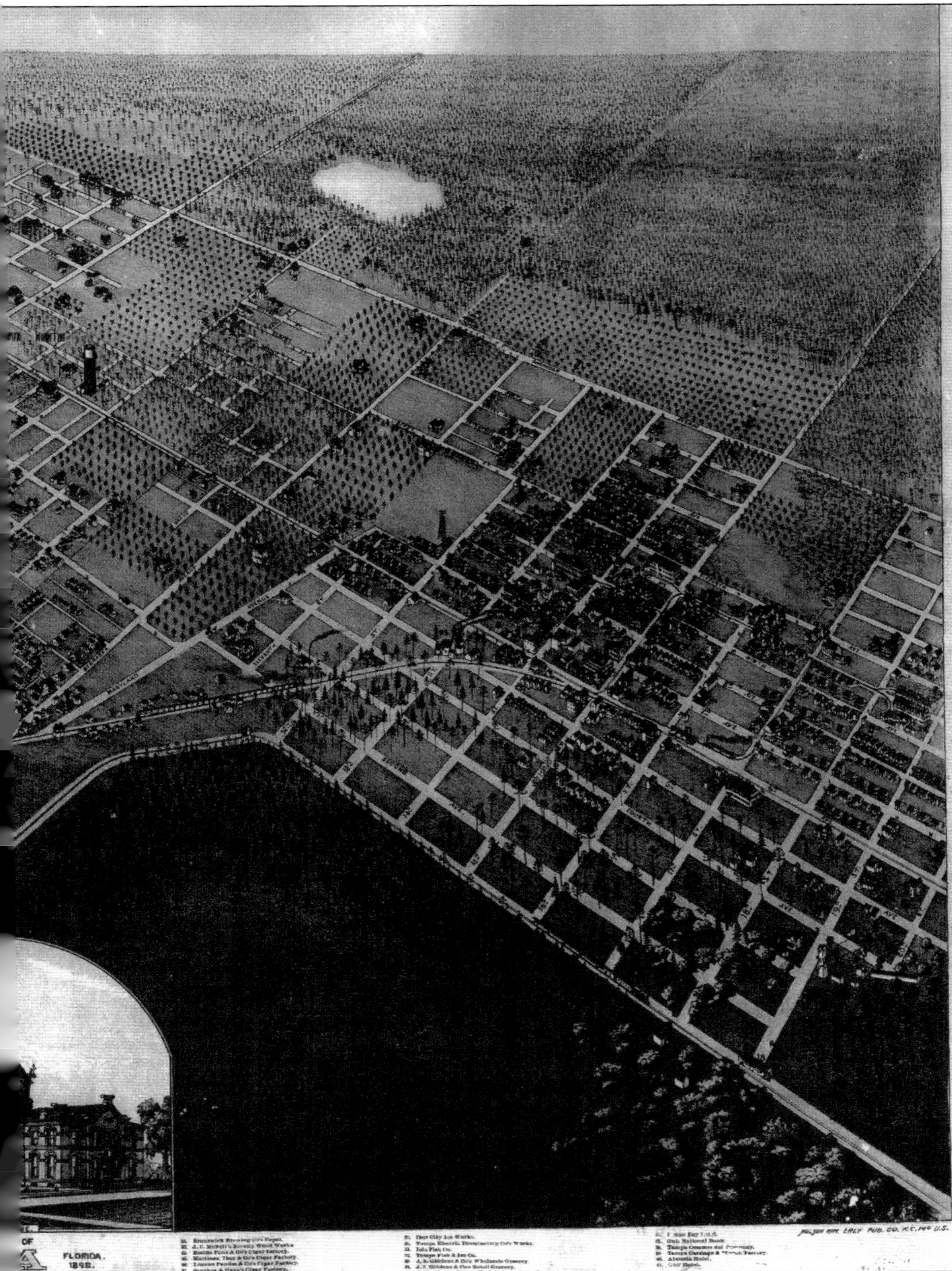

years after the opening of the bridge, over 75 homes were built in Hyde Park. This map, drawn by Augustus Koch and printed by Hudson Publishing Co. of Kansas City, Missouri, provides the best record of Tampa's first growth spurt. (Private collection of J. Fraser Himes.)

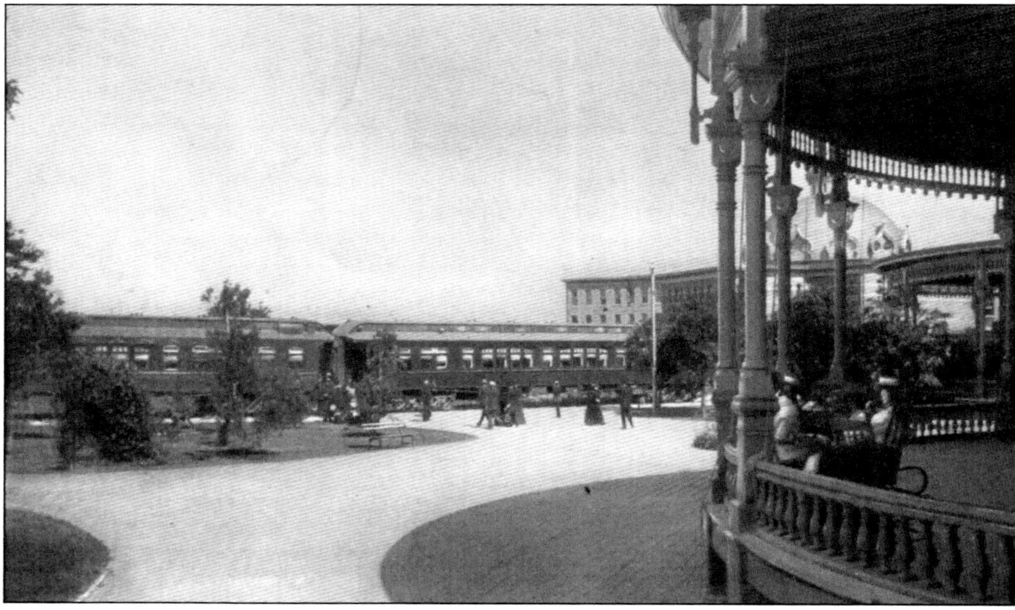

Guests arriving at the Tampa Bay Hotel in 1893 would have arrived on a train owned and operated by Henry B. Plant. Those arriving from the northern United States would have made the journey entirely by rail, often in private railcars. Individuals that disembarked from Key West, Havana, or Mobile would have traveled on a Plant Line steamer to Port Tampa and then taken the train to the hotel. (Henry B. Plant Museum Archives, Tampa, Florida.)

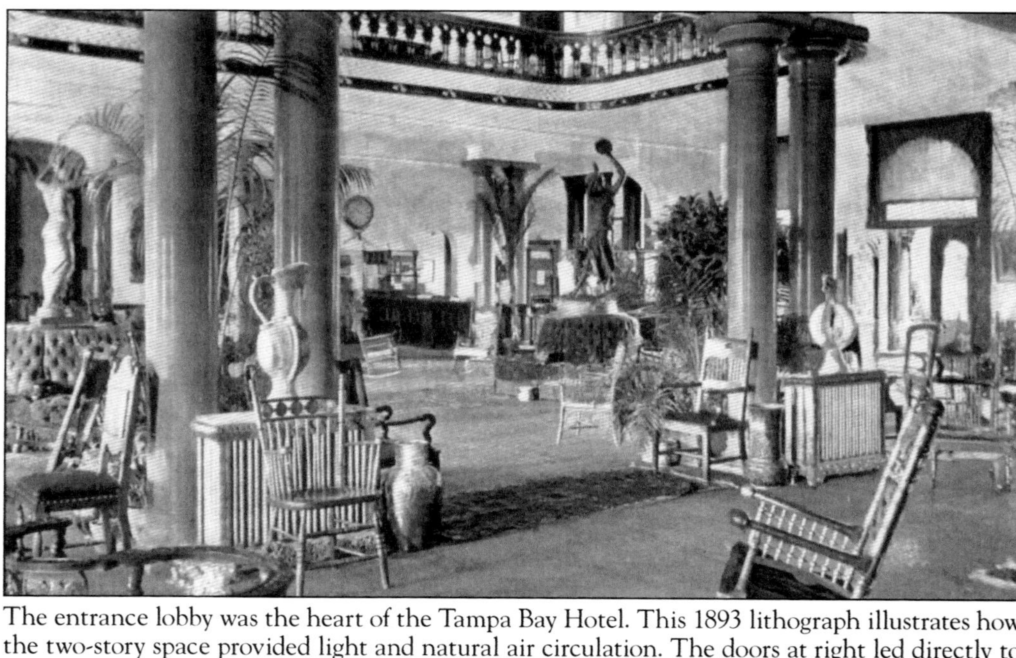

The entrance lobby was the heart of the Tampa Bay Hotel. This 1893 lithograph illustrates how the two-story space provided light and natural air circulation. The doors at right led directly to the area where railroad cars arrived. The atrium was enclosed after the hotel ceased operating in 1932. (Henry B. Plant Museum Archives, Tampa, Florida.)

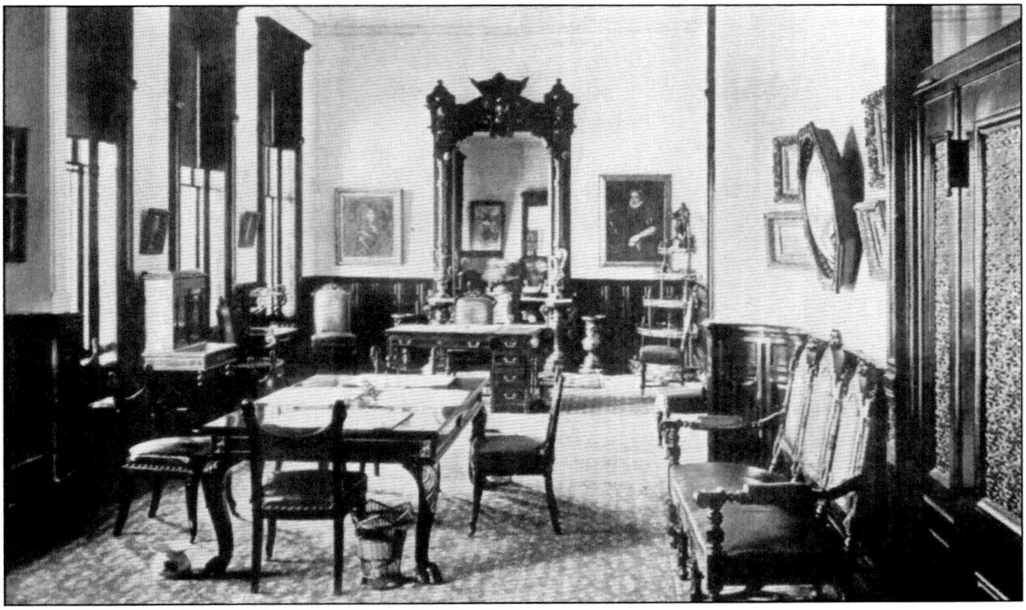

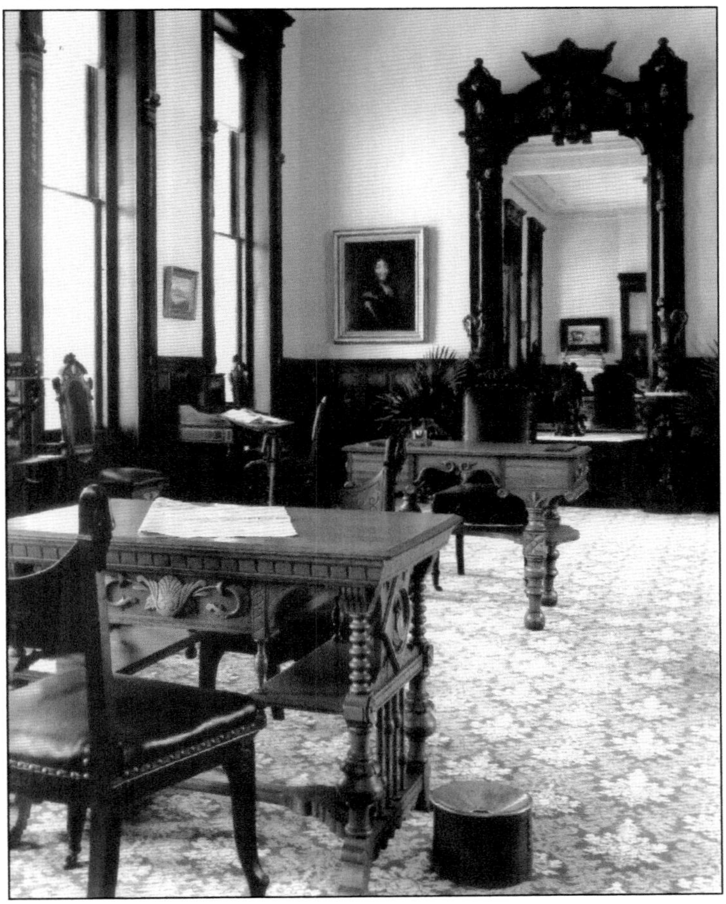

The Writing and Reading Room of the Tampa Bay Hotel, depicted in the 1893 lithograph above, was a private retreat for male guests. Each day, the room was stocked with newspapers, periodicals, and writing materials. Now part of the Henry B. Plant Museum, the room has been preserved and remains historically accurate, as shown at right. All of the furnishings are original, the original yellow color of the walls was discovered by microscopic analysis, and the electric lighting is re-created with reproduction Edison carbon-filament bulbs. (Both, Henry B. Plant Museum Archives, Tampa, Florida.)

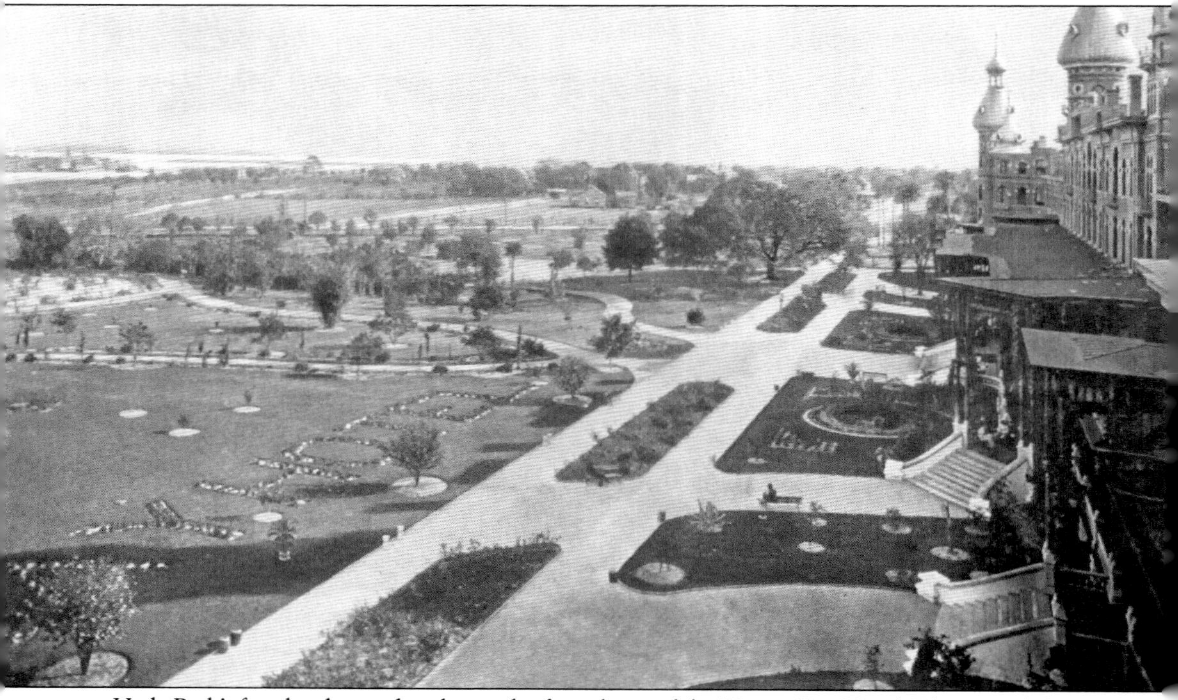

Hyde Park's first landscaped park was the front lawn of the Tampa Bay Hotel. This 1896 lithograph illustrates the Victorian exuberance of the hotel's front lawn or, as it was called in the hotel's promotional literature, the Esplanade. Hyde Park residents had free run of the hotel grounds, except during the hotel's winter season. Today, the area is known as Plant Park. (Henry B. Plant Museum Archives, Tampa, Florida.)

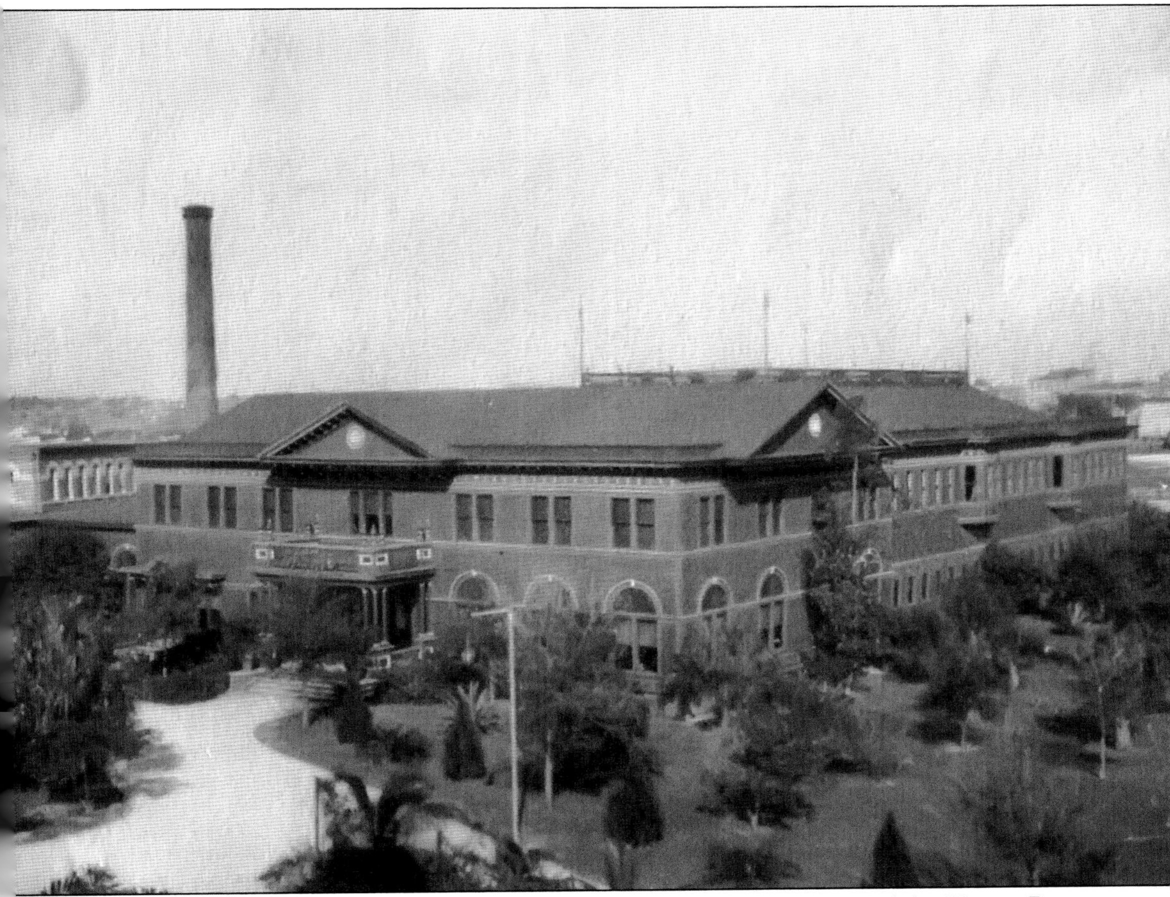

Several other buildings and structures were erected to expand the services of the Tampa Bay Hotel. The Casino, the large wooden building in the center of the photograph, was completed in 1896 and included an indoor swimming pool, theater, and other ancillary facilities. The building remained empty after the hotel closed in 1932 and was lost in a 1940 fire. Another important building that was part of the original hotel complex was the coal-fueled power plant that provided electricity for the hotel. The power plant's smokestack is visible in the left background of the photograph. (Henry B. Plant Museum Archives, Tampa, Florida.)

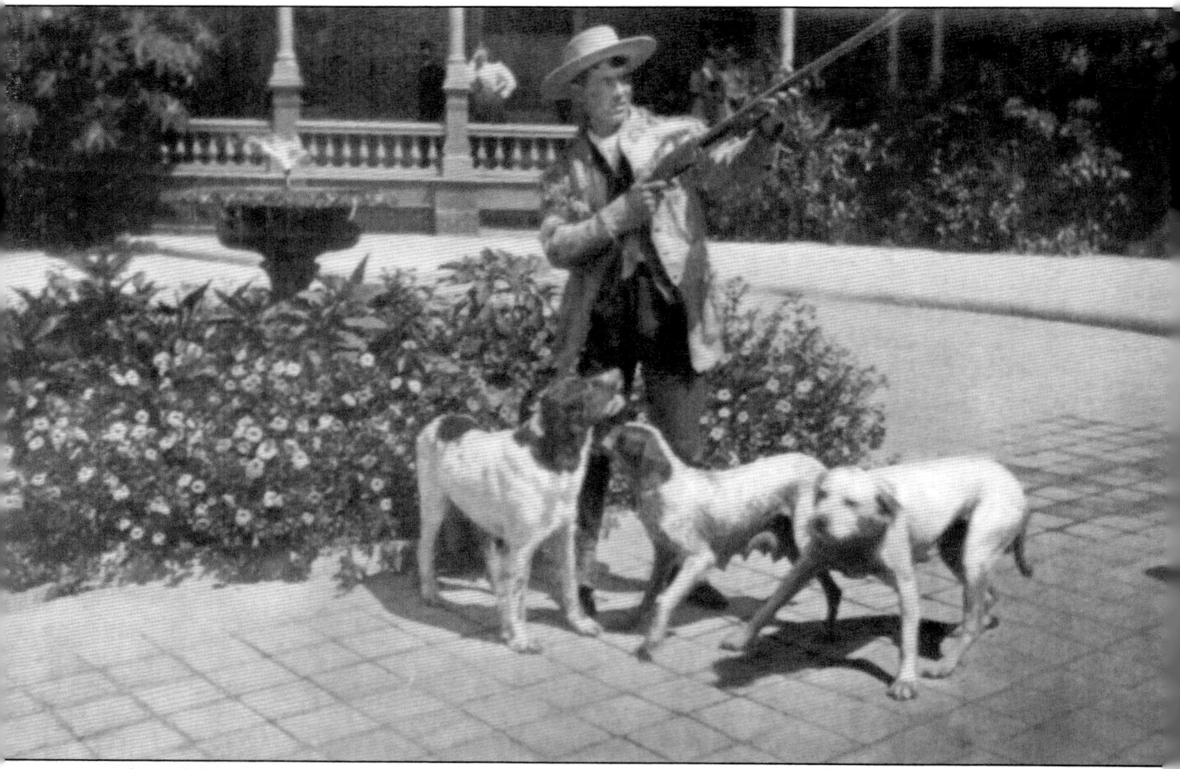

Plentiful hunting was available to early residents of Hyde Park as well as to the guests of the Tampa Bay Hotel. The untamed wilderness and marshy areas surrounding the area's first buildings abounded with snipe, quail, plover, and other varieties of birds. The game made its way to the dinner table. (Henry B. Plant Museum Archives, Tampa, Florida.)

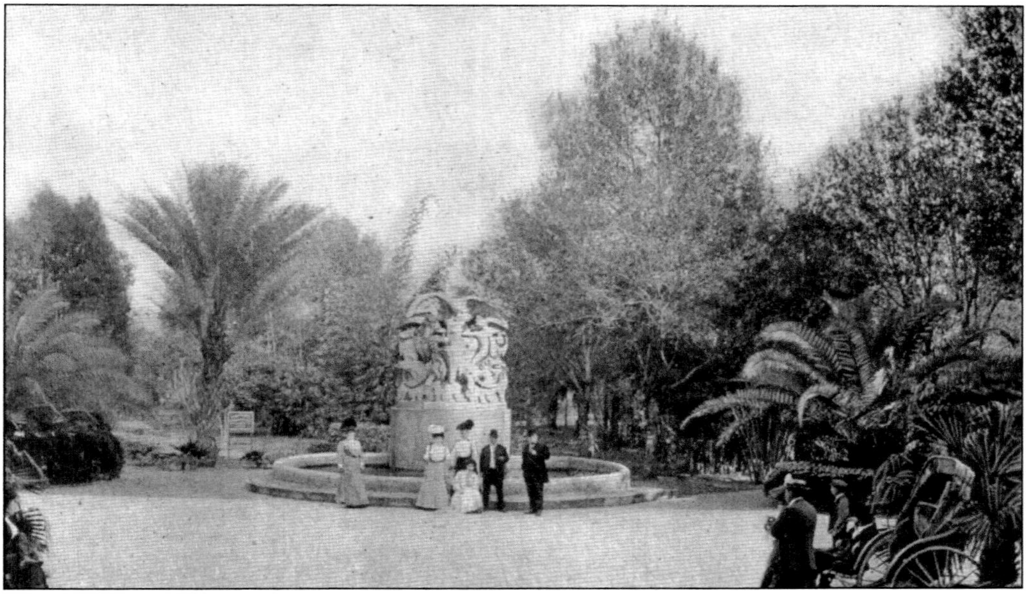

After Henry B. Plant's death in 1899, his widow, Margaret, commissioned this memorial fountain in his memory. Created by renowned sculptor George Grey Barnard, the memorial was called *Transportation* as a tribute to Henry Plant's successful system of trains and ships. The sculpture was placed on the front lawn of the hotel and is the oldest public art in Tampa. (Henry B. Plant Museum Archives, Tampa, Florida.)

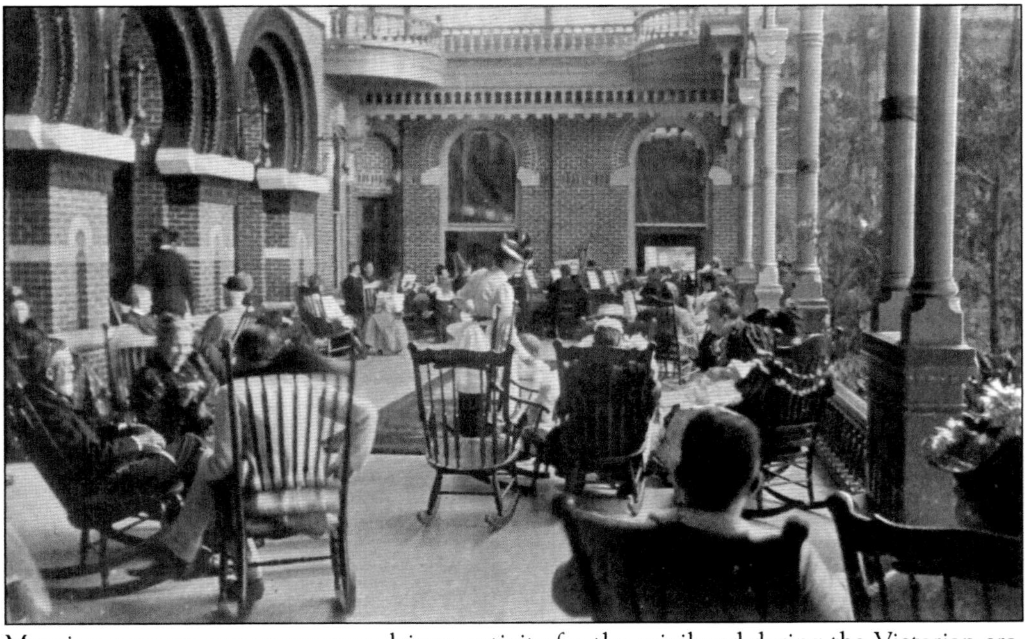

Morning concerts were a common leisure activity for the privileged during the Victorian era. In a time before radio and other mass forms of communication, listening to live music was as widespread and popular as listening to an iPod is today. Enjoyment of the music was interrupted by lively conversations and/or reading the newspaper. (Henry B. Plant Museum Archives, Tampa, Florida.)

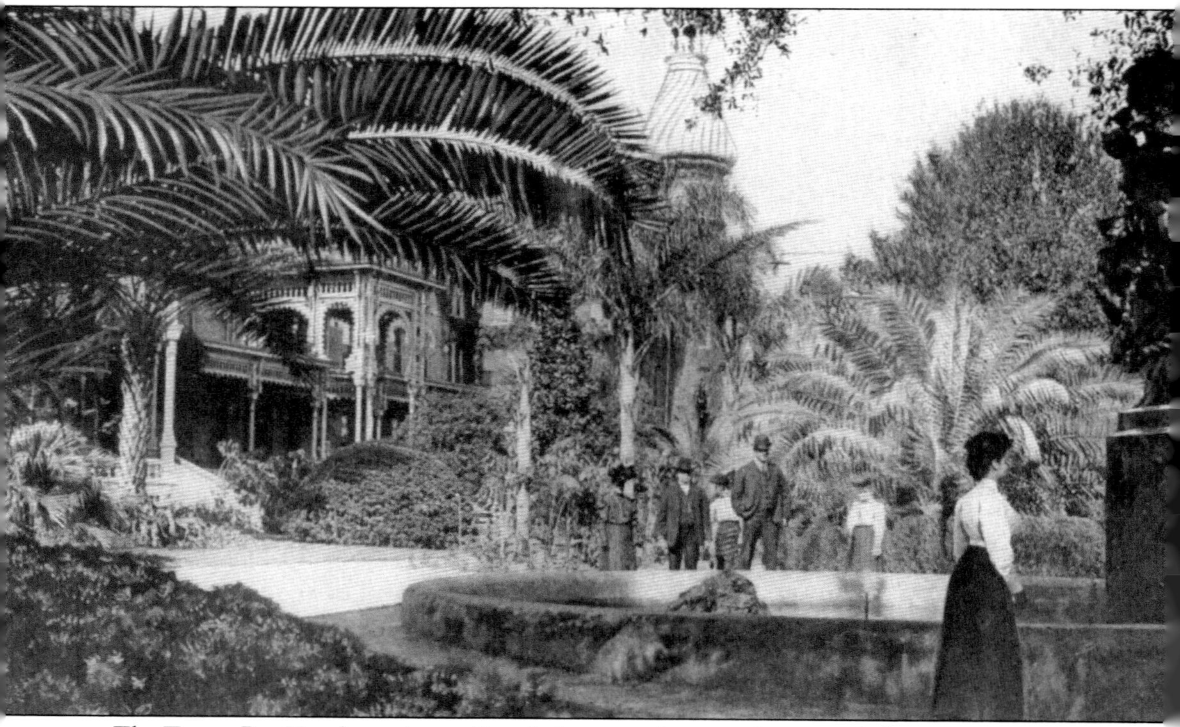

The Tampa Bay Hotel was situated in a lush, tropical setting that provided an extensive variety of outdoor activities. Exotic plants were imported in keeping with the hotel's goal to expose guests to garden materials they had never seen. Today, the gardens are a public park, and the memorial fountain, seen at far right in the photograph, has been restored and remains in the same location. (Henry B. Plant Museum Archives, Tampa, Florida.)

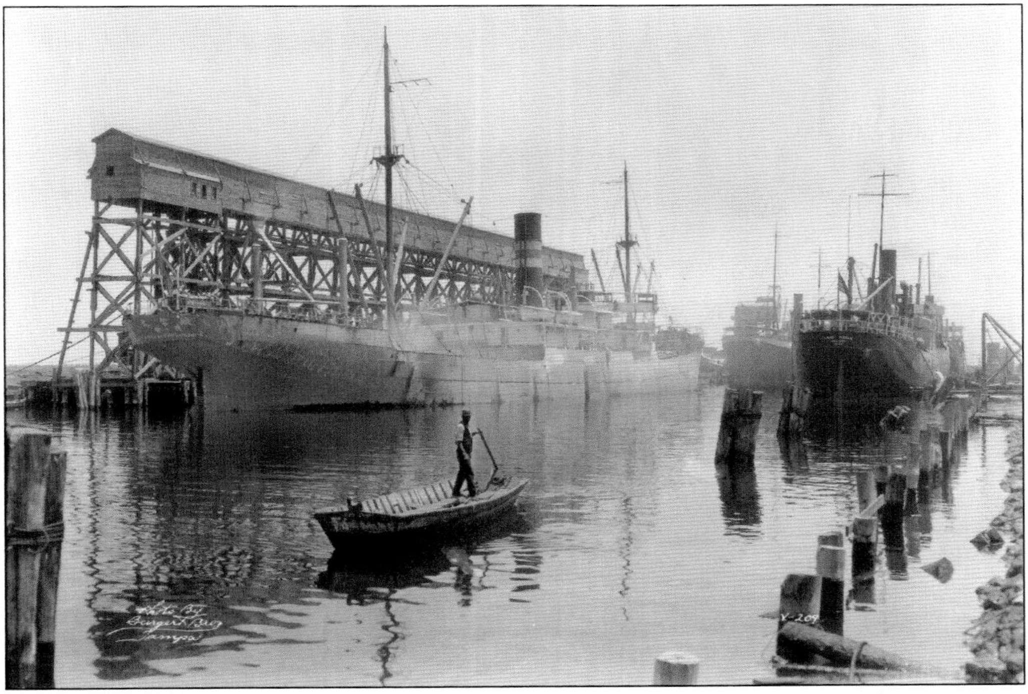

After bringing the railroad to Tampa in 1884, Henry B. Plant initiated two significant projects that changed Tampa forever—the construction of the Tampa Bay Hotel and, six miles away, the construction of a deepwater port at Old Tampa Bay, on the western edge of the Tampa peninsula. Within a decade, the new port became one of the busiest in the United States. One of several phosphate loading facilities is illustrated above; the Port Tampa Inn is in the photograph below. The inn was built by the Plant Investment Company entirely over the waters of Old Tampa Bay. Legend has it that hotel guests would fish from the hotel's porches and have the chef prepare the catch for dinner that same day.

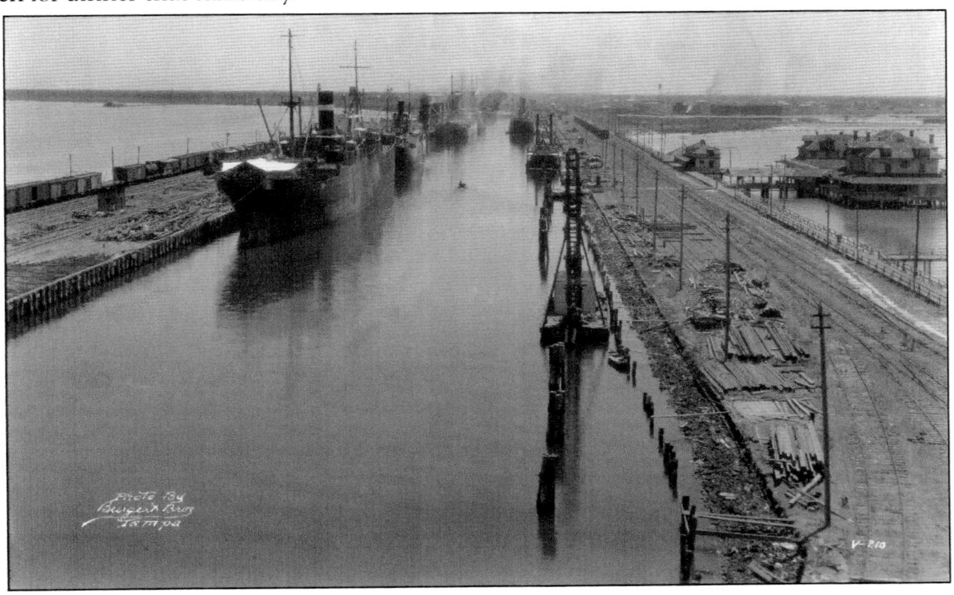

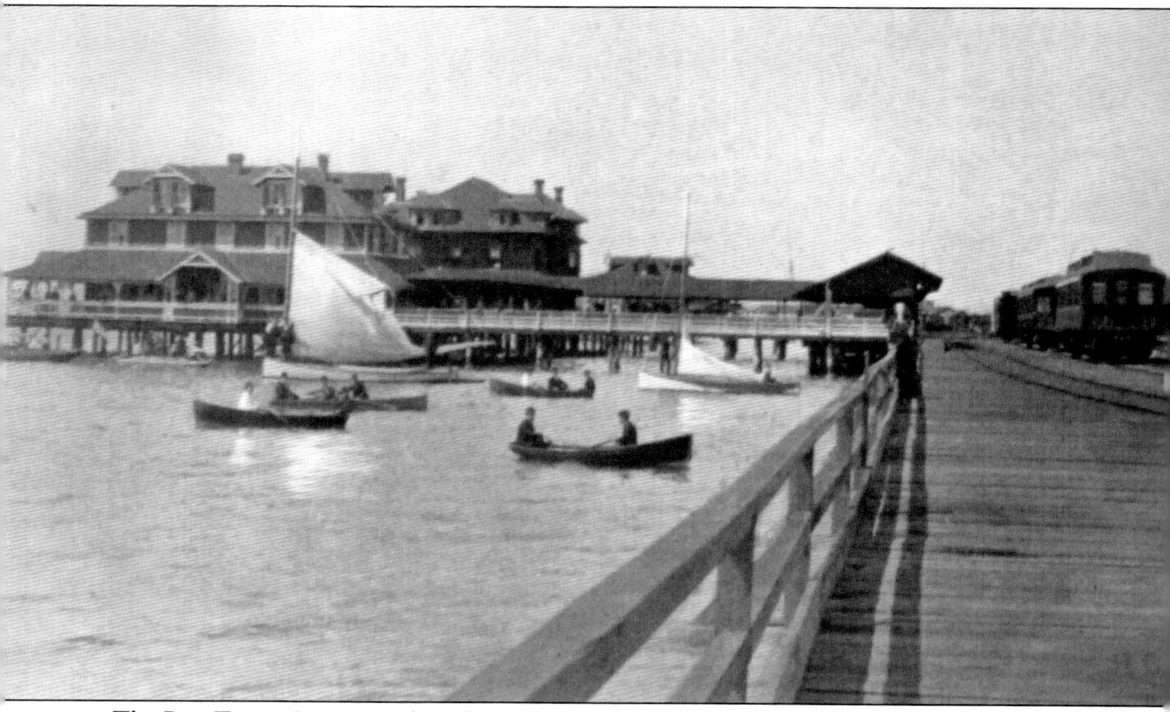

The Port Tampa Inn not only welcomed guests from Havana, Key West, and other seaport cities along the Gulf Coast, but residents of Tampa. Local guests would likely take the train, unless they were willing to travel the untamed roads. Upon arrival, the inn provided a quick escape to boating, fishing, swimming, and possibly the only local waterfront dining room available at the time.

Two

HALCYON DAYS

Tampa's official US Census population in 1900 was 15,839. In a little more than a generation, it had become the fastest growing city in Florida (and one of the fastest growing cities in the country). Tampa and Hyde Park welcomed the 20th century with optimism and a spirit of enthusiasm and civic pride.

The staid formality of the Victorian period ended as the new century was greeted with unabashed anticipation. The emerging architectural designs of the Arts and Crafts Movement ventured beyond the mere creation of new styles; the modern movement redefined the renewed American democratic philosophy of social reform through design. Advances in technology and rapid economic expansion fostered the creation of a larger and more prosperous middle class, and it became possible for the expanding population to live in an attractive, affordable environment.

Fresh styles ushered in the first wave of architectural modernism in Hyde Park. Craftsman and Prairie styles dominated new construction between the first two decades of the 20th century. The modernism included innovative laborsaving appliances in homes, affordable and hygienic plumbing, electricity, and money-saving construction techniques. Smooth roads were built to accommodate automobiles, and front-yard fences were abandoned in favor of pedestrian-friendly sidewalks that connected public byways with wide front porches.

The physical expansion of Hyde Park at the beginning of the 20th century was greatly influenced by the City Beautiful Movement. The movement's inspiration was the 1893 World's Columbian Exposition in Chicago. Based on the concept that a pleasant and attractive environment fosters a higher quality of life for inhabitants, the movement's effect on Tampa led to the evolution of Bayshore Boulevard, parkways planted with trees, the construction of an obelisk to honor the veterans of World War I, and the purchase of the Tampa Bay Hotel by the City of Tampa.

Eclectic architectural styles also emerged during this time, replacing the exuberant detailing of Victorian homes. Hyde Park's expanding population vied with one another in friendly competition for architectural modernity. By the 1920s, Mediterranean Revival architecture had become popular for both family homes and commercial buildings; many of these are still standing today.

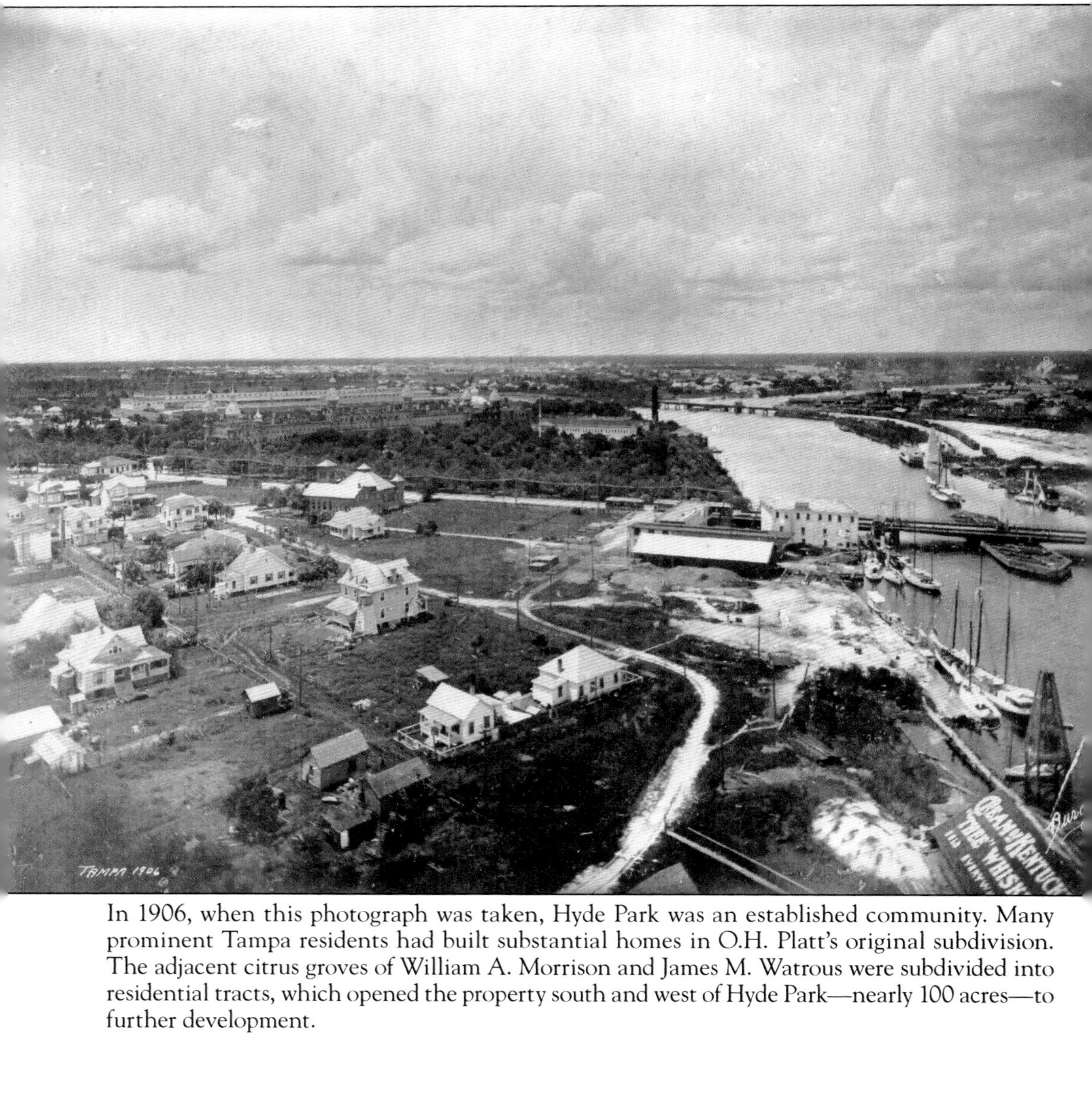

In 1906, when this photograph was taken, Hyde Park was an established community. Many prominent Tampa residents had built substantial homes in O.H. Platt's original subdivision. The adjacent citrus groves of William A. Morrison and James M. Watrous were subdivided into residential tracts, which opened the property south and west of Hyde Park—nearly 100 acres—to further development.

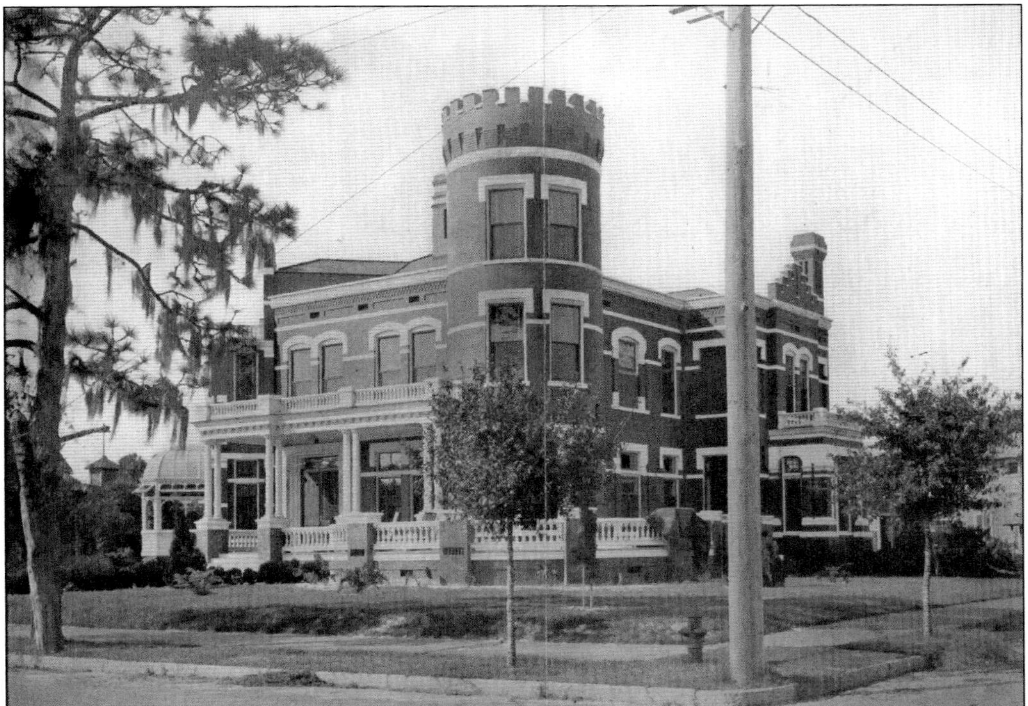

The Knight mansion, owned by Peter O. and Lillie Knight, was completed in 1895 and was one of Tampa's largest and most imposing early private residences. (The Knights' intermediary residence, the Knight cottage, was pictured in chapter one.) Sold in 1946 and occupied by the Tampa Jewish Community Center until 1960, the building was demolished in 1963. A few years later, a condominium was constructed on the site. (Tampa Historical Society.)

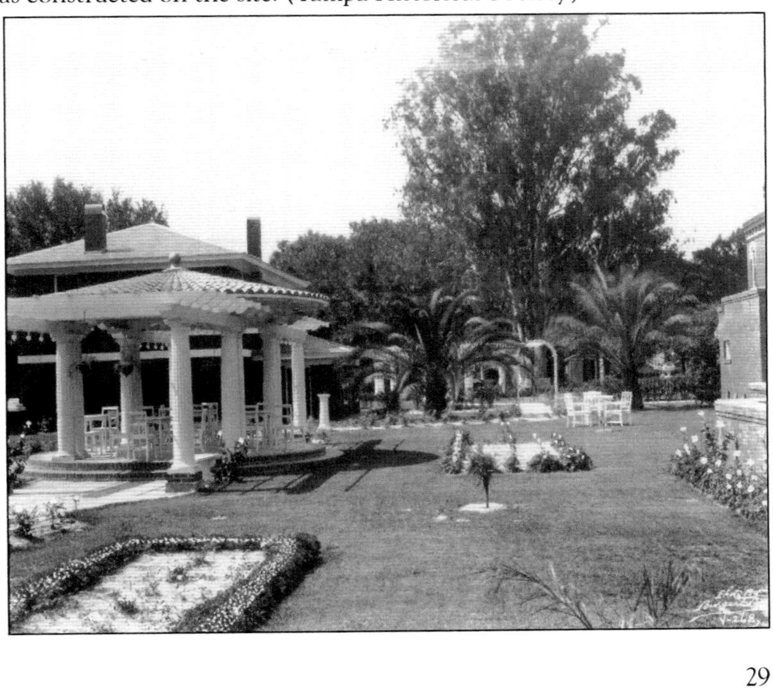

Lush planted areas and formal gardens home surrounded the Knight home. This 1921 photograph shows the portion of the garden that served as an outdoor extension of the conservatory. The Knights frequently entertained, and their Hyde Park estate became the hub of Tampa's social and cultural life. Outdoor activities were held in the gardens throughout most of the year.

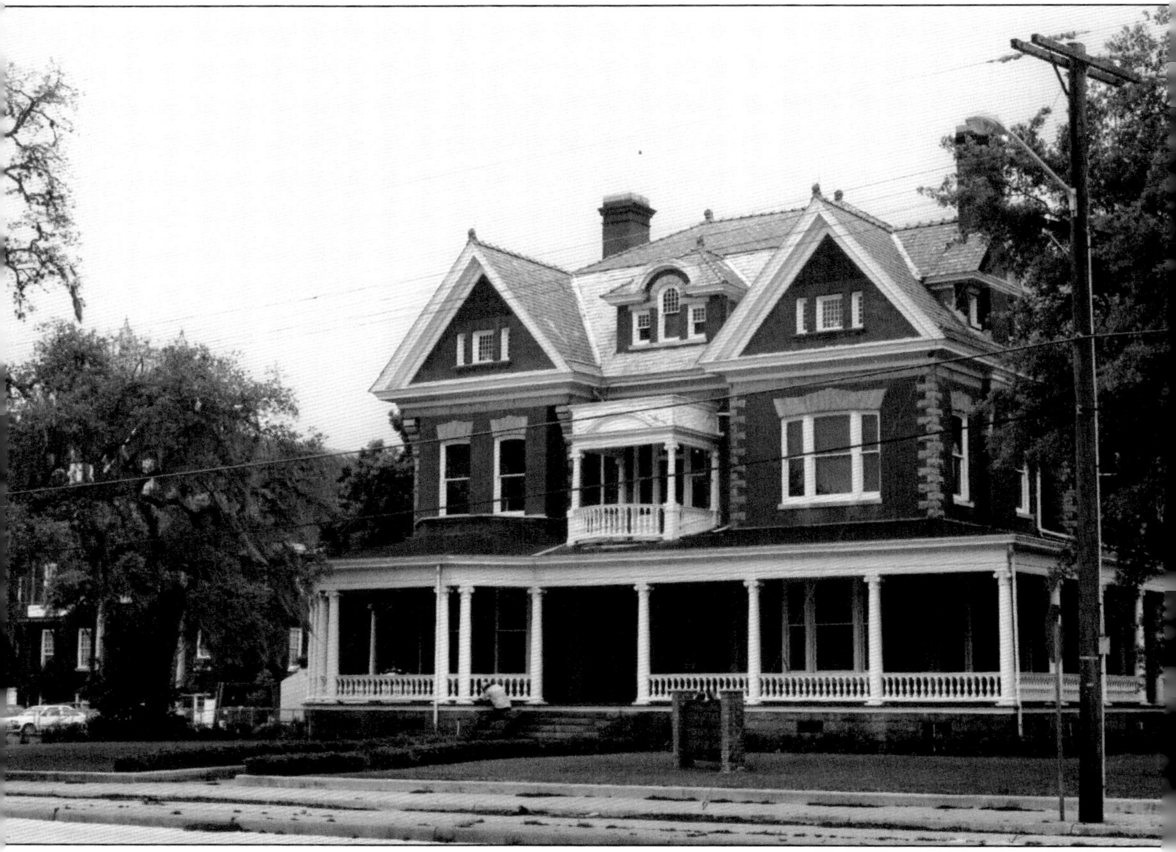

The James B. Anderson house was one of the first Hyde Park homes designed by a local architect, Francis J. Kennard. The home was constructed in 1898 with redbrick and granite that was transported from Georgia. The building currently houses professional offices. (Florida Bureau of Historic Preservation.)

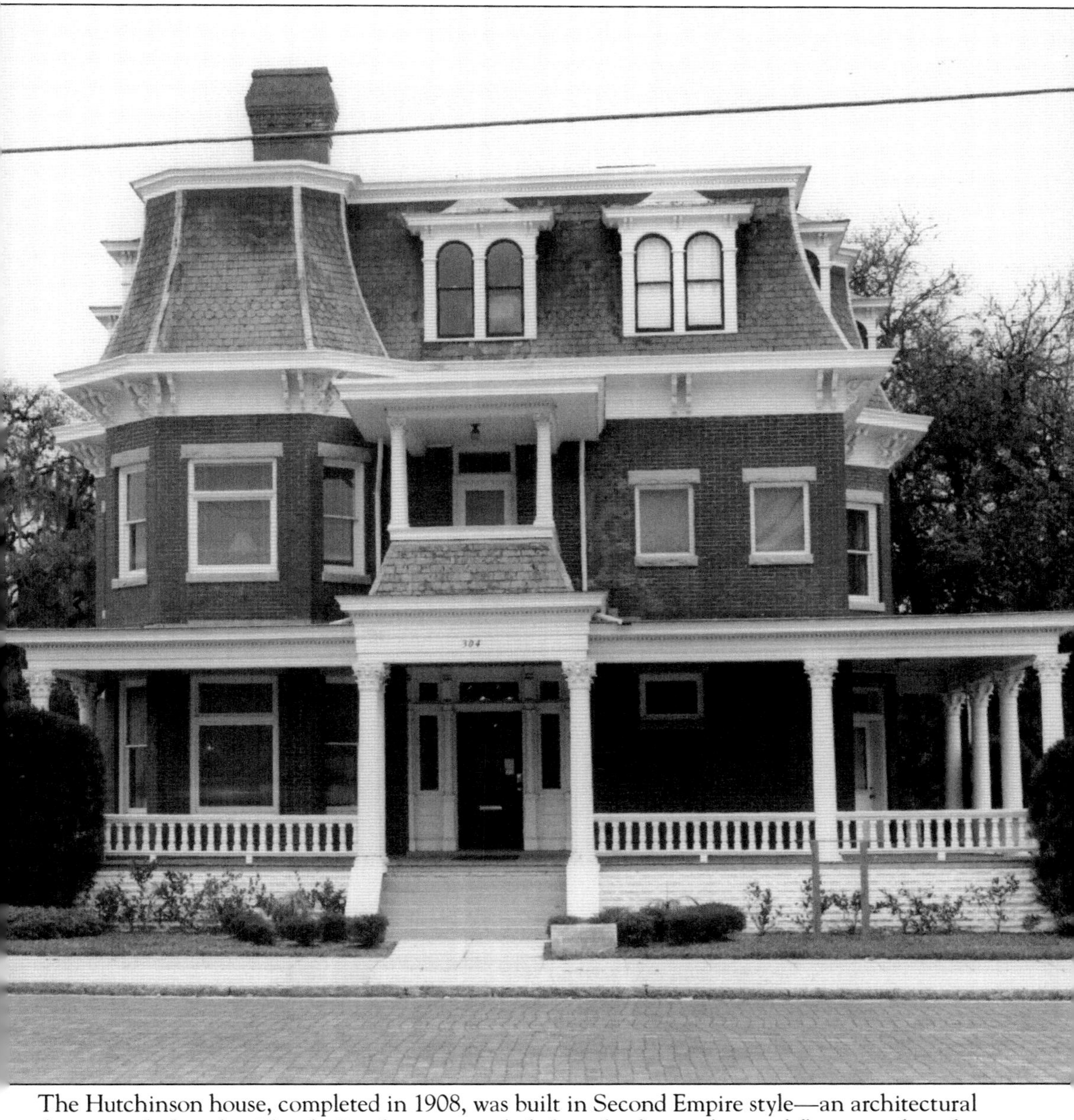

The Hutchinson house, completed in 1908, was built in Second Empire style—an architectural design rarely found in Florida. Porches were included on the first and second floors to adapt the house to the area's subtropical climate. Currie J. Hutchinson and his wife, Harriet Mae, moved to Hyde Park from Ohio and reportedly wanted a house that was reminiscent of their home state. (Florida Bureau of Historic Preservation.)

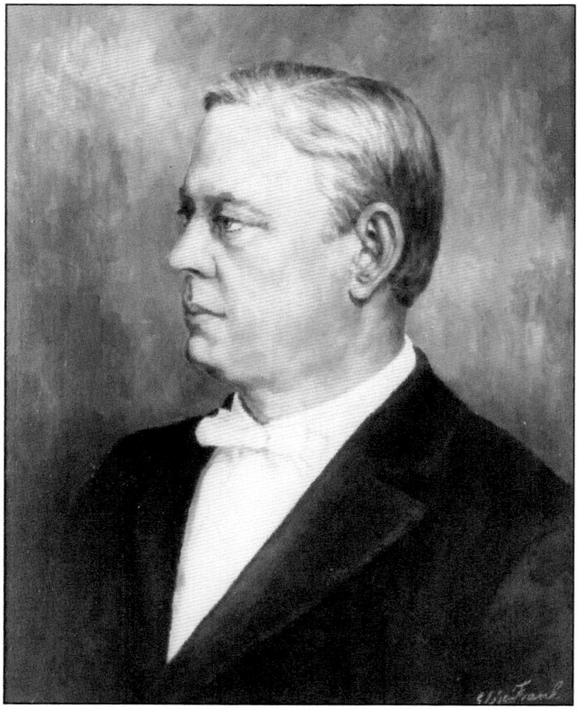

D.B. McKay was born in Tampa in 1868. The descendant of a wealthy Tampa pioneer, he became owner and publisher of the *Tampa Daily Times* and was elected mayor of Tampa five times. McKay, appointed county historian in 1949, chronicled the early history of Tampa-Hillsborough County.

On October 7, 1900, D.B. McKay married Aurora P.F. Gutierrez, the daughter of Gavino Gutierrez, a pioneer in Tampa's early Spanish community and a leader in the establishment of the cigar industry in Tampa's Ybor City. They are pictured around 1923 with their 10 children on the porch of their Victorian period home on Horatio Street. (Tampa Bay History Center.)

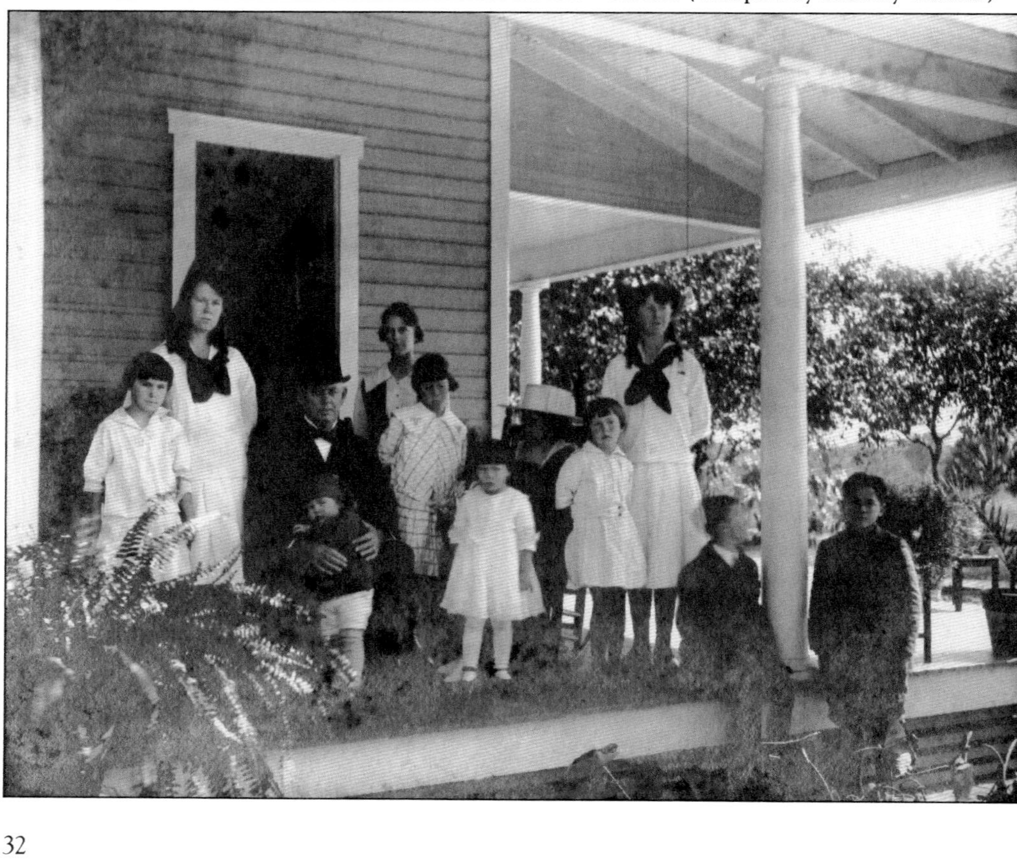

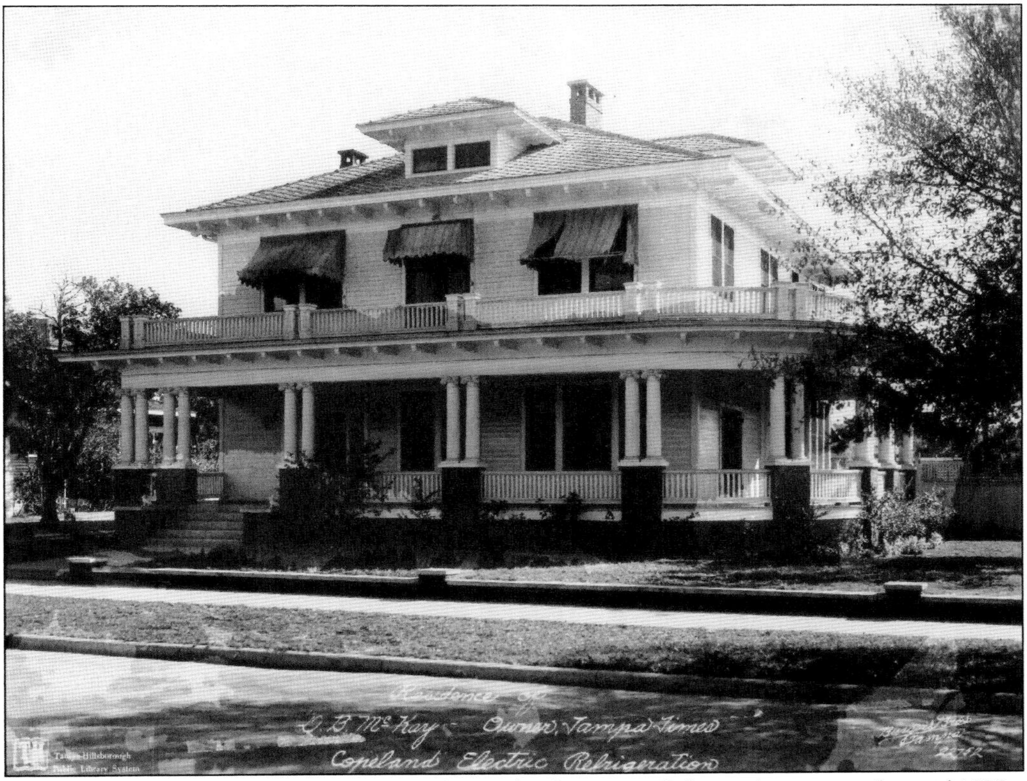

D.B. McKay and his wife, Aurora, moved into this house on Orleans Avenue in the mid-1920s. Craftsman was the dominant architectural style for upwardly mobile upper/middle-class families during the first half of the 20th century.

The McKay home represented the height of suitability for a prominent family in the years between the two world wars. The interior was an appropriate setting to raise a family and to entertain civic and business leaders. This 1931 photograph of the vestibule and staircase depicts a home that was light and airy, free of clutter, restrained, and absent gilded furniture.

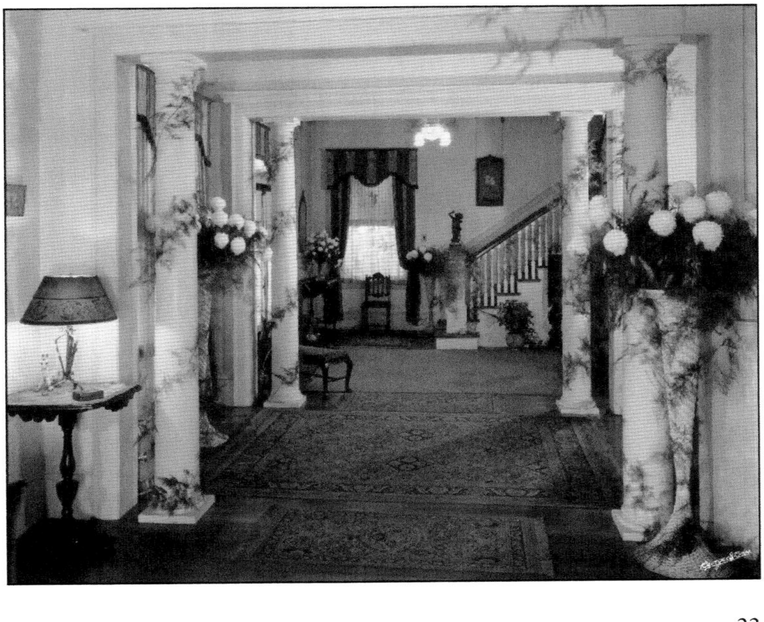

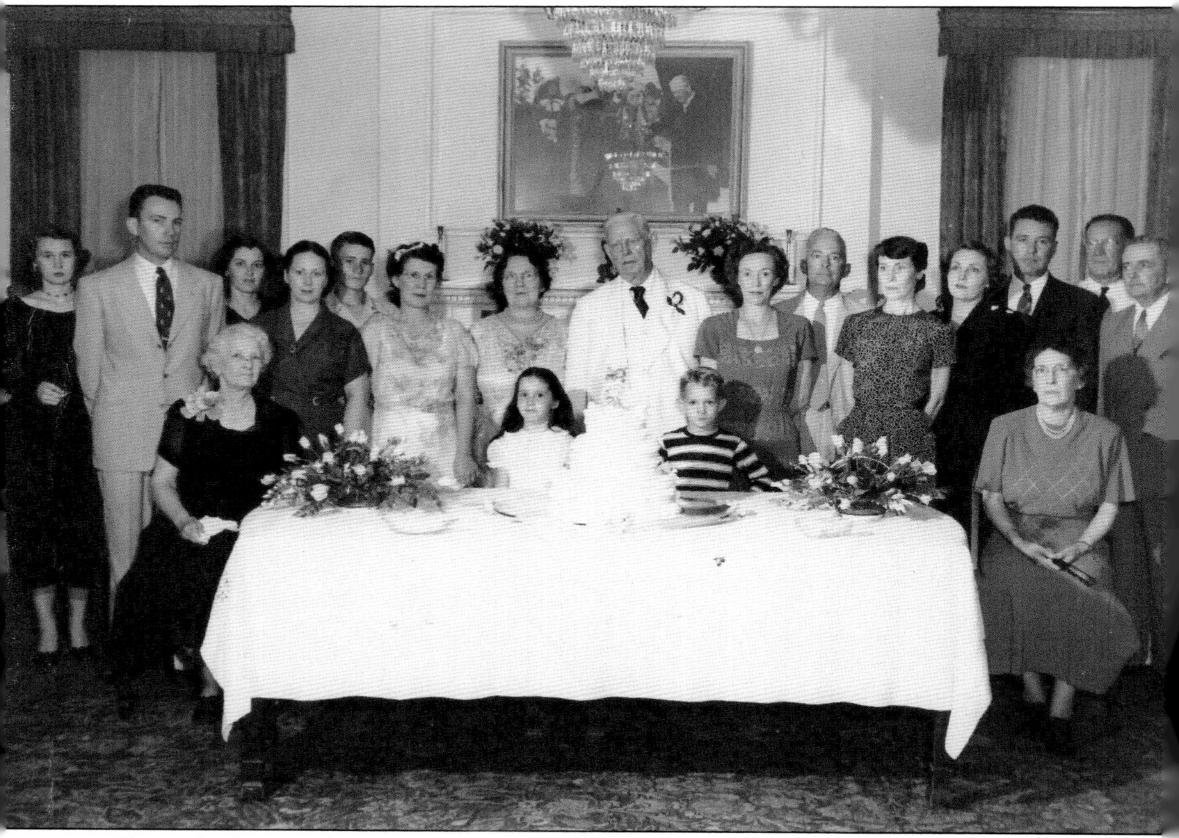

This 1950 photograph was taken at Aurora and D.B. McKay's Bayshore Boulevard home during the celebration of their 50th wedding anniversary. Children, grandchildren, and other family members surround the McKays, who stand in the center of the photograph. (Tampa Bay History Center.)

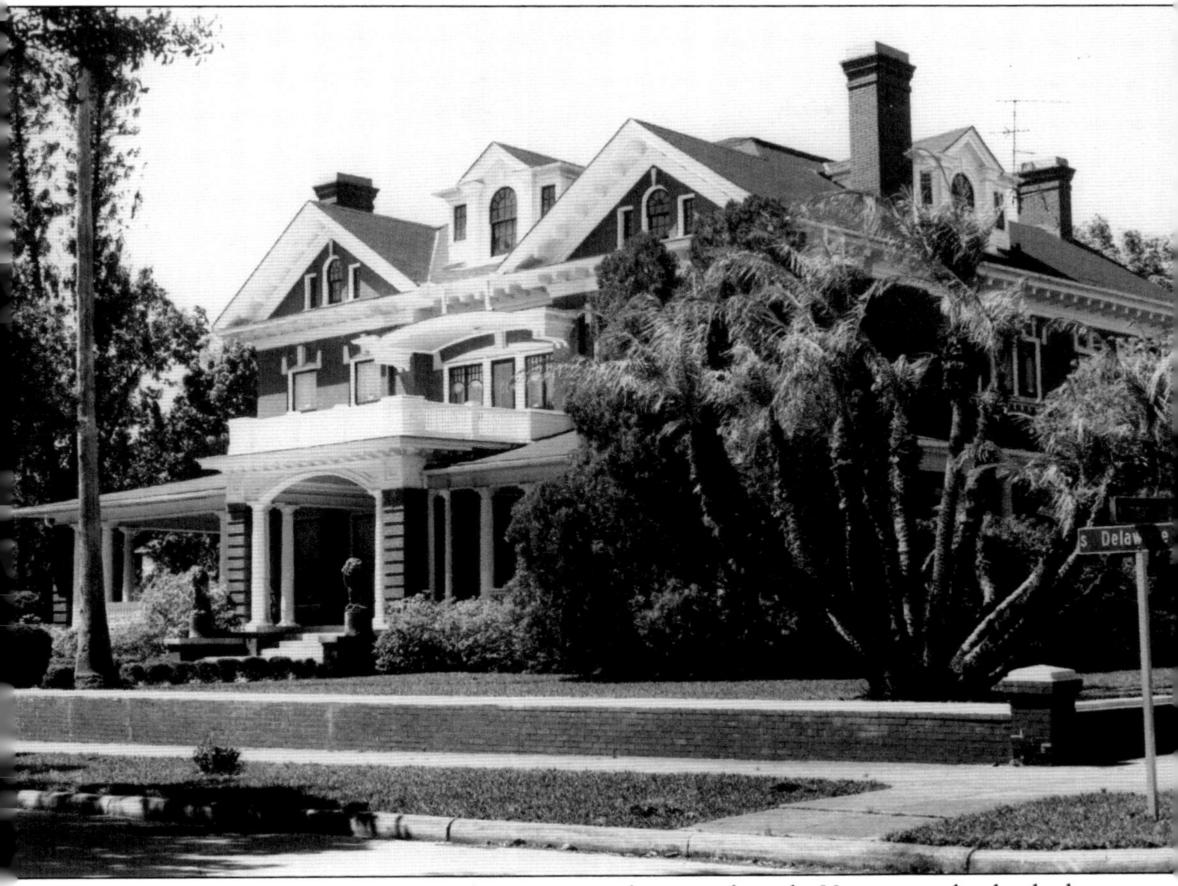

The Himes home, built in 1911, was another impressive departure from the Victorian styles that had been preferred in Hyde Park in the first decade of the 20th century. The redbrick home is dominated by the front porch, symmetrically balanced windows and center door, and the low balustrade around the platform porch. The large and impressive structure reinforced Hyde Park's status as one of Tampa's most desirable residential locations. (Florida Bureau of Historic Preservation.)

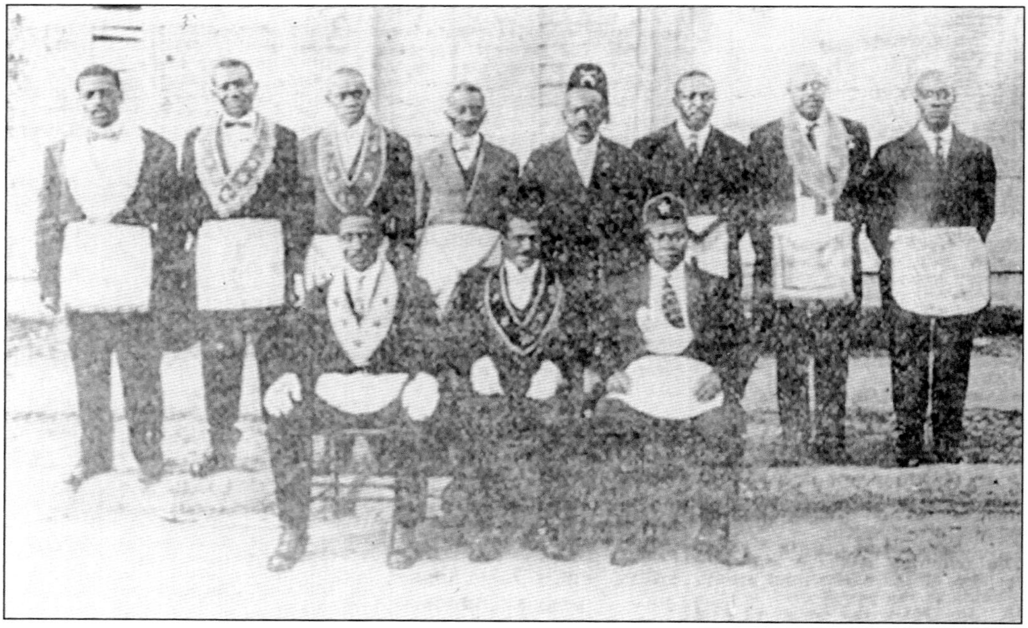

This photograph of the West Hyde Park Lodge No. 327 was taken on January 28, 1915, in a section of Hyde Park known as Dobyville. Named after prominent longtime resident Richard Cornelius Doby, Dobyville contained a mixture of residential, industrial, and commercial buildings that developed on both sides of Henry B. Plant's rail line through Hyde Park. (Tampa Bay History Center.)

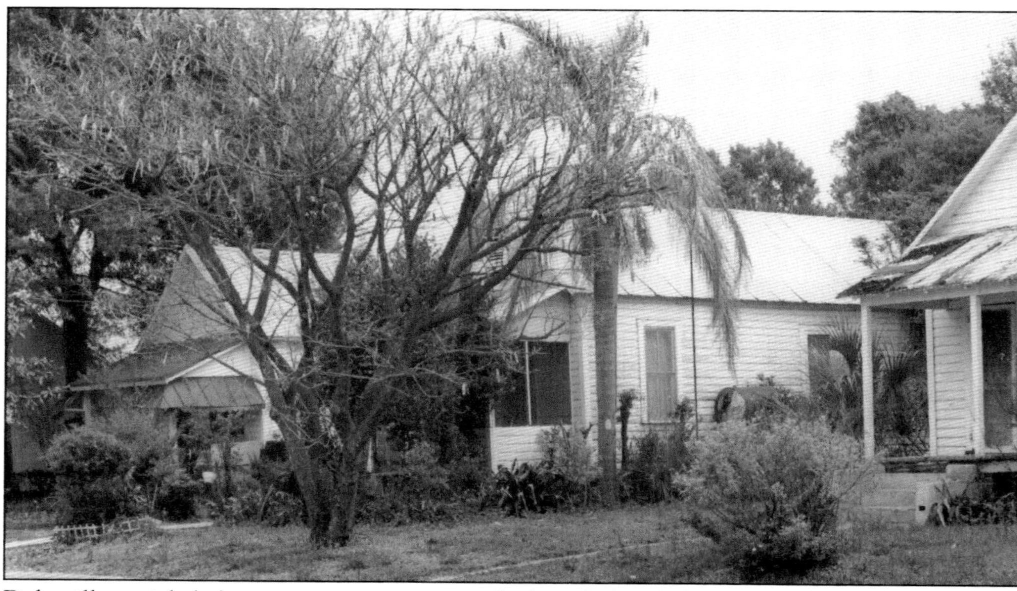

Dobyville, a tightly knit community, consisted of single-family homes, churches, retail stores, a public and a private school, and various industrial buildings. It was an active community during Tampa's period of racial segregation. By the 1920s, Dobyville's population accounted for 10 percent of Tampa's black population. This 1982 photograph reflects the simple home styles prevalent in the Dobyville area. (Florida Bureau of Historic Preservation.)

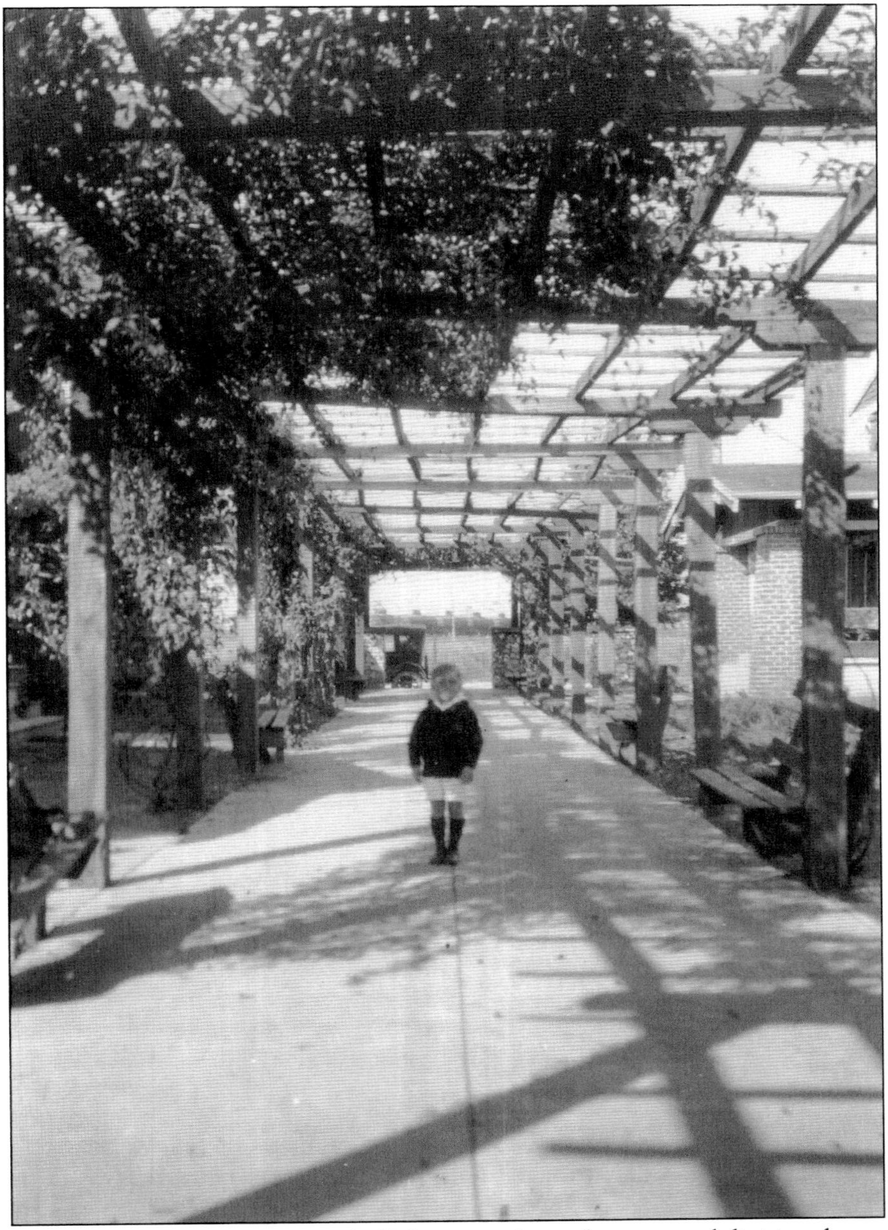

Hyde Park's Bungalow Terrace is an early-20th-century bungalow court subdivision that provided affordable Craftsman-style housing for the rapidly emerging middle class. Developed in 1913 by Alfred Swann and Eugene Holtsinger, the first homes were sold for $4,500, including the land. The low-maintenance bungalows were built on small lots and centered on a generous common sidewalk. Small garages were accessed from rear alleys. The 345-foot pergola pictured above was constructed in 1918 and spanned the length of the bungalow court, providing individual covered archways to each bungalow. In 1924, the pergola was removed because of rot caused by the invasive bougainvillea that had been planted to cover the structure. Through the years, Bungalow Terrace's homes have attracted writers (including best-selling author Alec Waugh), artists, and even professional athletes. (Private collection of Craig Shatto.)

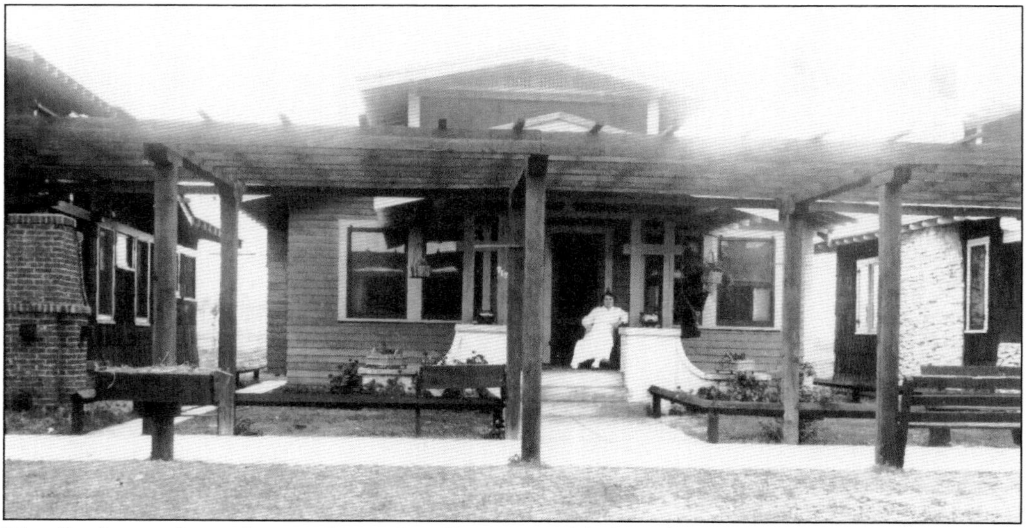

The Craftsman bungalows in Bungalow Terrace enabled residents to own a finely constructed home that provided the most modern features available at the time. Each home included a front porch, built-in interior cabinets, modern kitchens, and full bathrooms. (Private collection of Craig Shatto.)

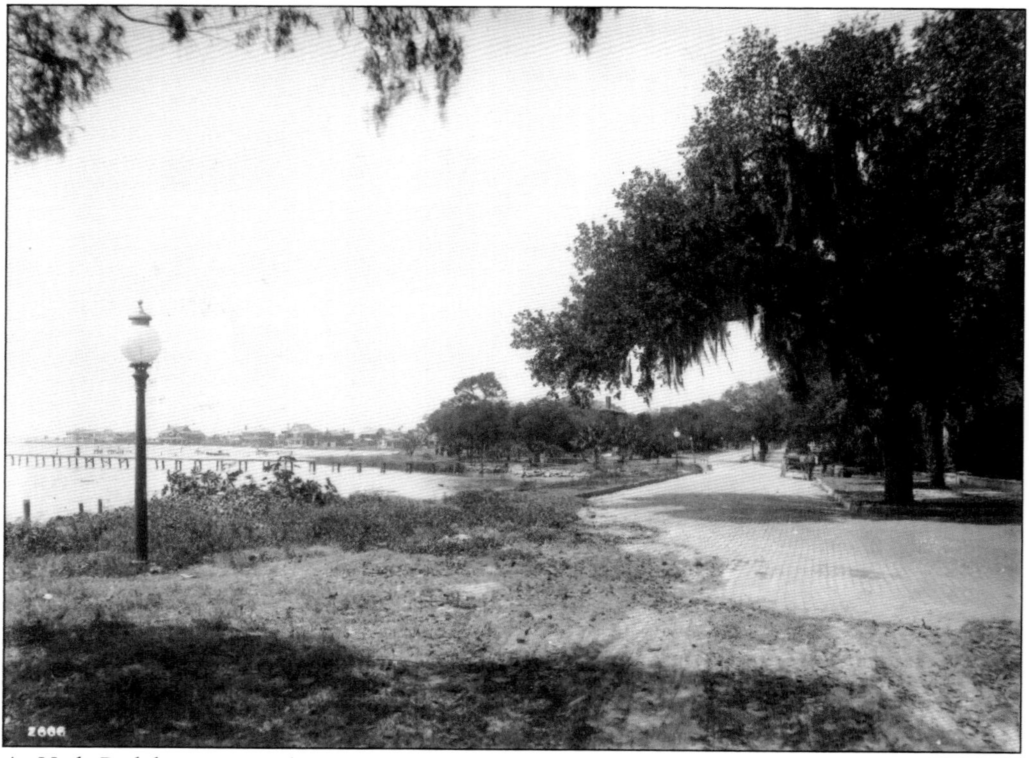

As Hyde Park began to evolve into a residential community, civic leaders were intent on keeping the bay accessible to all. The early developers of Hyde Park, principally Alfred Swann and Eugene Holtsinger, converted the dreary shore into an open space by building a mile of seawall and opening Bayshore Boulevard to the community.

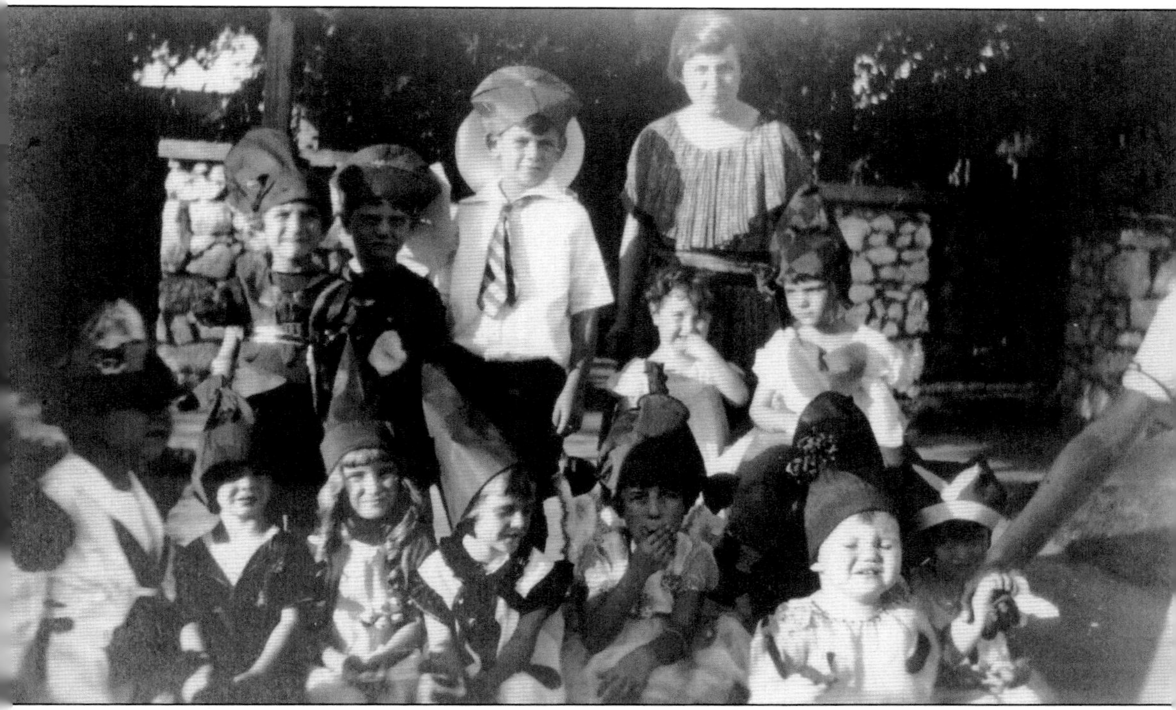

Hyde Park was a closely knitted community that provided numerous amenities for children living in the neighborhood. This early-1920s photograph was taken before a costume parade down Bungalow Terrace's wide sidewalk. The happenstance parade was followed by a party at a nearby home. (Private collection of Craig Shatto.)

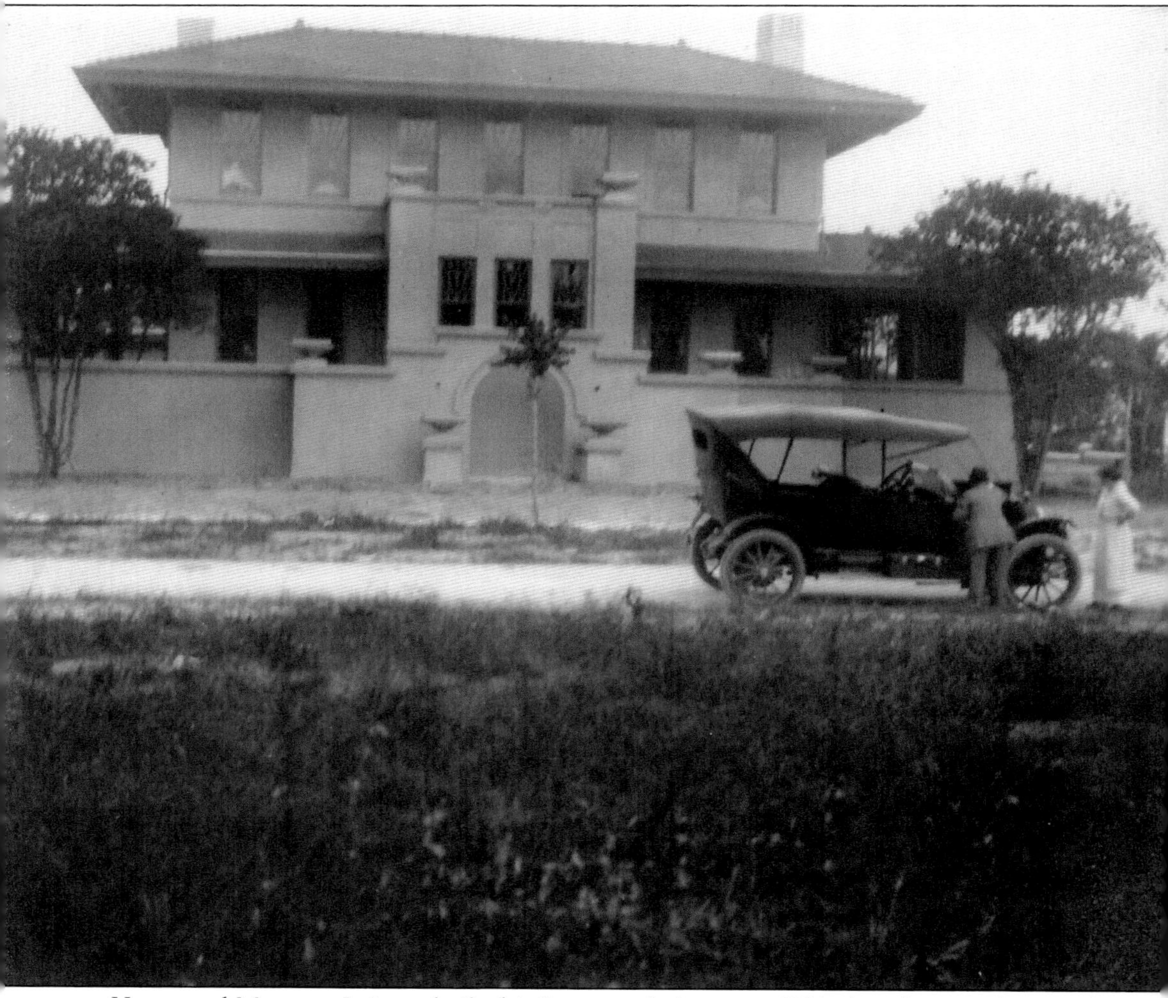

Henry and Margaret Leiman built this Prairie-style house in 1914; this photograph was taken when construction was nearly complete. The Leimans moved to Tampa from New York City in 1894, just as Tampa's Ybor City was becoming the largest center for cigar manufacturing in the world. Henry Leiman's training in the fabrication of wooden boxes enabled his quick success in the business of supplying cigar boxes to Ybor City's booming cigar factories. By 1902, Leiman had formed the Tampa Box Company, which soon became the largest manufacturer of wooden cigar boxes and cigar accessories in the world. The success of the company provided the resources for the Leimans to commission the most modern home built in Tampa to date. As owners of a successful box manufacturing company, they also had the ability to import exotic mahogany, teak, and walnut from around the world for their extraordinary new home.

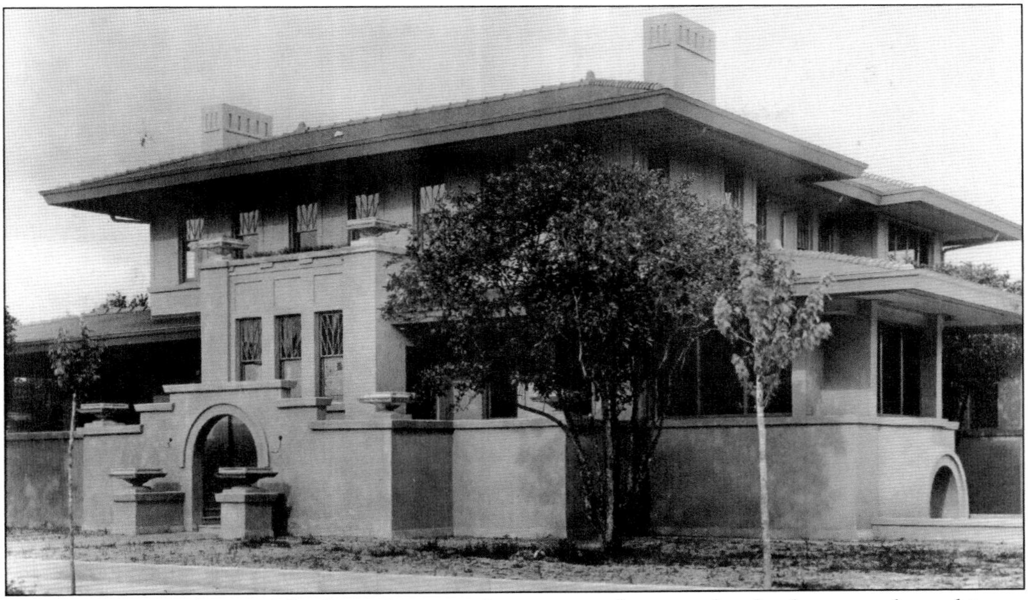

The Prairie School, one of the few indigenous American architectural styles, began under architects Louis Sullivan and Frank Lloyd Wright. In terms of the Leiman house, this style influenced the hipped, low-pitched roof extending to wide overhanging eaves and the exterior details of the home, which emphasized horizontal lines with square architectural features.

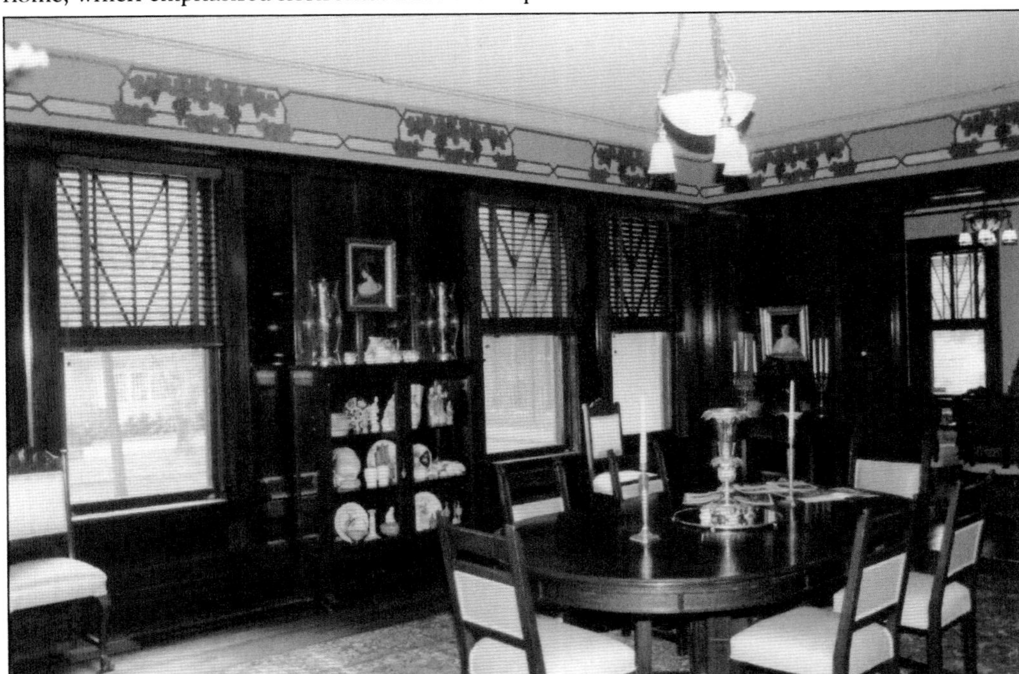

The dining room of the Leiman house is a masterpiece of the Arts and Crafts Movement, dominated by vertical elements and a variety of imported woods. The room exemplifies the home's large, well-lit spaces with windows that open to continuous views of the grounds. (City of Tampa Historic Preservation.)

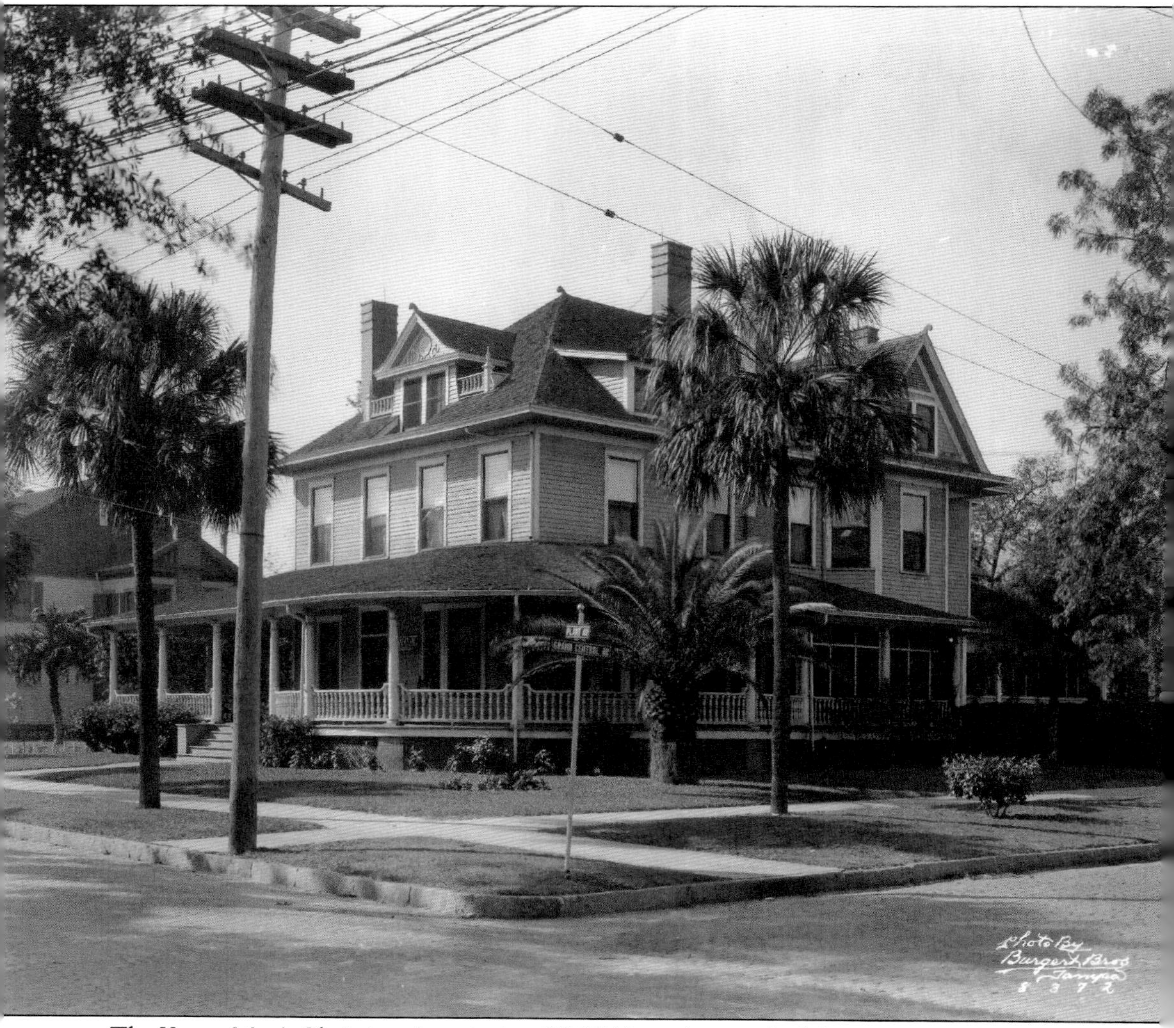

The Young Men's Christian Association (YMCA) was bequeathed this impressive home on Plant Avenue. The building provided overnight accommodations and other programs for young men who were relocating to or visiting Tampa. Many of the new arrivals experienced their first taste of urban living here.

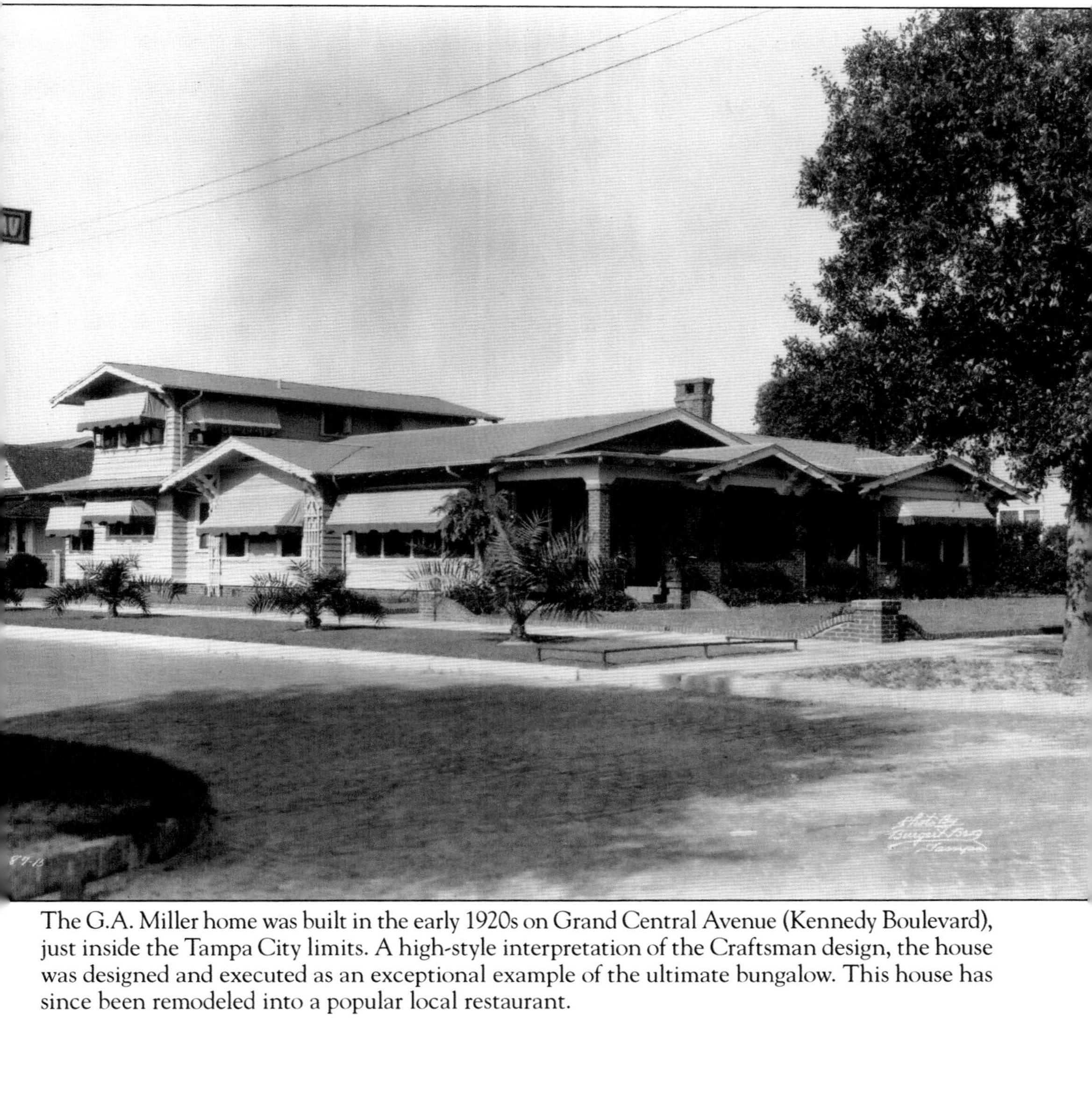

The G.A. Miller home was built in the early 1920s on Grand Central Avenue (Kennedy Boulevard), just inside the Tampa City limits. A high-style interpretation of the Craftsman design, the house was designed and executed as an exceptional example of the ultimate bungalow. This house has since been remodeled into a popular local restaurant.

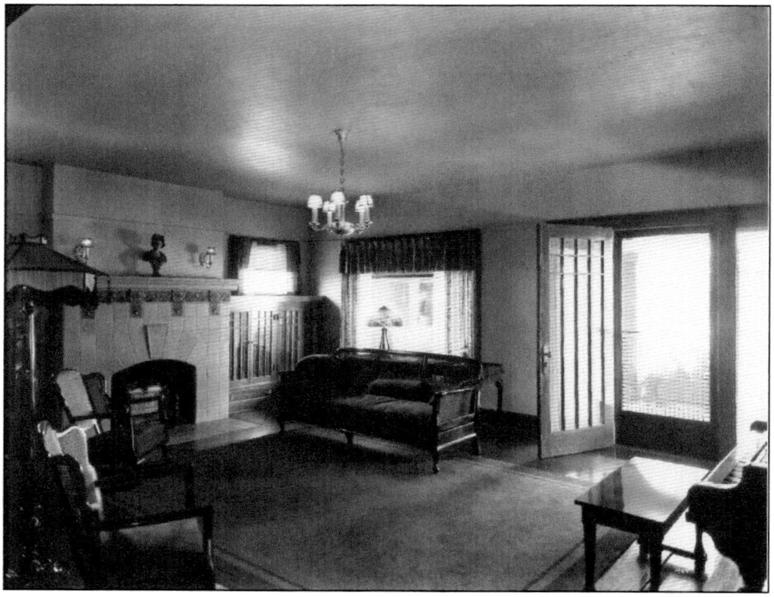

The richness of the living room in the G.A. Miller home is due to deep wood tones, and the Arts and Crafts form of the fireplace is highlighted by imported ceramic tile. The room was not brightly lit and revealed a hushed, contemplative environment. The front door was complemented with a simple screen door.

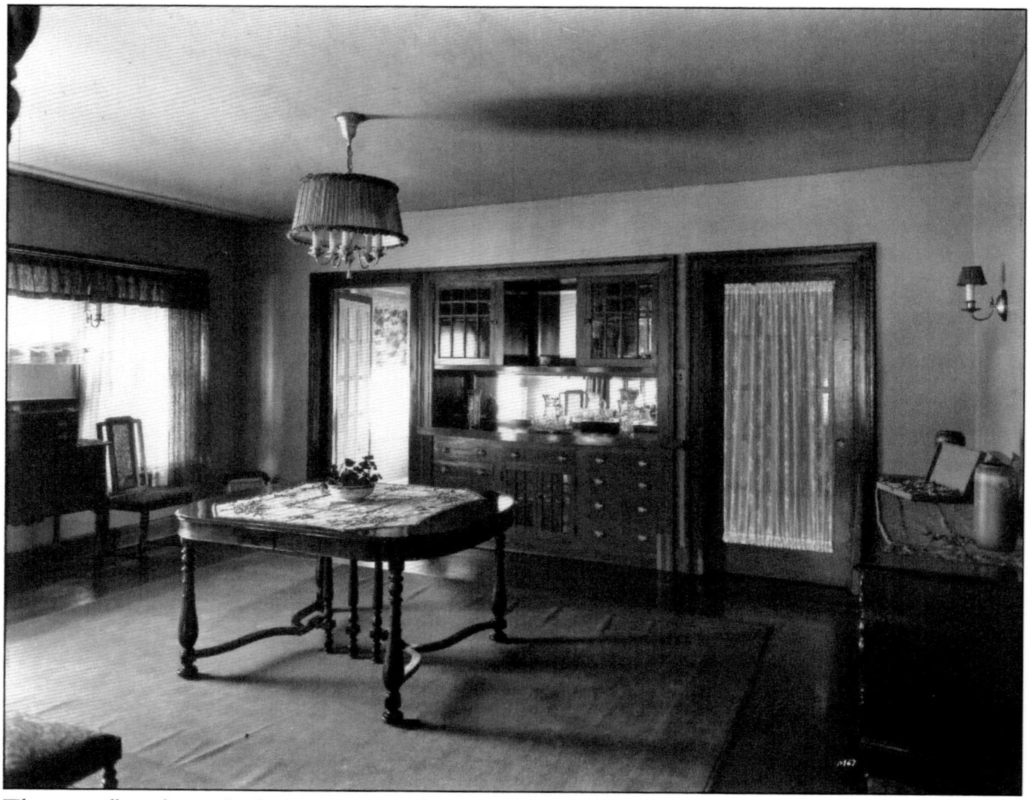

The easy flow from the living room to dining room of the Miller home was influenced by Frank Lloyd Wright's Prairie style. Oriental carpets covered the wood floors and helped define the living spaces. Miller was a contractor and president of G.A. Miller Builder, Inc., and this home reflects his pride in craftsmanship.

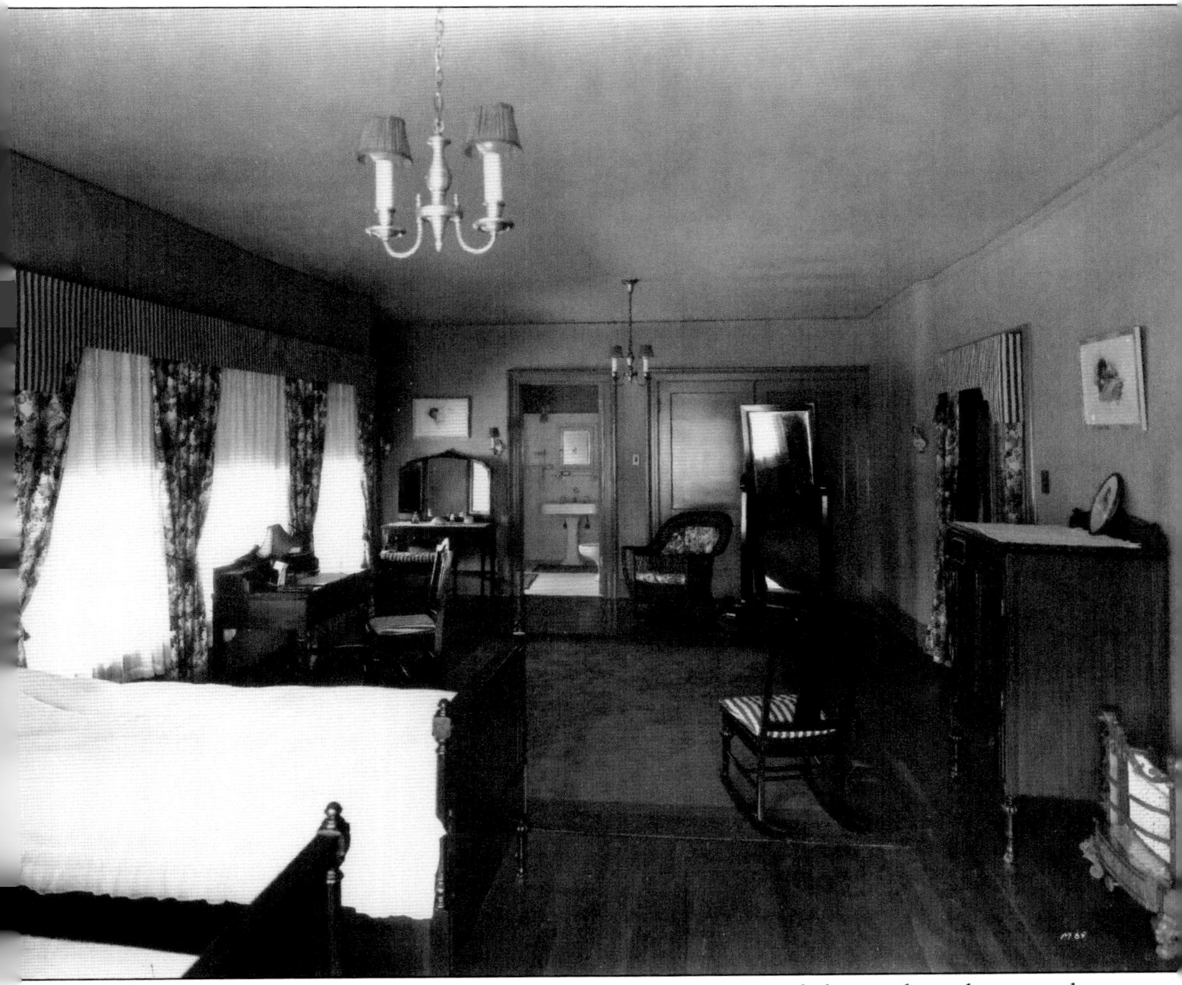

The expansive master bedroom of the G.A. Miller house was much larger than the typical bedroom found in Hyde Park in the early 1920s. The private bathroom attached to the bedroom was a modern and uncommon luxury of the period.

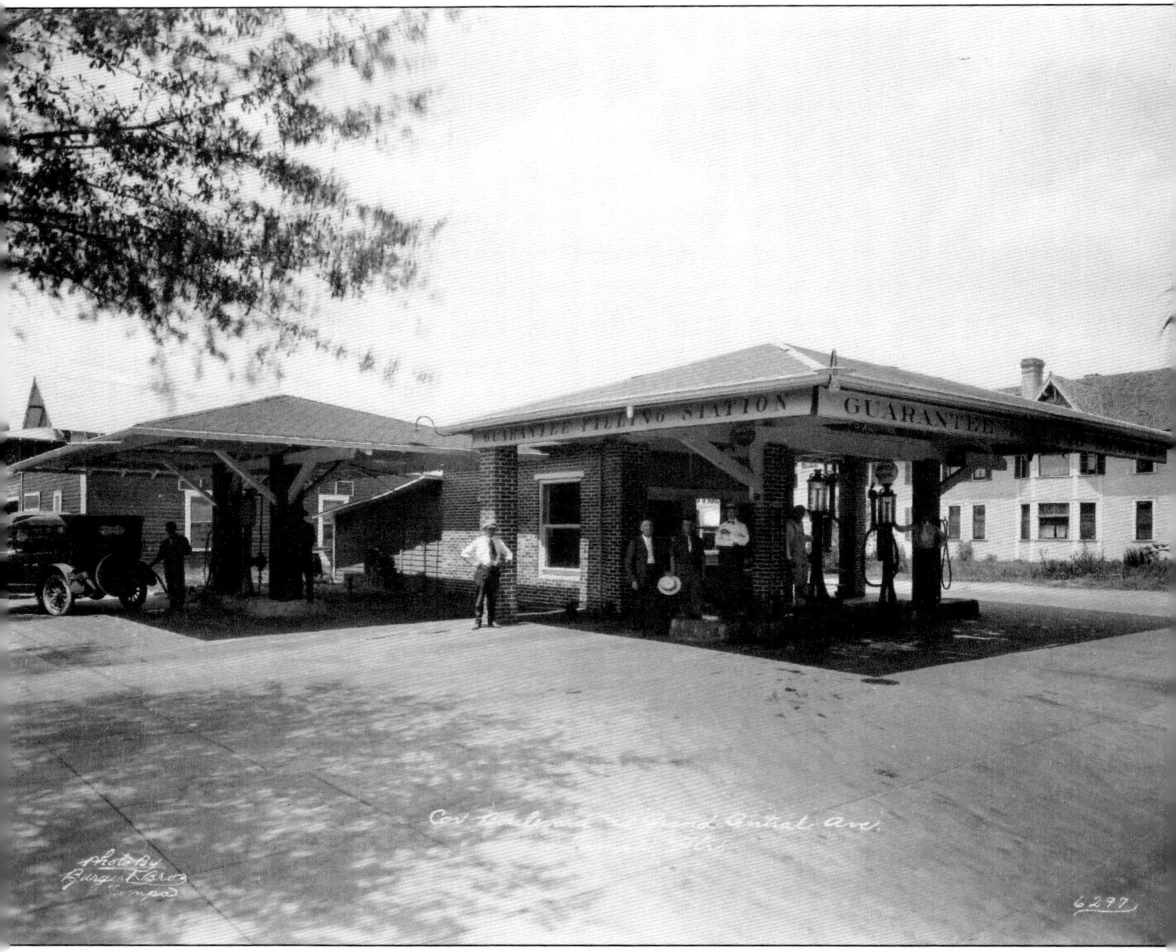

The automobile became a popular mode of travel at the beginning of the 20th century. At first, gasoline was available at very limited locations. Affluent families had gas pumps attached to private garages behind their homes. As the automobile became more affordable, service stations began to appear in residential neighborhoods. This Guarantee Filling Station was designed to loosely resemble the Craftsman-style homes that were popular at the time.

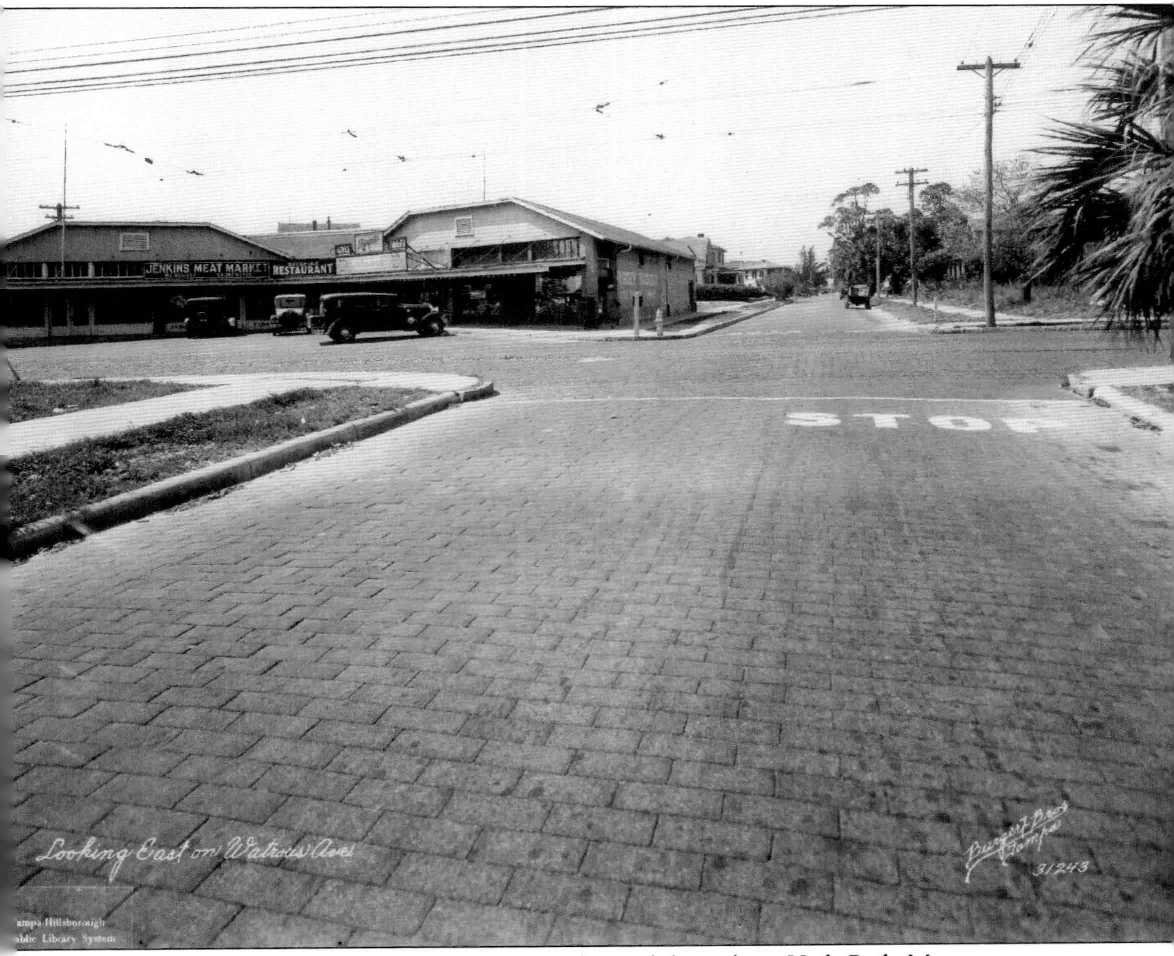

Neighborhood commercial shopping centers were located throughout Hyde Park. Most customers either walked to the center to shop or had merchandise delivered to their homes. This center, located on the corner of Rome and Watrous Avenues, included the Piggly Wiggly, Bayshore Pharmacy, Bayshore Restaurant, and Jenkins Meats.

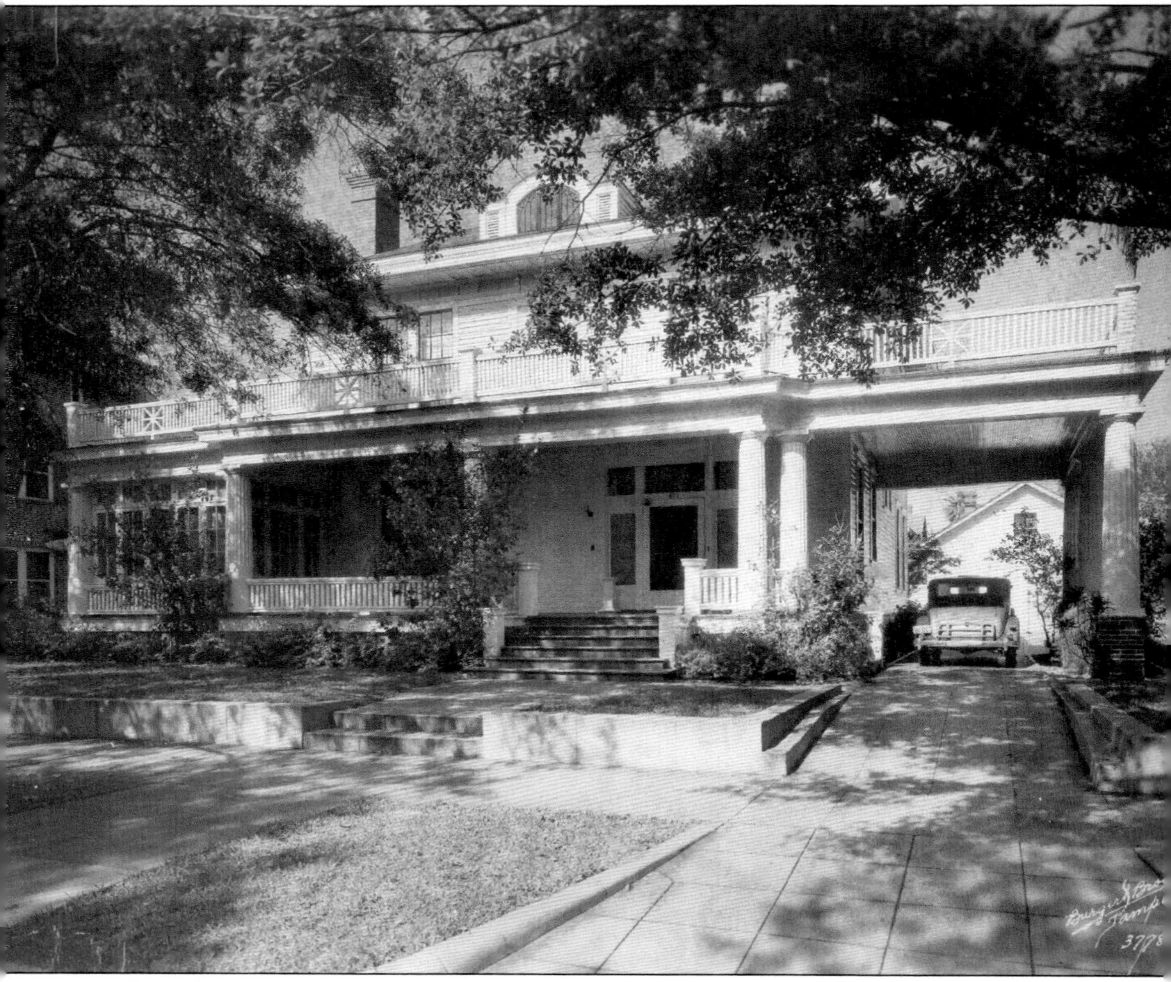

The Robert W. Miller home shows the close relationship of the Craftsman and Prairie homes built in the foursquare shape. This 1921 photograph was taken soon after the house was completed. Miller was the president of Miller-Lenfestey Dairy Supply Company and prominent in the civic affairs of Tampa. (City of Tampa Historic Preservation.)

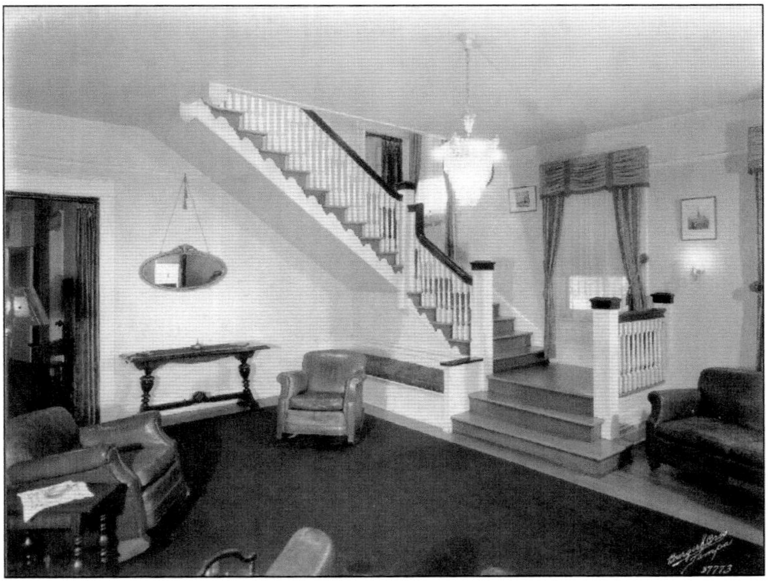

The front room of the R.W. Miller home has high ceilings with a centered chandelier. The home was very modern, yet retained a distinctive reference to a wholesome American lineage. Decorative details were significantly simpler than they would have been in previous generations. (City of Tampa Historic Preservation.)

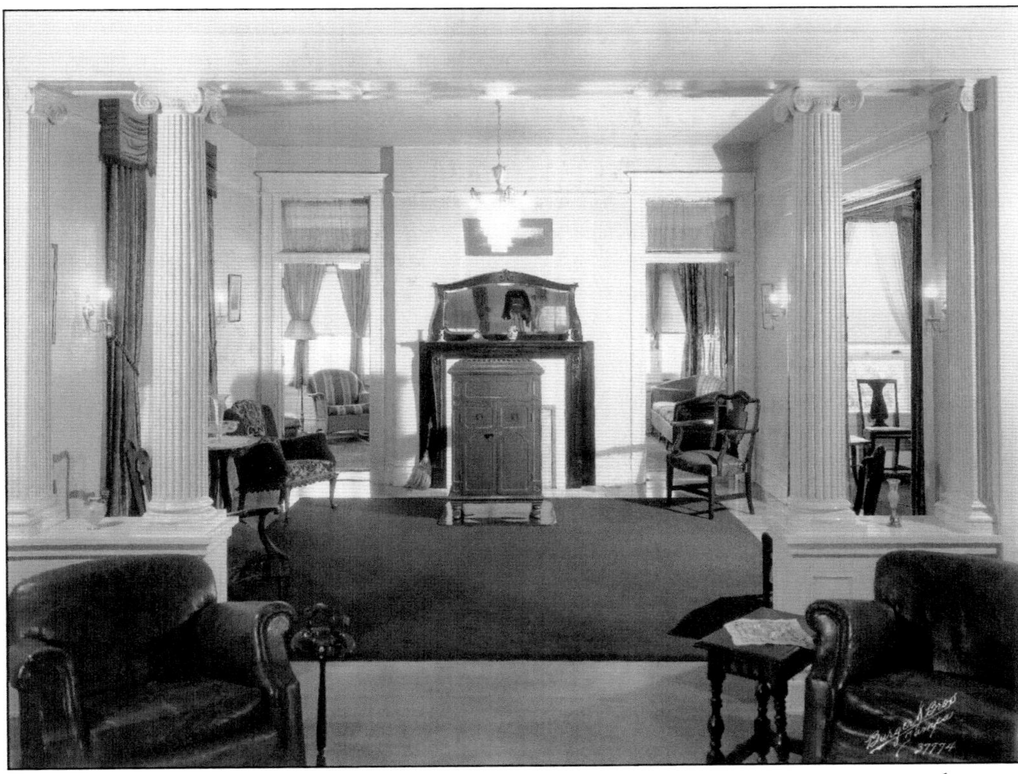

The Miller home was featured in a 1921 issue of *Country Homes* magazine—a spring edition of homes in different parts of Florida. Hyde Park was rapidly developing, and architects and builders were able to feature new technological improvements in a comfortable environment. Florida homes supplanted the heavy draperies and dark colors of the Victorian era with light colors and an airy feeling. (City of Tampa Historic Preservation.)

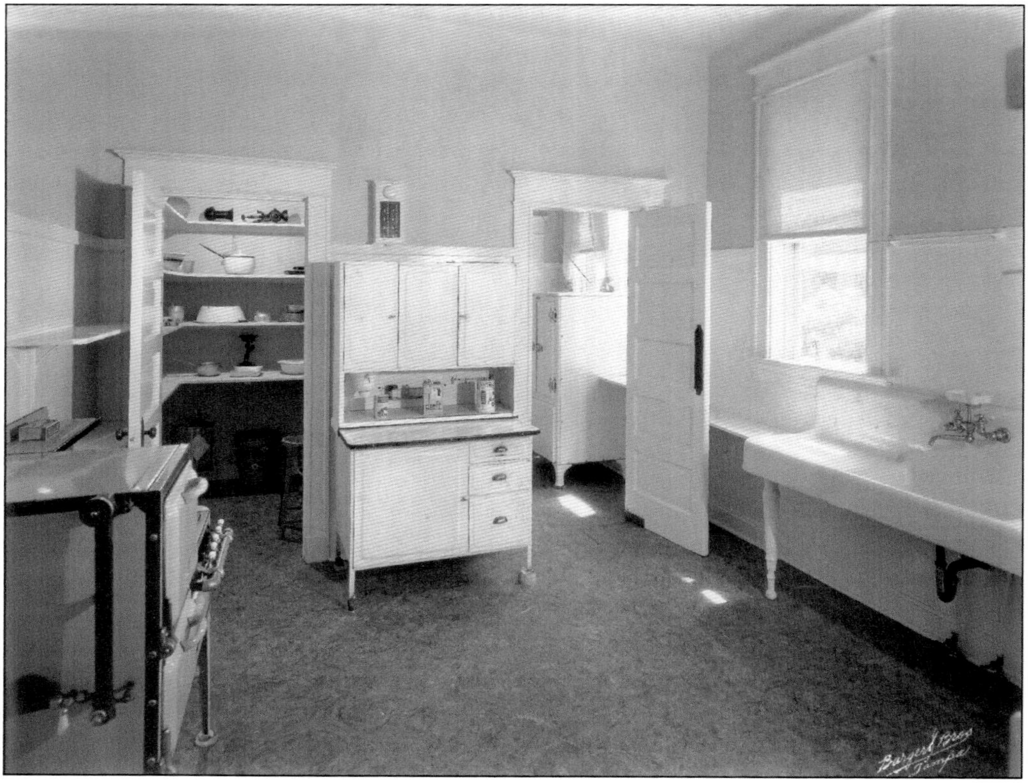

During the first decades of the 20th century, most of the domestic construction in Hyde Park employed the newest available consumer products. This kitchen, in the R.W. Miller home, was designed to be an integral part of the home and furnished so that a modern family could use the kitchen and enjoy the home without domestic help. The kitchen sink (with hot and cold water), gas stove, and electric refrigerator were hygienic and easy to use. In 1921, when this kitchen was installed, the electric refrigerator in the icebox room at the back would have cost, on average, more than a new car. (City of Tampa Historic Preservation.)

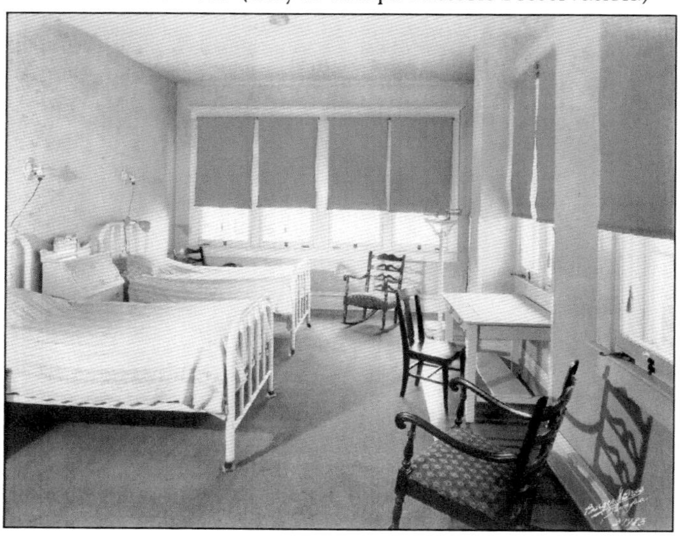

Sleeping porches were common appendages to bedrooms in Hyde Park as well as throughout the southern United States. They were usually located at the back of the house, as shown in this 1921 photograph of the R.W. Miller home. The sleeping porch started to appear in domestic construction as modern science began to understand the benefits of fresh air and the importance of maintaining a hygienic home. (City of Tampa Historic Preservation.)

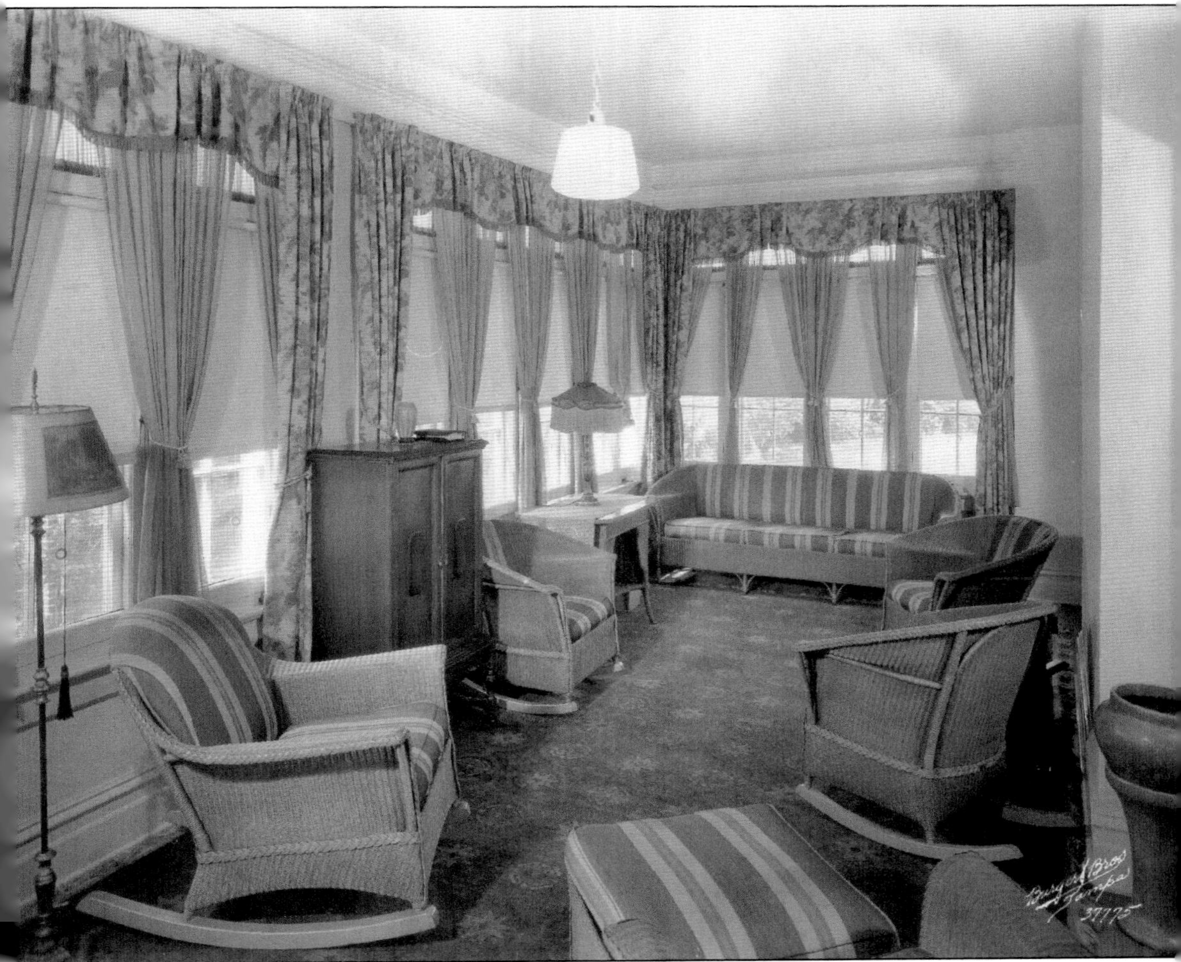

The sunroom of the R.W. Miller home was a bright and airy room that provided a comfortable settting for family and guests, especially during the warmer months of the year. Sunrooms, which began to appear in domestic architecture at the beginning of the 20th century, were the forerunner of the family room that became a standard feature in suburban homes after World War II. (City of Tampa Historic Preservation.)

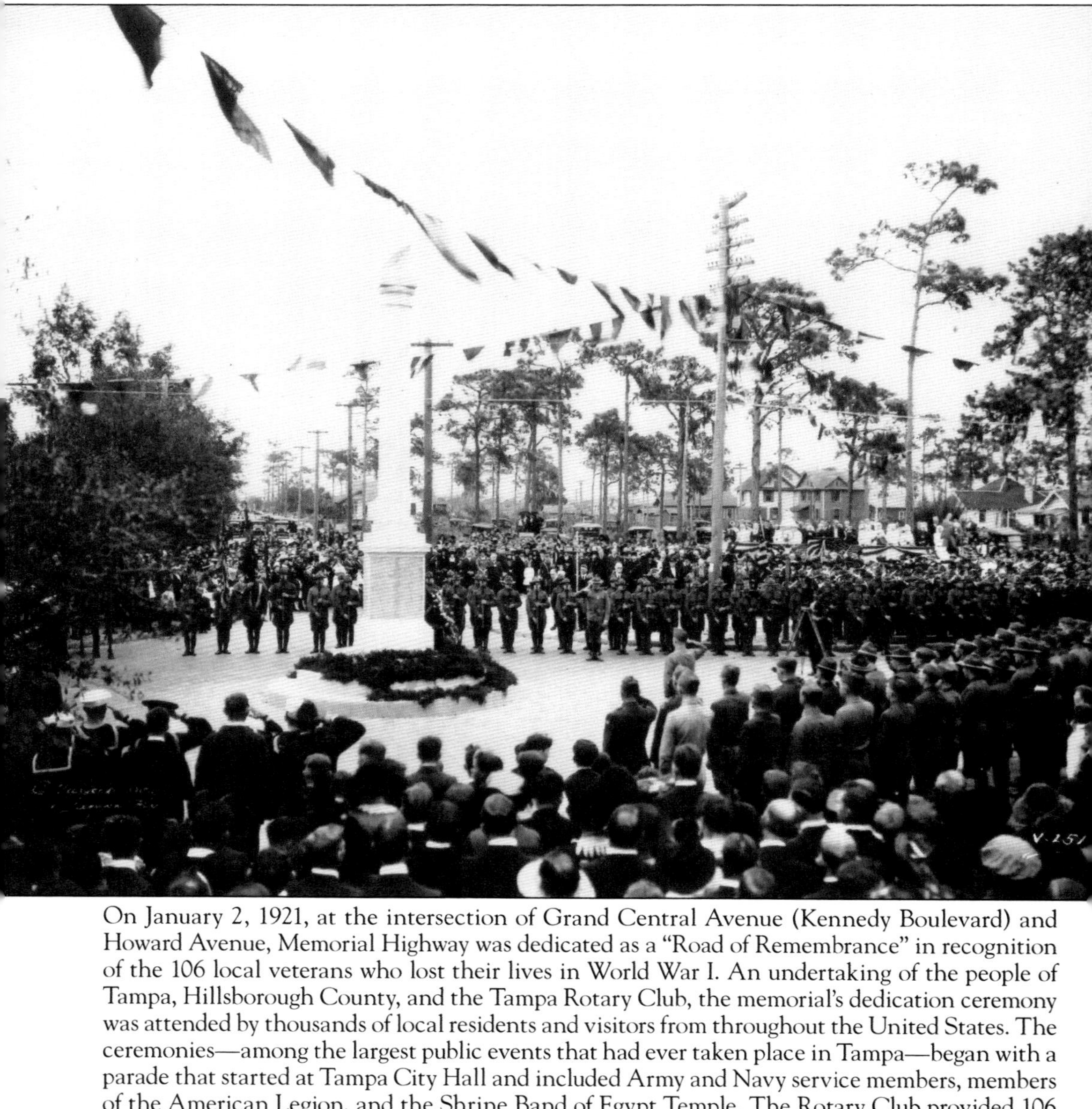

On January 2, 1921, at the intersection of Grand Central Avenue (Kennedy Boulevard) and Howard Avenue, Memorial Highway was dedicated as a "Road of Remembrance" in recognition of the 106 local veterans who lost their lives in World War I. An undertaking of the people of Tampa, Hillsborough County, and the Tampa Rotary Club, the memorial's dedication ceremony was attended by thousands of local residents and visitors from throughout the United States. The ceremonies—among the largest public events that had ever taken place in Tampa—began with a parade that started at Tampa City Hall and included Army and Navy service members, members of the American Legion, and the Shrine Band of Egypt Temple. The Rotary Club provided 106 wreaths that were laid at the monument. This was one of the first US memorials dedicated to those who died in World War I.

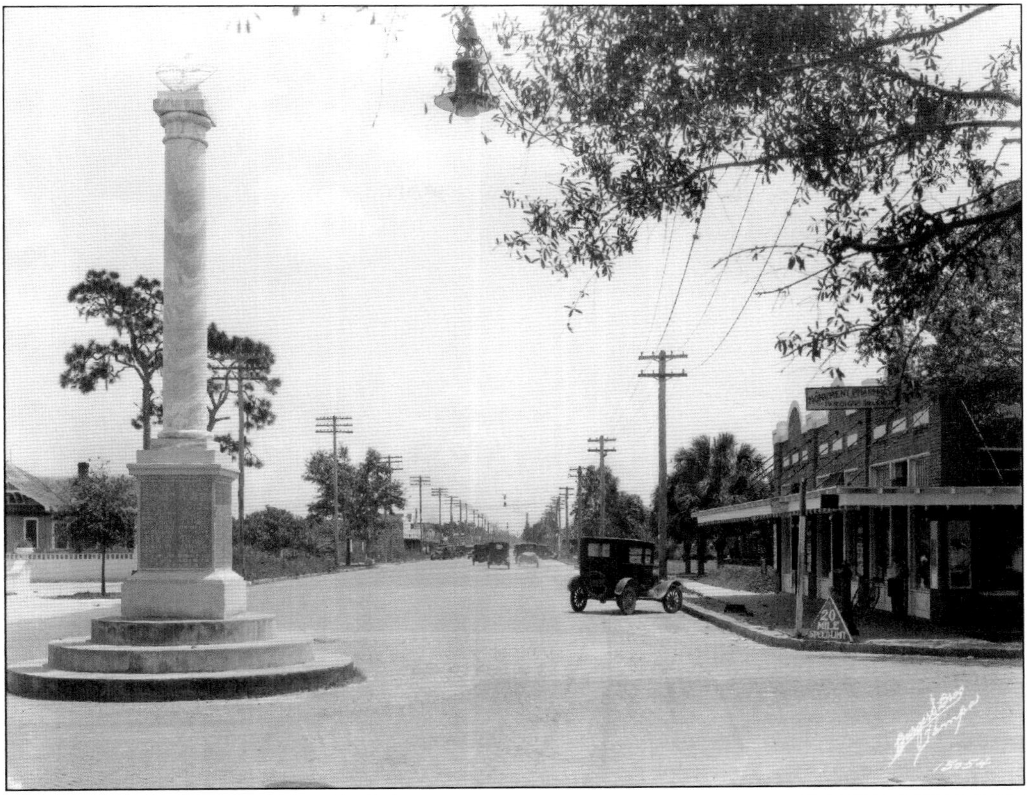

The World War I memorial included two identical statues—one located in Hyde Park at Grand Central Avenue (Kennedy Boulevard) at Howard Avenue and the other at the Pinellas County line at the city of Oldsmar. Both statues were created by August R. Fox, who immigrated to Tampa from Carrera, Italy. This photograph looks east toward Hyde Park.

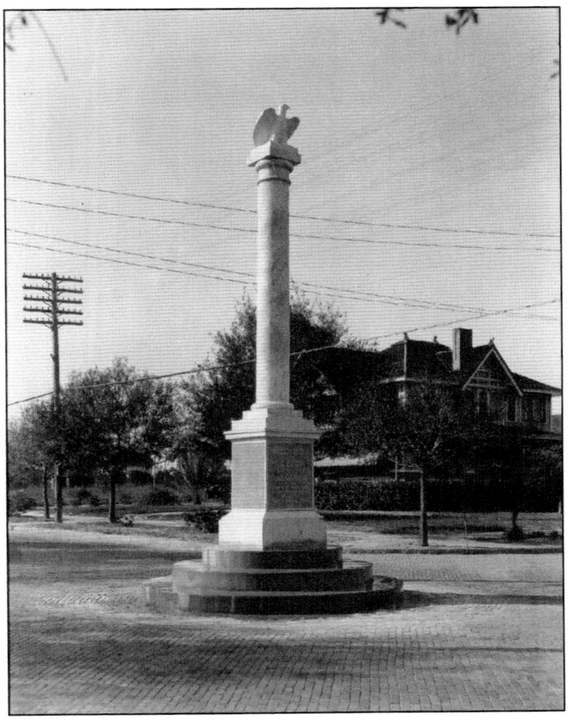

The two memorial statues were connected by Memorial Highway, a 13.5-mile, brick-paved road that linked Tampa to Oldsmar. Along the roadway, live oak trees, flowering oleander shrubs, and 12 memorial markers were placed. The memorial markers were inscribed with the names of the 106 Tampa and Hillsborough County citizens that lost their lives during the war. The two statues and 12 memorial markers have been relocated along Kennedy Boulevard, west of Hyde Park.

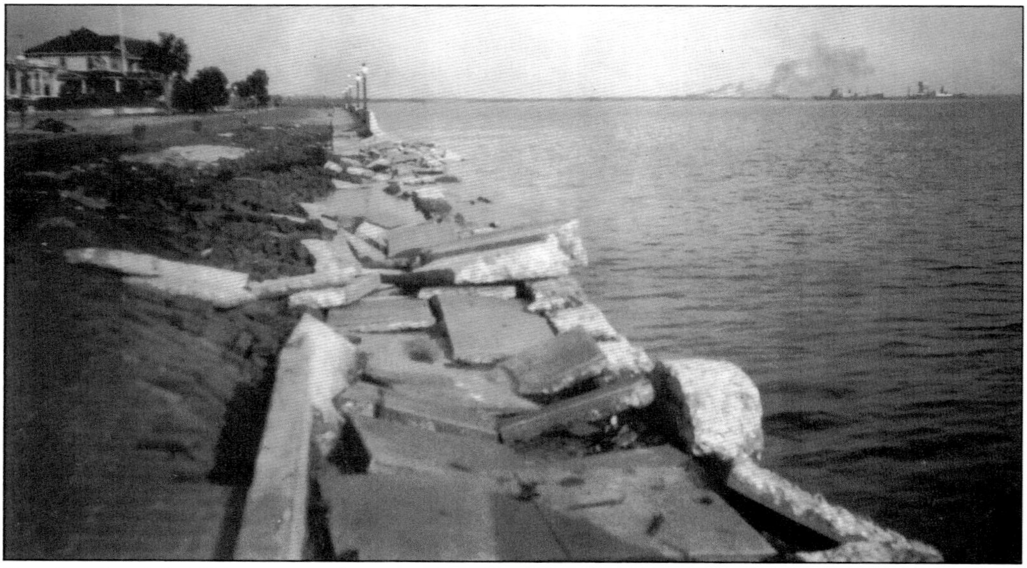

On October 25, 1921, a severe hurricane ravaged Bayshore Boulevard. Winds in excess of 100 miles per hour pounded the seawall, causing destruction and flooding of the low-lying areas of Hyde Park. The trolley cars and tracks that extended along Hillsborough Bay were extensively damaged, and several bay-front homes were destroyed. (Ferman family archives.)

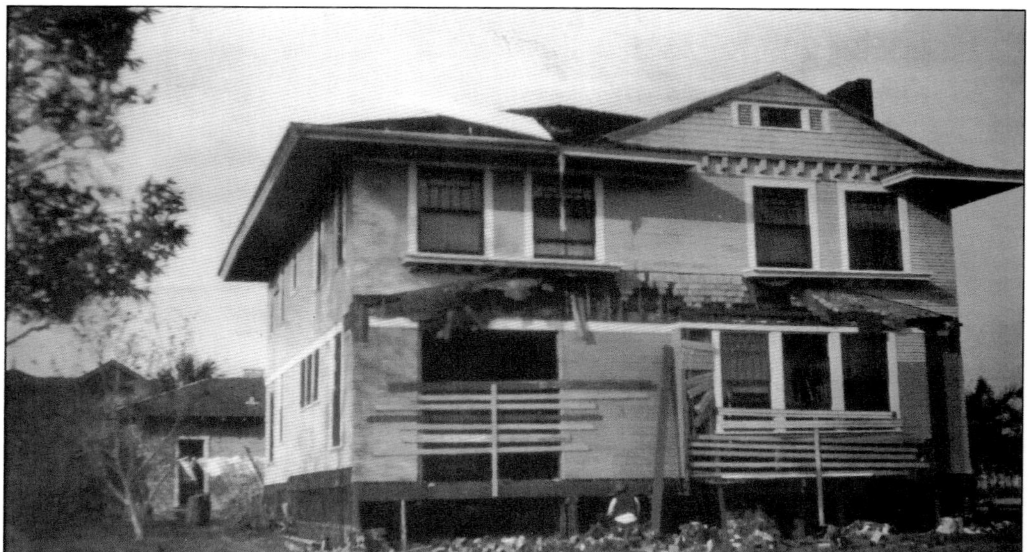

The 1921 hurricane dumped six inches of rain in a 24-hour period, causing widespread flooding. Many streets were flooded, and electric power was disrupted. The Bayshore Boulevard home in this photograph was severely damaged, as were neighboring buildings. Soon after the destructive storm, both this home and Bayshore Boulevard were rebuilt.

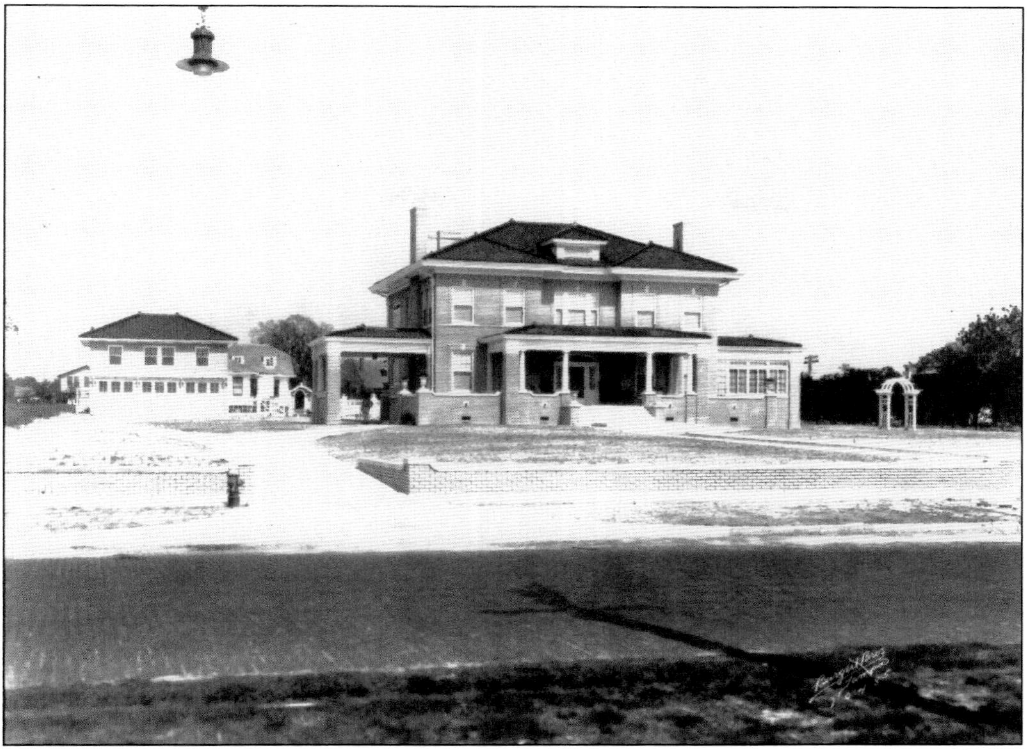

Fred Ferman, a prominent Tampa businessman, selected the site for his Bayshore Boulevard home immediately after the hurricane of 1921. He took a hard look at all the properties along Bayshore Boulevard after the severe storm and selected this parcel, which had remained high and dry. The home he shared with his wife, Bess, and their family, along with another home Ferman built behind the Bayshore Boulevard home, remain in the family. (Ferman family archives.)

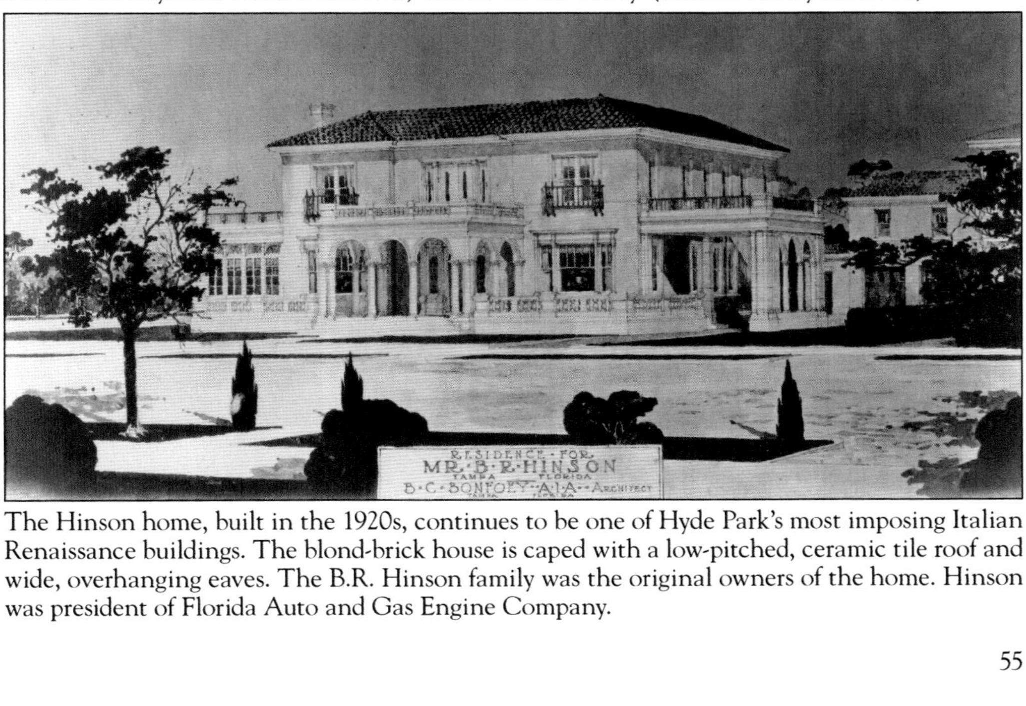

The Hinson home, built in the 1920s, continues to be one of Hyde Park's most imposing Italian Renaissance buildings. The blond-brick house is caped with a low-pitched, ceramic tile roof and wide, overhanging eaves. The B.R. Hinson family was the original owners of the home. Hinson was president of Florida Auto and Gas Engine Company.

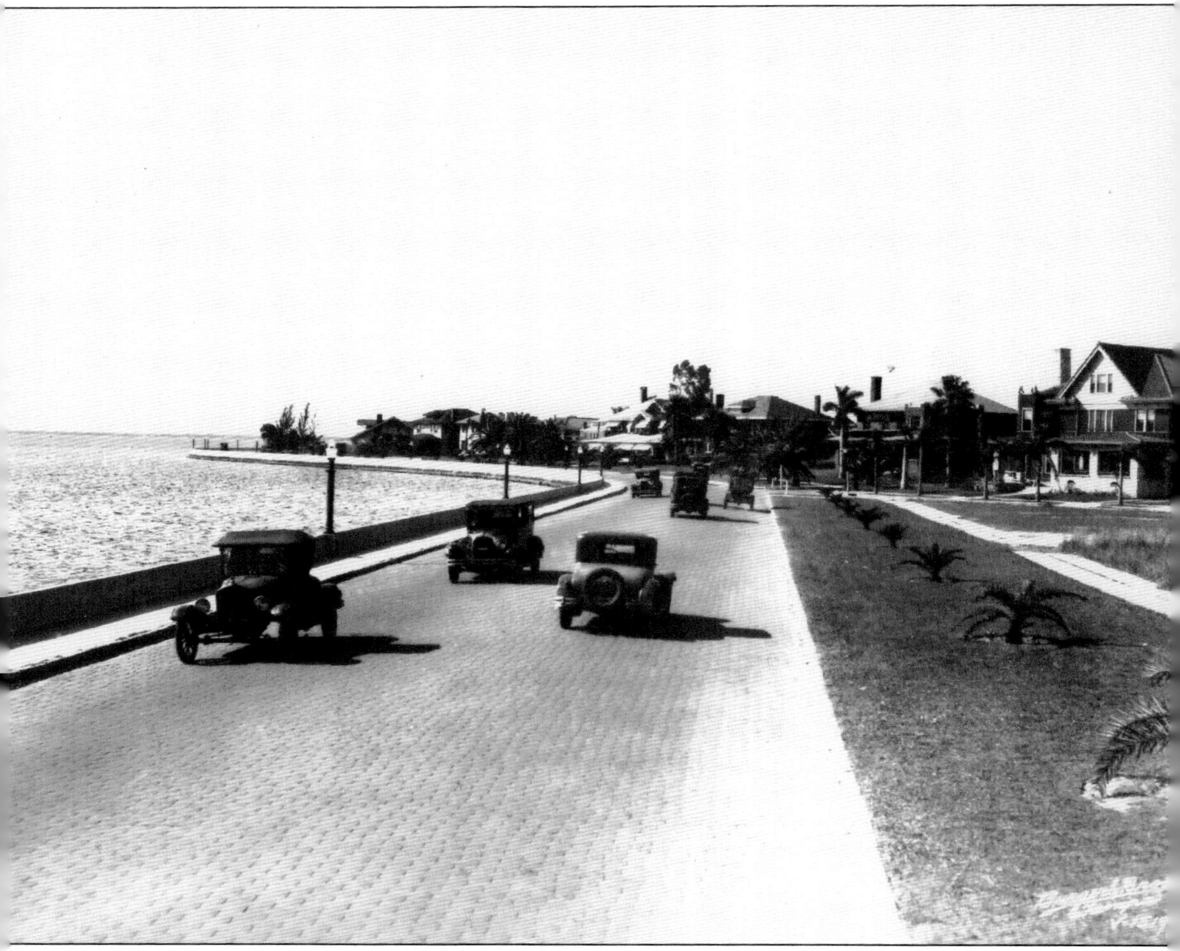

The completion of the section of Bayshore Boulevard from Swann Avenue to Rome Avenue made travel possible along Hillsborough Bay to Ballast Point, located at the southern end of the Interbay Peninsula. The scenic roadway is a testament to Hyde Park's early developers and their commitment to not build homes along Hillsborough Bay.

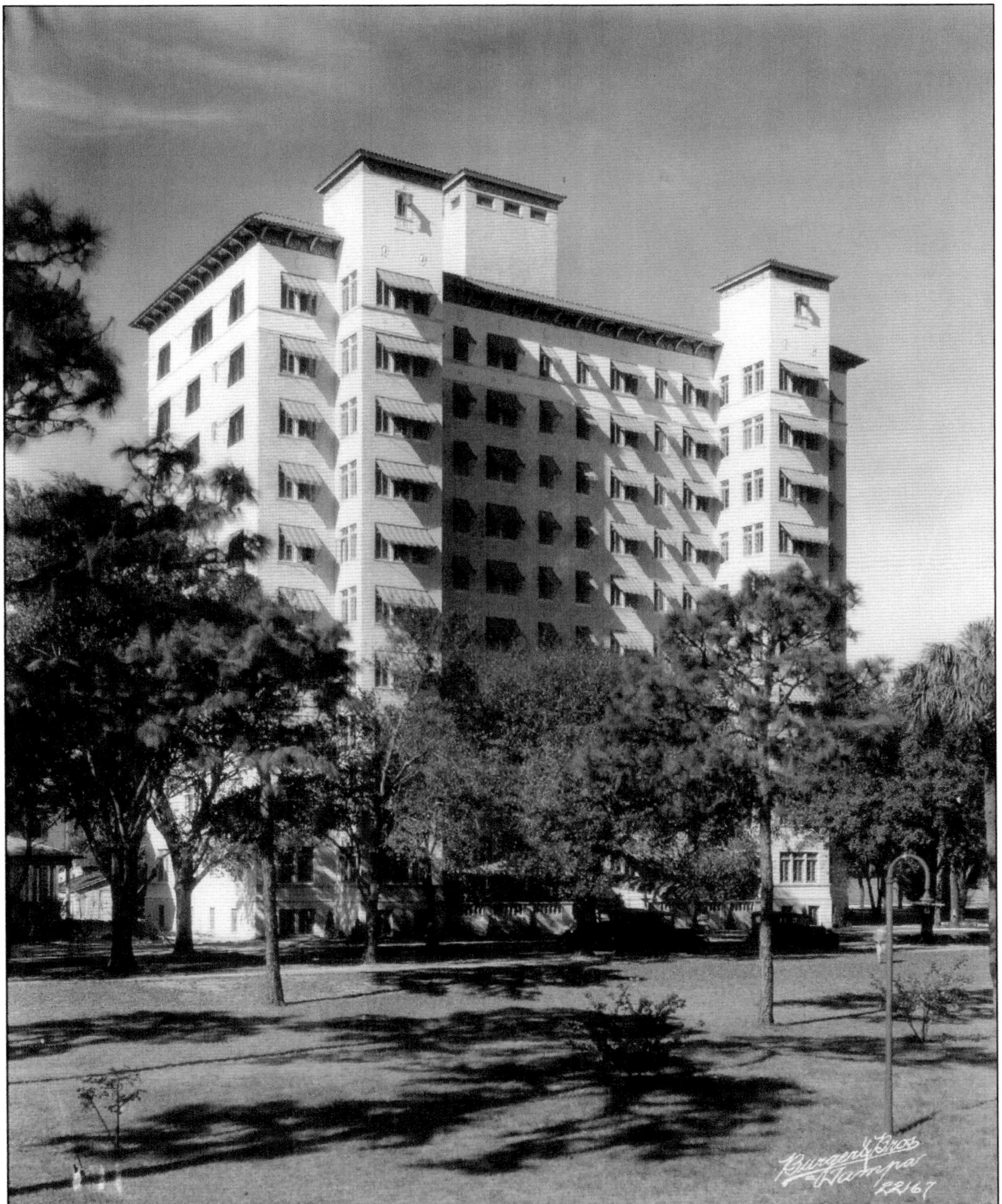

Multistory apartment buildings—or vertical housing, as this type of housing was called in Victorian jargon—began to appear in Hyde Park in the 1920s. The Myeyaron Apartments, later renamed the Embassy Apartments, were built on a section of the original Tampa Bay Hotel grounds. In Victorian-era Tampa, apartment living was not considered socially acceptable by the middle class. The social and cultural changes of the 20th century embraced luxury apartments for single people, senior citizens, and people seeking a second home that required minimal upkeep, and early apartments were often leased as fully furnished units. Several multistory apartment buildings were constructed in Hyde Park before the Depression. This building, which was demolished, served several generations of residents before it became housing for University of Tampa students.

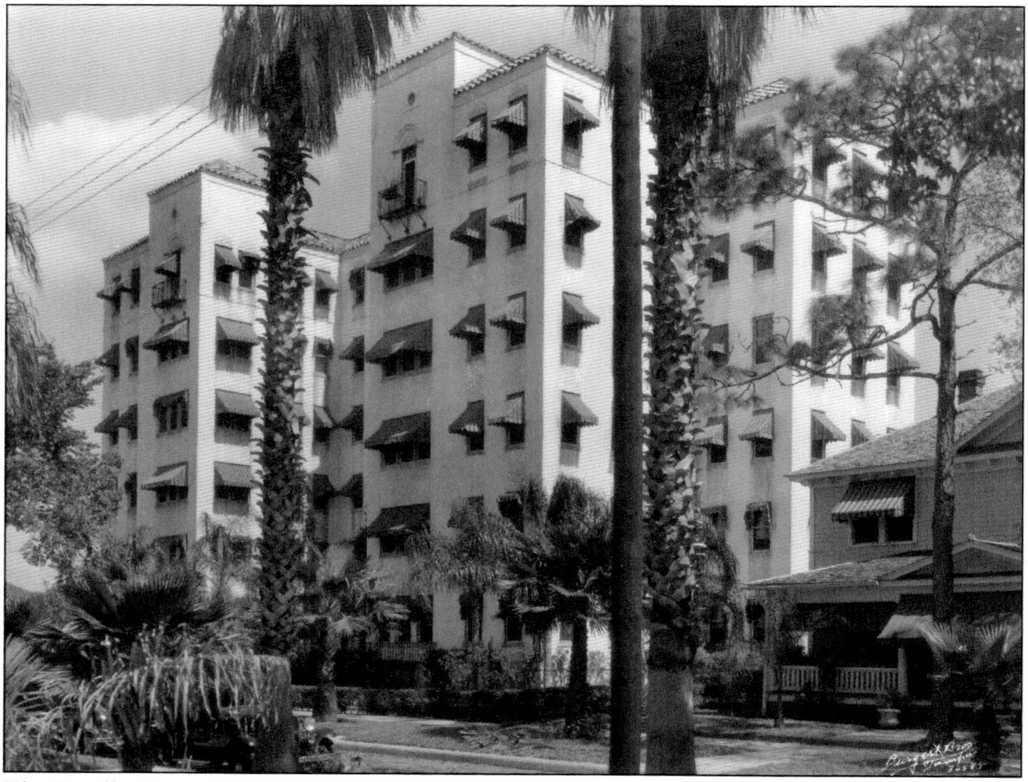

The Seville Apartment building was constructed during the mid-1920s. Two apartments were located on each floor with windows on all four elevations permitting cross ventilation similar to a detached home. The window awnings were common on the residential and commercial buildings of Hyde Park before air-conditioning became available.

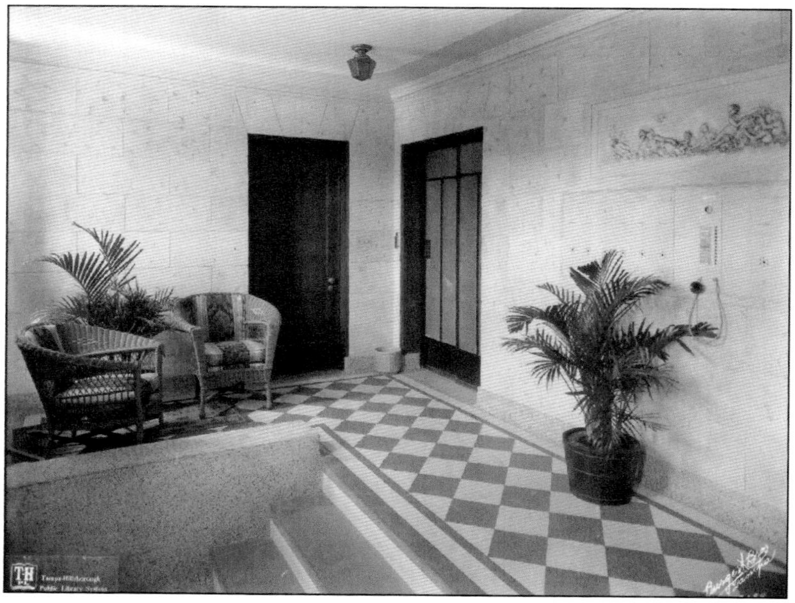

The lobby of the Seville Apartment building, the first residential condominium in Tampa, offered an interior space for neighbors to interact with one another and to welcome guests.

The floor plans of the Seville apartments were similar to those of the bungalows in the surrounding neighborhood. Each unit had separate front and back doors with separate elevator service. The fireplace shown here was a decorative detail and was not functional.

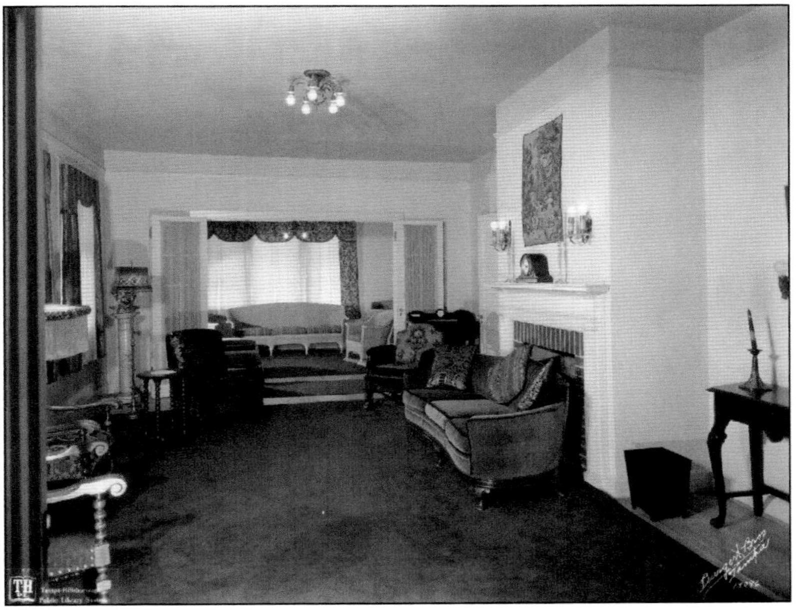

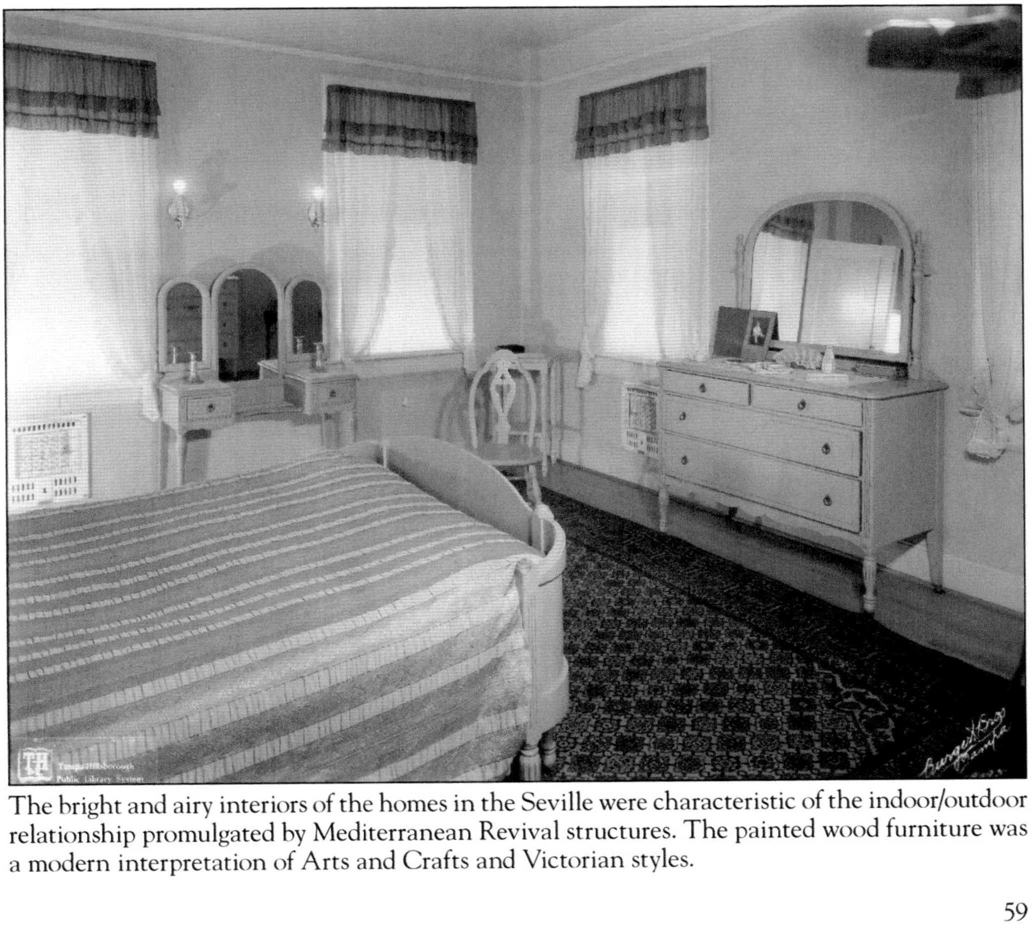

The bright and airy interiors of the homes in the Seville were characteristic of the indoor/outdoor relationship promulgated by Mediterranean Revival structures. The painted wood furniture was a modern interpretation of Arts and Crafts and Victorian styles.

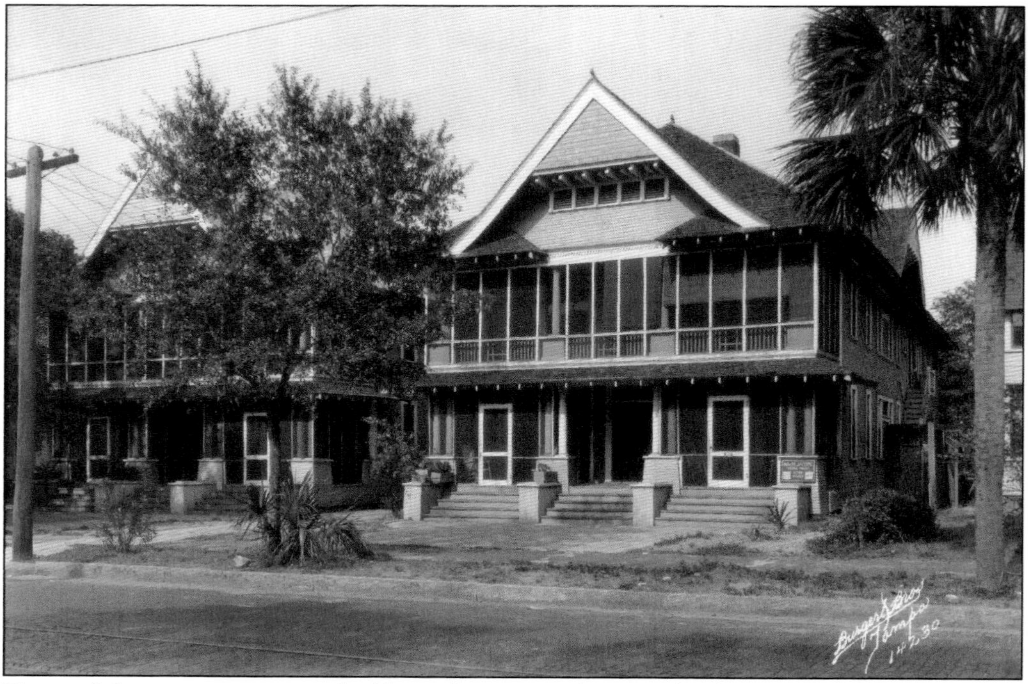

Two- and three-story apartment buildings, featuring architectural styles commonly associated with single-family homes, can be found throughout Hyde Park. These residential units were smaller and less luxurious than the mid-rise structures. Many of these were constructed alongside single-family homes, enabling population diversity that continues in the present day.

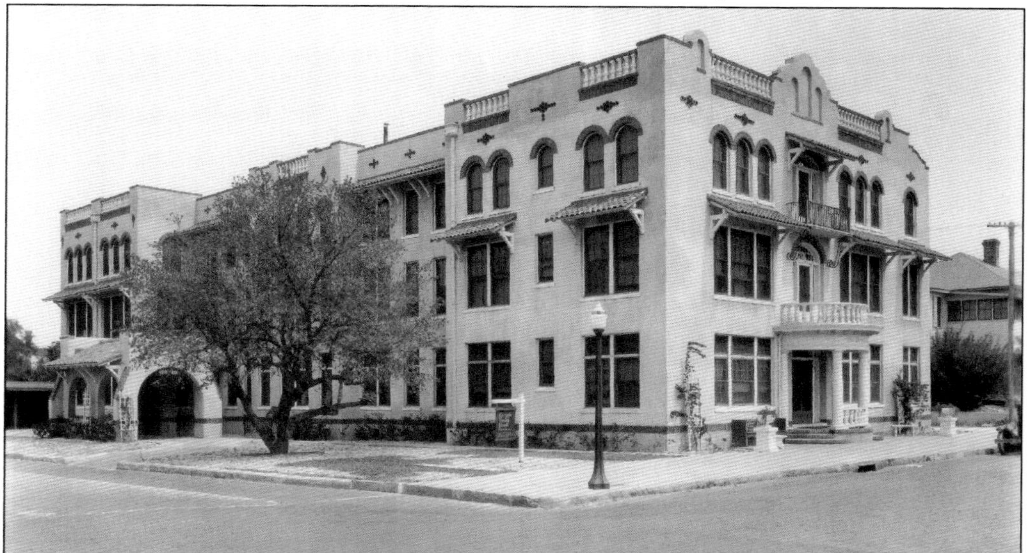

The 1920s also saw the development of small inns and hotels. The Carlyle Inn (later renamed the Edgewater Hotel) was known for its dining room and luxurious accommodations. The hotel closed several times during the Depression, enjoyed a renaissance during World War II, and closed for good in the late 1960s; the building was empty for several years. The exterior has been rehabilitated to its former appearance, and this is currently an office building.

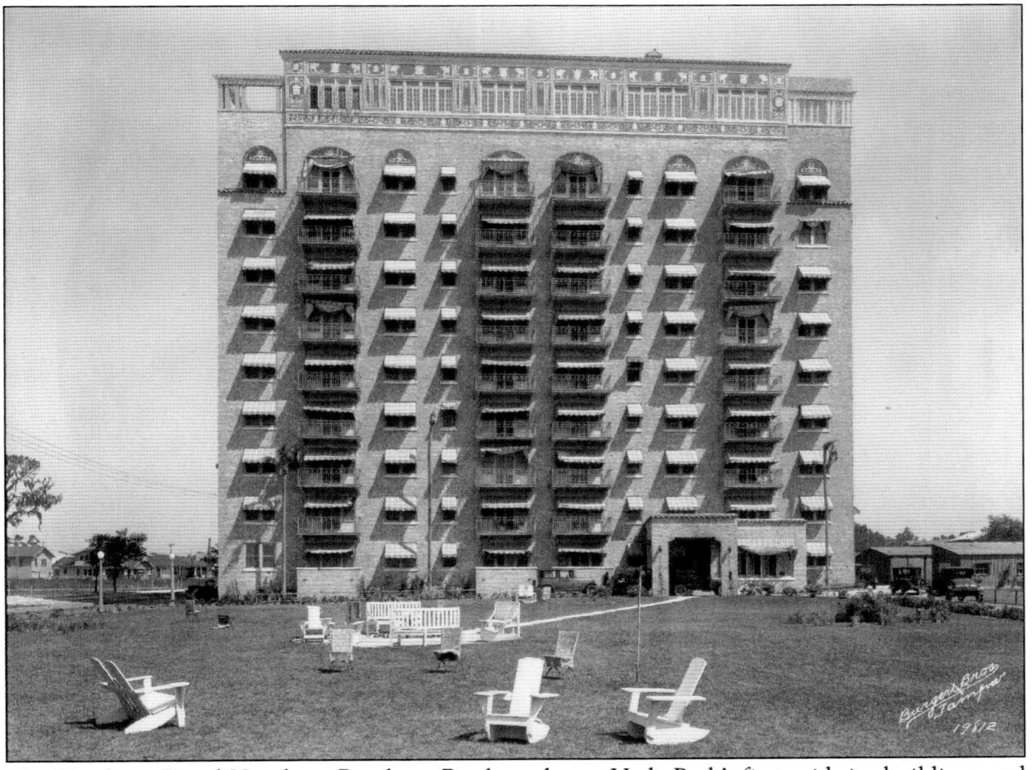

The Bayshore Royal Hotel, on Bayshore Boulevard, was Hyde Park's first mid-rise building, and it remained the area's tallest structure until the late 1990s. The hotel opened in 1924 and was one of several luxury hotels built in Tampa during the Florida land boom. Each guest room had a private balcony looking out on Hillsborough Bay or the peninsula, in addition to a variety of modern amenities. The top floor of the Bayshore Royal was an elegant and expansive ballroom with panoramic views of the Tampa peninsula. The building was converted to a residential condominium in the early 1980s.

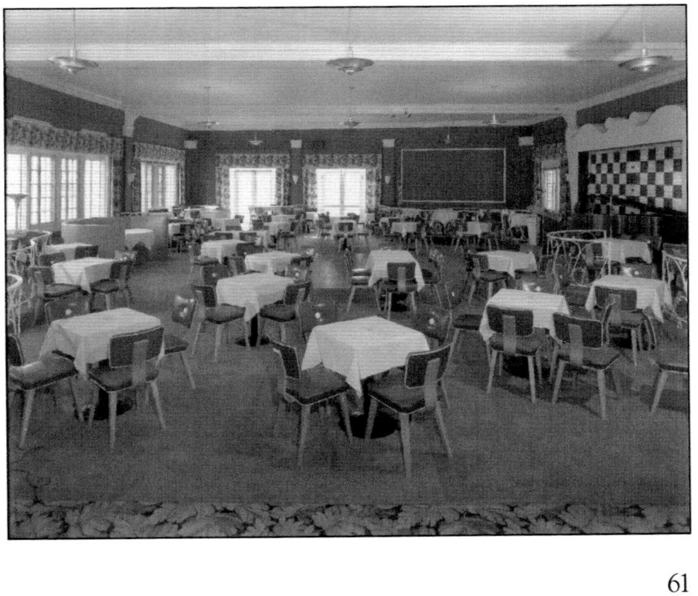

The Skyline Room on the top floor of the Bayshore Royal Hotel was a premier supper club that featured a wide variety of guest artists on a regular basis. The room provided unobstructed views of the Tampa Bay area and hosted many social and business events and activities. The room was divided into penthouses when the building was converted into a condominium.

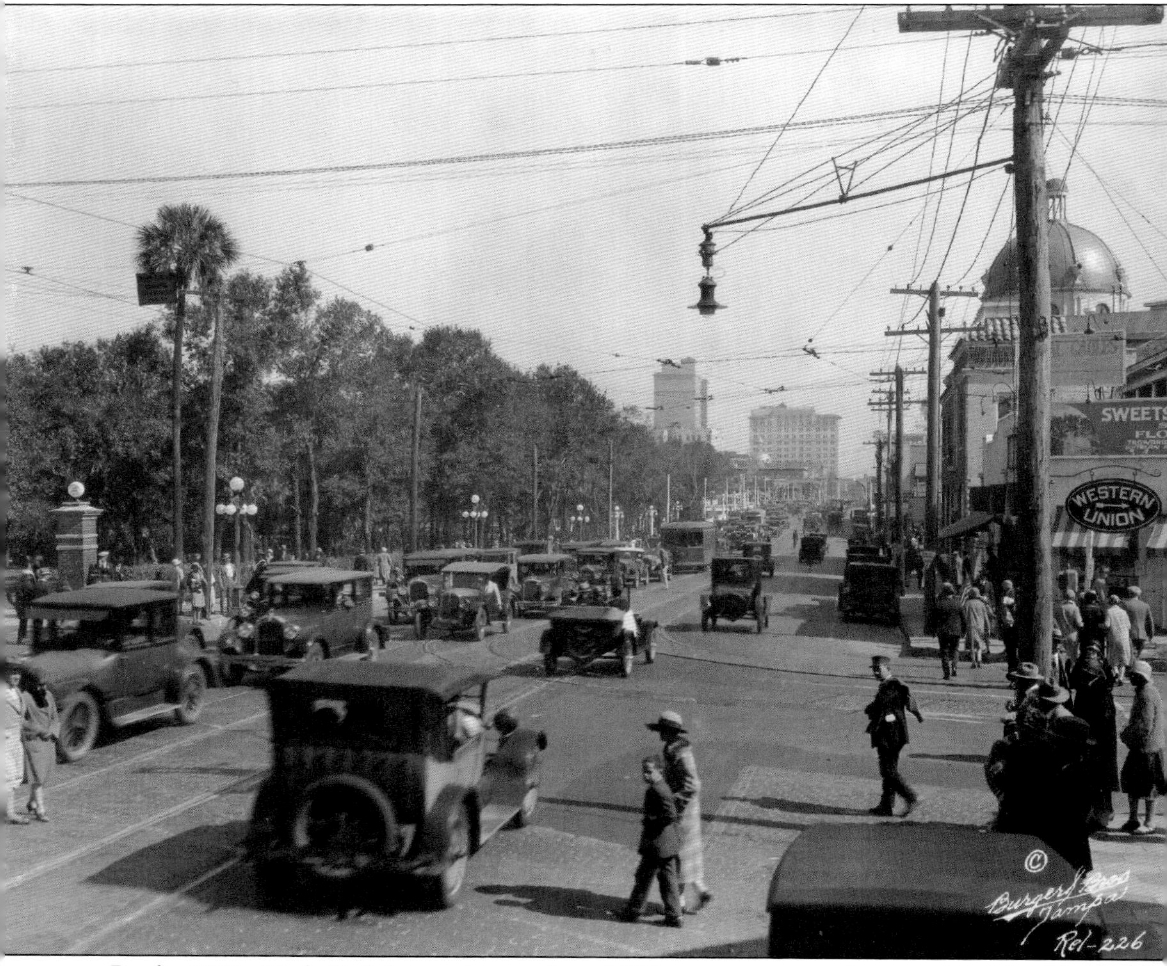

By the 1920s, Hyde Park boasted more than 1,200 guest rooms at places such as the splendid Tampa Bay Hotel, the Crescent, the Carlyle Inn, and the Bayshore Royal Hotel. This photograph was taken looking down Lafayette Street (Kennedy Boulevard) during the height of the tourist season in 1923. Pedestrians far outnumbered automobiles. Both tourists and residents could enjoy a wide variety of dining options in local restaurants, visit specialty retail shops, and attend live performances at the theater. The City of Tampa and local businesses provided recreational attractions and activities in Plant Park, including horseshoe and shuffleboard competitions, tennis courts, and concerts throughout the winter season.

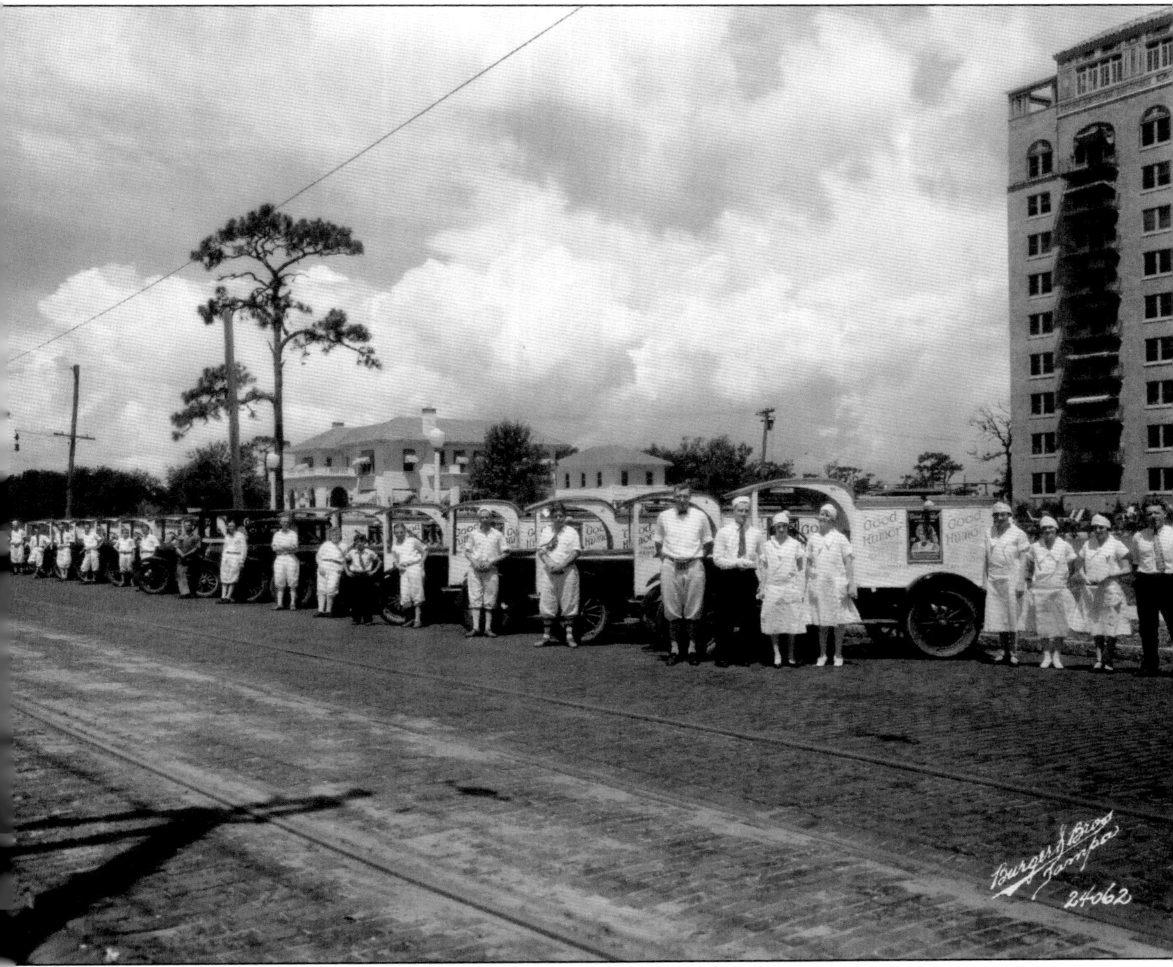

Good Humor ice-cream trucks lined up on Bayshore Boulevard, in front of the Bayshore Royal Hotel, for this 1920s promotional photograph. The Good Humor manufacturing plant was located several blocks away, adjacent to the railroad line, along Hyde Park's industrial corridor. Ice-cream trucks were especially popular before residential refrigeration could adequately ensure consistent freezing.

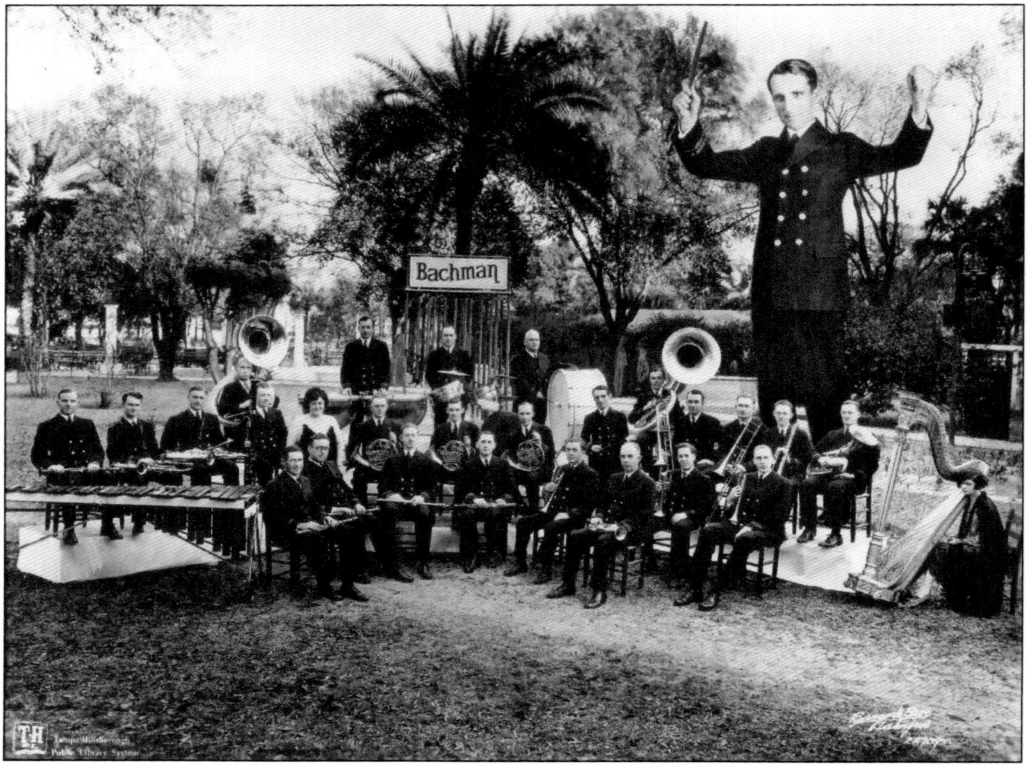

Plant Park was the location of numerous outdoor concerts and church services. Col. Harold Bachman and his "Million Dollar Band" traveled throughout the eastern United States performing in concert halls, at fairs, and outdoors in communities with suitable weather. Tourists and residents alike anticipated the band's frequent visits to Plant Park. Spectators were also frequently engaged in horseshoe, tennis, and shuffleboard competitions, as shown in the 1922 photograph below.

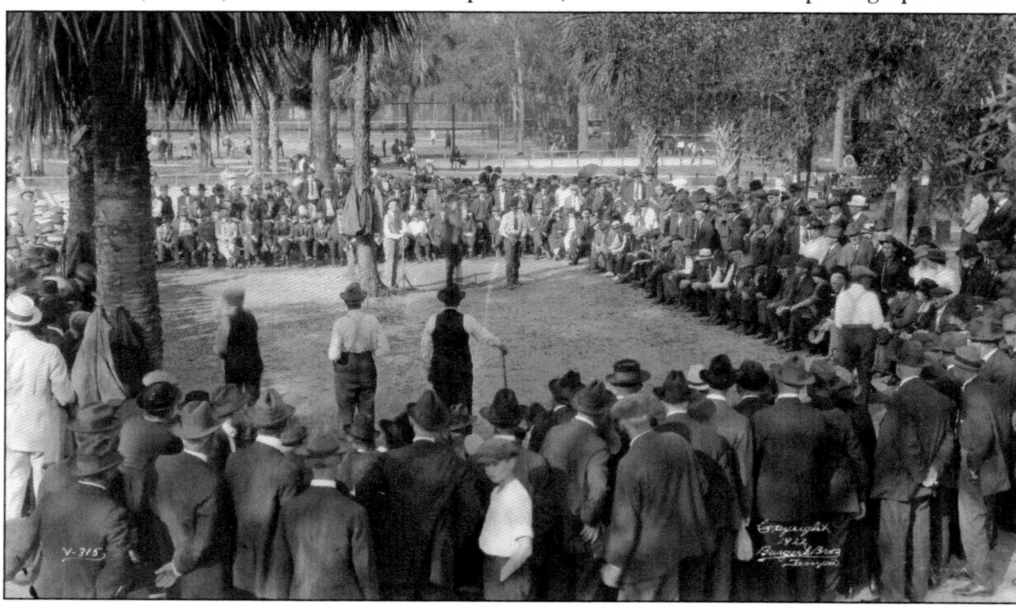

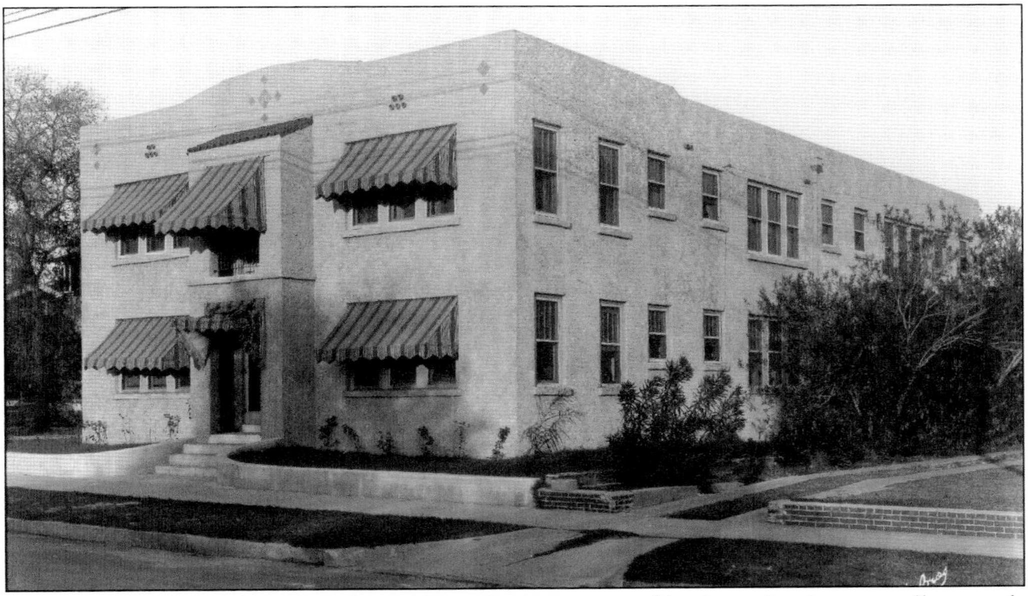

The desirability of Hyde Park in the 1920s resulted in increased land-use density on smaller parcels of land. The popularity of Mediterranean Revival buildings resulted in the construction of this two-story apartment structure on Rome Avenue. The building provided modest accommodations for young singles and retired individuals.

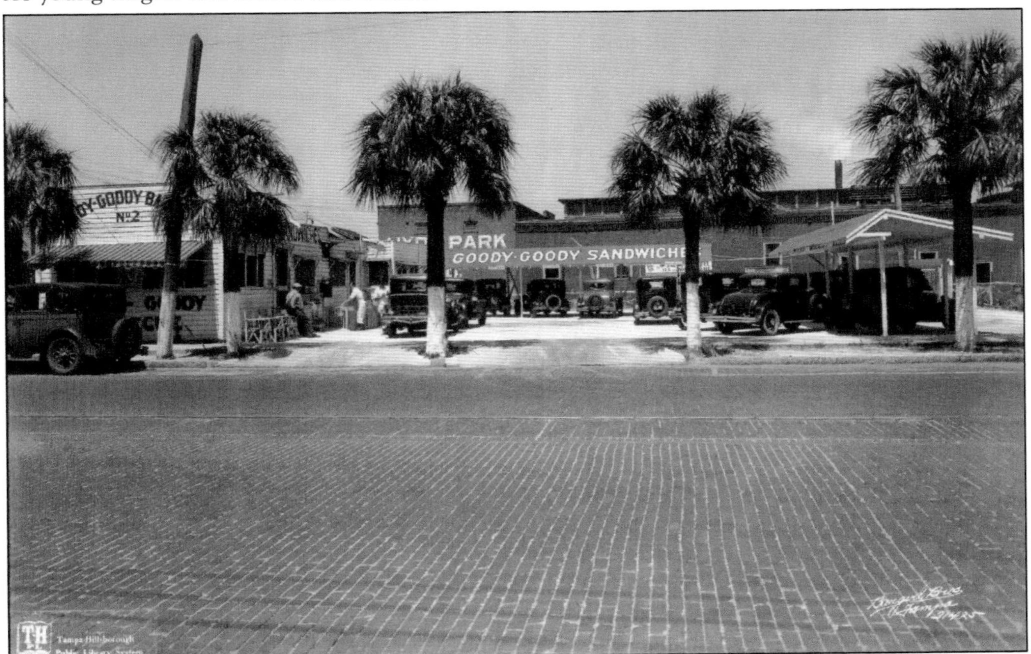

The Goody Goody opened in 1925 as a drive-in restaurant on Grand Central Avenue (Kennedy Boulevard). The restaurant's success triggered the opening of a second location north of downtown Tampa, on Florida Avenue, in 1929. The Hyde Park location closed during the Depression, but the larger and more modern Florida Avenue location was a Tampa landmark until it closed in 2005.

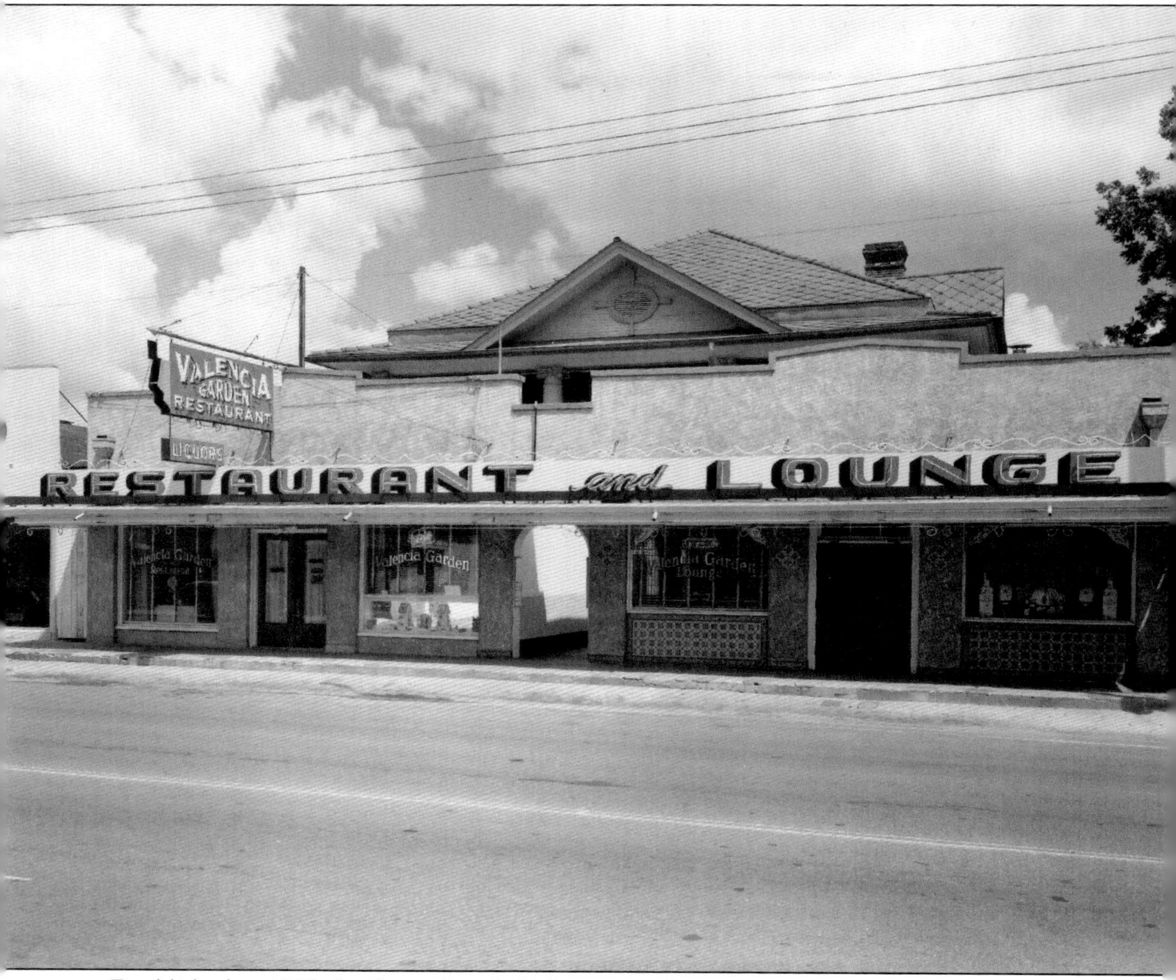

Established in 1927, the Spanish-style Valencia Garden restaurant was a popular destination for tourists and a lunching place for Tampa's political elite. Manuel Beiro, the restaurant's charismatic owner, was a Tampa institution. Beiro was the spokesperson for the restaurant and regularly appeared on local late-night television, ending his Friday evening commercials by raising a glass of wine and wishing the viewer "salud and happy days." The restaurant was closed in 2009, and the building has been demolished.

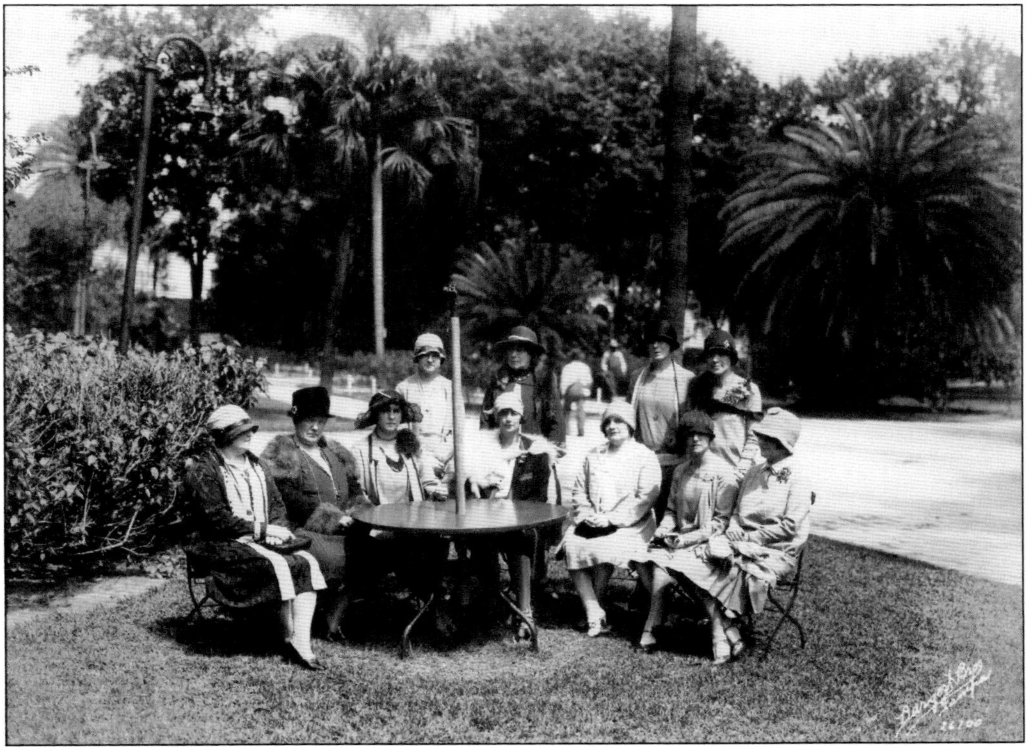

The east garden of the Tampa Bay Hotel—now known as Plant Park—always played an important role in the social and business communities. This March 20, 1928, photograph shows a group of prominent women entertaining Mrs. Don Alejandro Padilla (seated, second from right), wife of Spain's ambassador to the United States, and her daughter (standing, far right). The hosts were wives and daughters of cigar manufacturers who owned factories in the Ybor City and West Tampa sections of Tampa. (Tampa Bay History Center.)

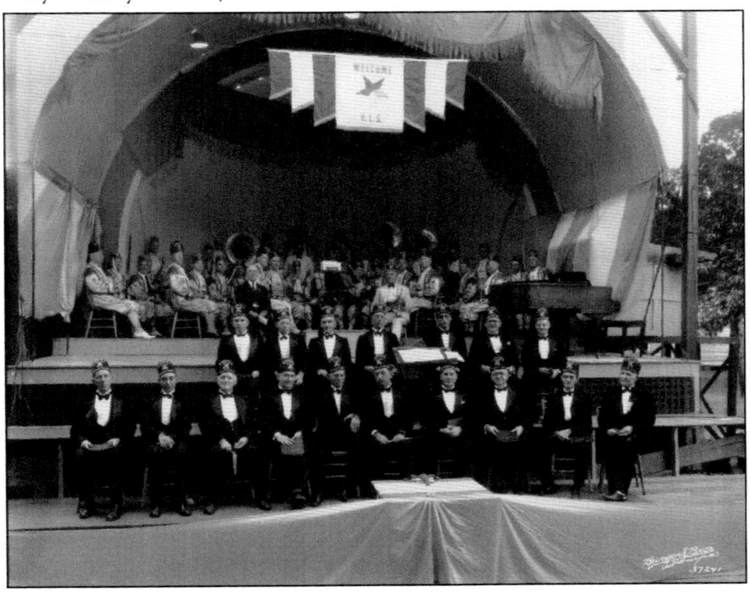

A band shell was erected in Plant Park to welcome special guests and to celebrate civic events. The Shrine Band of Egypt Temple is featured in this photograph from the 1920s.

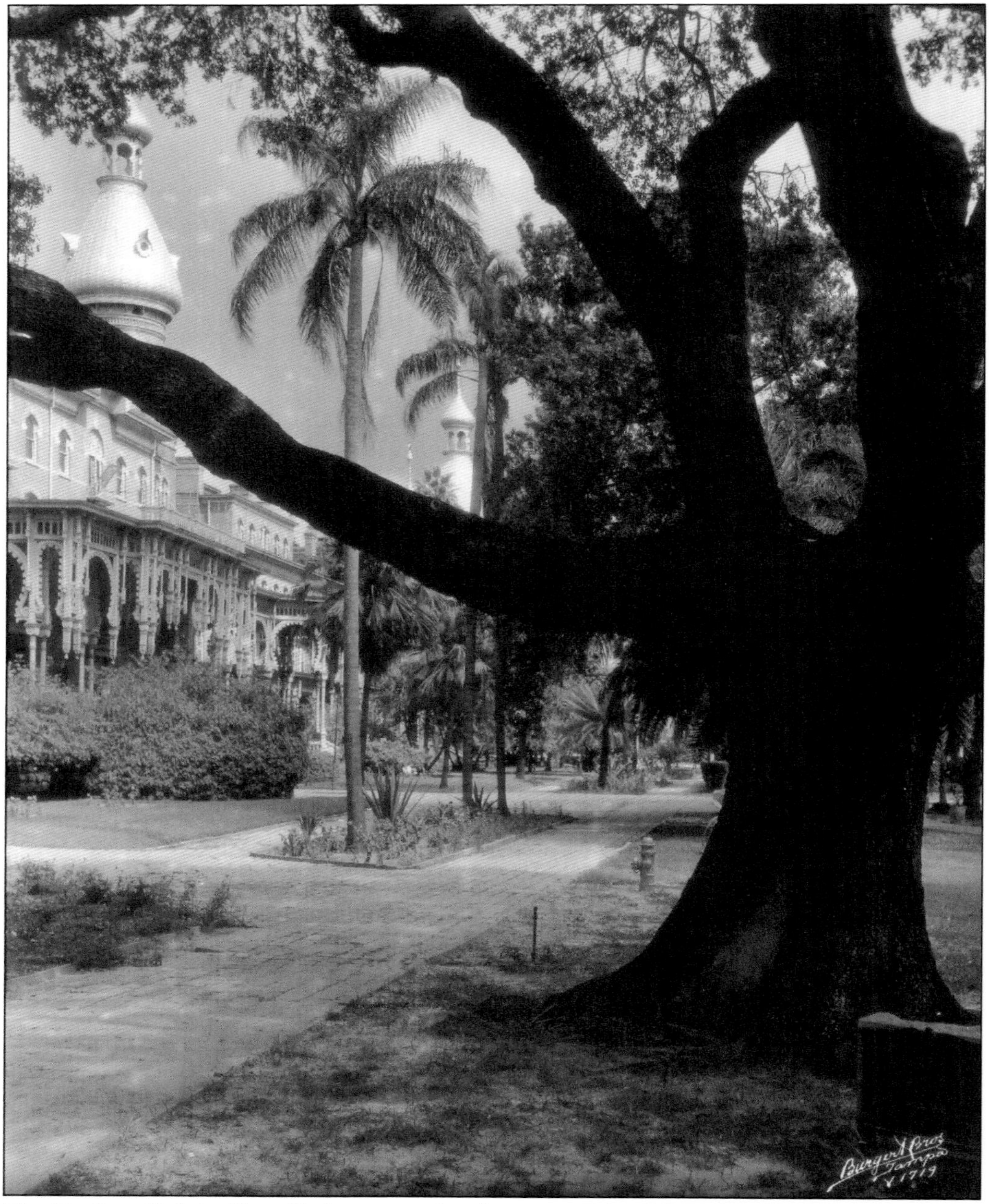

The De Soto Oak in Plant Park is steeped in history and local lore. In 1539, Spanish explorer and conquistador Hernando de Soto—leading one of the first European expeditions into the west coast of Florida with a flotilla of 9 ships, over 620 men, and 220 horses—came ashore in Tampa Bay. Soon after landing, he made his way into Hillsborough Bay and began his land travels northward, possibly from this site in Plant Park. Rumor has it that de Soto and his men met with local Native Americans at the site of the oak tree. In 1926, the local chapter of the Daughters of the American Revolution placed a tablet on the site to recognize de Soto's contribution to local history. Generations of teachers have stood under the towering tree to describe de Soto's exploration of Florida's west coast—and beyond—to inquisitive students.

Three

Schools, Houses of Worship, and Cultural Facilities

Community and public investment in Hyde Park in the first two decades of the 20th century reinforced the neighborhood's desirability as a place to visit and to live. The City of Tampa purchased Henry B. Plant's luxurious Tampa Bay Hotel in 1905, several years after Plant's death. The exotic hotel gardens became a municipal park, and the facilities in the Casino became available for community events. Public and social functions that define the present-day community emerged using the various facilities of the hotel. The annual Gasparilla festivities, the Florida State Fair, and Tampa's first museum and zoo all originated on the hotel's property.

Residential construction flourished, necessitating the opening and expansion of public and private schools. Innovative educational programs were launched at John B. Gorrie Elementary School—with their school lunch program the first in Florida—and Woodrow Wilson Junior High was one of the first schools to establish a safety patrol program in the United States. The public schools were complemented with private schools and adult vocational education. The University of Tampa found a permanent home in Hyde Park, and the University of South Florida was born in yet another historic Hyde Park building.

Several professional orchestras were established, including the forerunner of the Florida Orchestra. Venues for professional and amateur dance and theater found permanent homes in Hyde Park. The diverse community that settled here also established houses of worship and a variety of social clubs. Many of the cultural traditions that began in the early 20th century are still enjoyed in Hyde Park today.

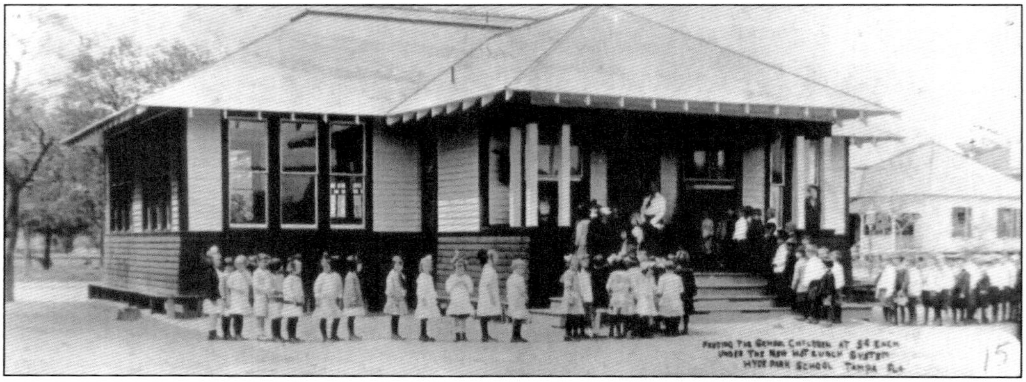

Hyde Park Grammar School (above) opened in September 1889 and is believed to be the oldest operating public elementary school in the state of Florida. The wood frame building opened with two classrooms and one teacher and was originally located on the corner of Platt Street and Magnolia Avenue—an area locals described as "a wilderness of rattlesnakes and cow pastures." The building was relocated at least twice. As the school grew, the original building became the lunchroom, offering the first hot lunch program in Florida. In 1921, the building was relocated to Swann Avenue and from 1922 to 1968 served as the Hyde Park Public Library. Since 1968, the building has been the Old Hyde Park Art Center, home of the Tampa Regional Artists. (Above, Gorrie School Archives.)

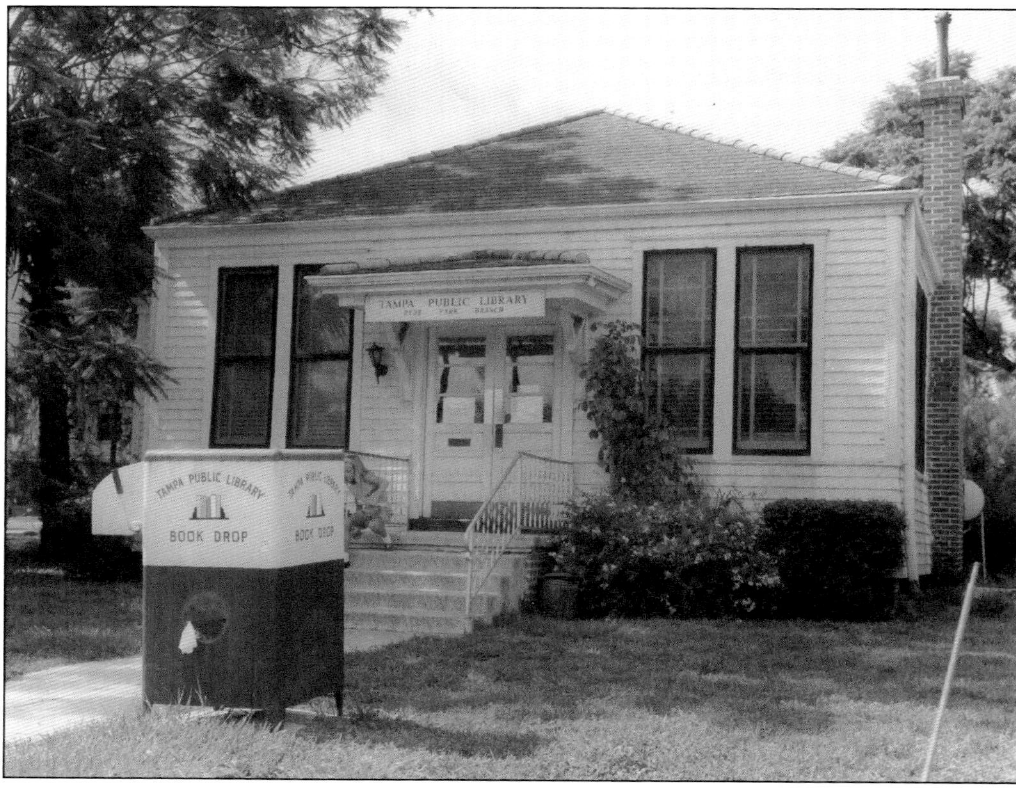

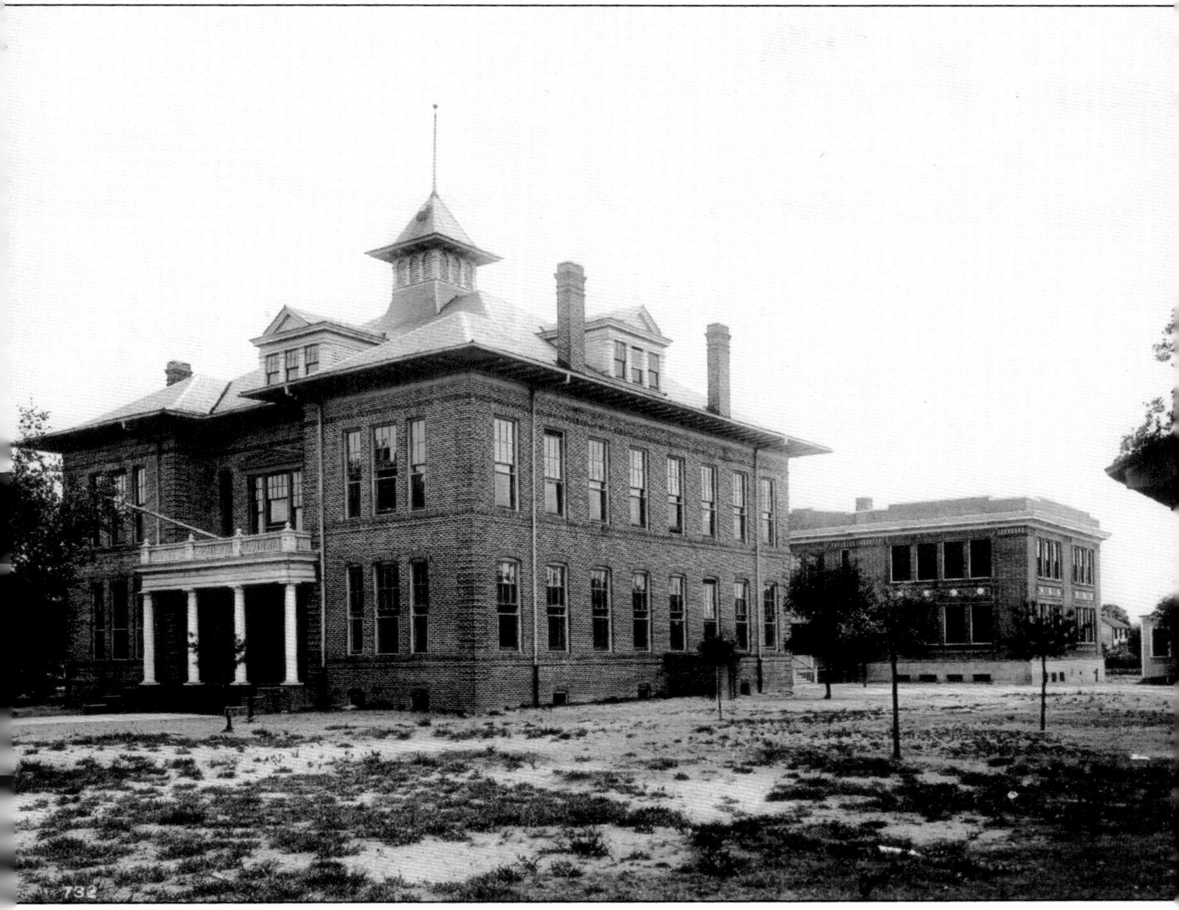

In 1903, Hyde Park Grammar School was relocated to a new brick building with eight classrooms (shown in the background at right). The first class had 240 students attend. In 1912, a second, larger brick building was constructed; it had a basement with indoor toilets as well as classroom fireplaces and cloakrooms. The school was renamed John B. Gorrie Elementary School in 1915 in honor of the Florida physician who invented the ice-making machine.

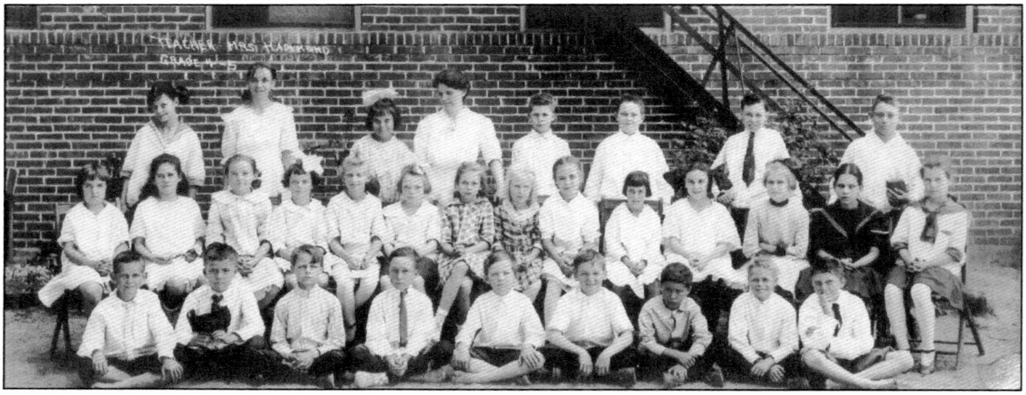

This 1916 photograph of Mrs. Hammond's fourth and fifth grade class was taken near the end of the school year. Each student was outfitted in their Sunday best, yet several of the boys came to school without shoes. When the weather was warm, it was not unusual for young children to attend school barefoot. (Gorrie School Archives.)

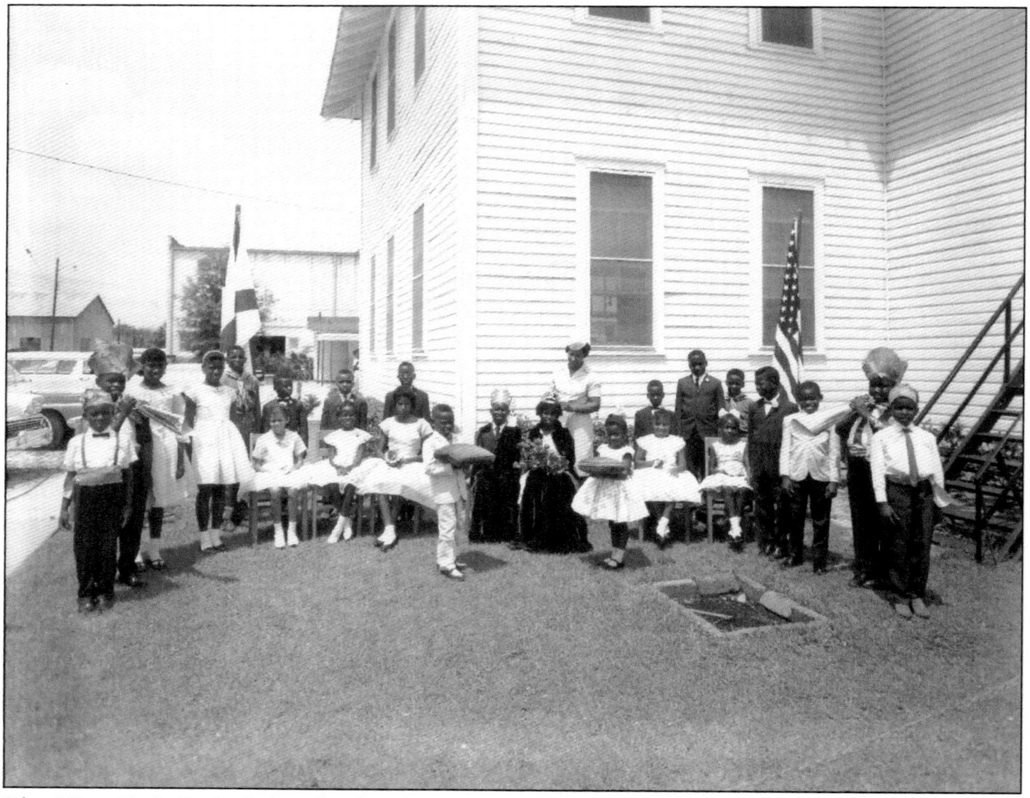

The West Hyde Park Colored School, established in 1910, was renamed for Richard Cornelius Doby, the civic leader who donated the land to the school board. Dobyville Elementary School was the core, along with several nearby churches, of Hyde Park's African American community. The spring coronation depicted in the photograph was an annual event that spanned several generations of students. The school was closed in 1996 and later razed.

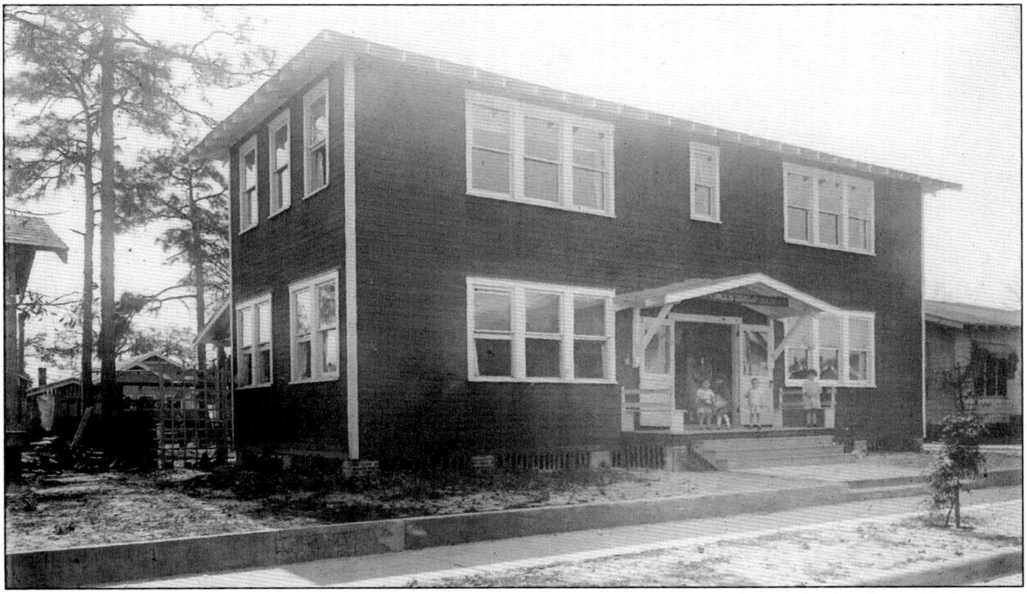

Helen Hill opened the Helen Hill Private School in 1913 as a nursery-through-third-grade facility. Originally located in a rented house next to Hill's Plant Avenue residence, the school soon served students in kindergarten through sixth grade. In 1925, the school relocated to this two-story building at 1908 Dekle Avenue, where it remained until it closed when Helen Hill retired in 1964. (Tampa Bay History Center.)

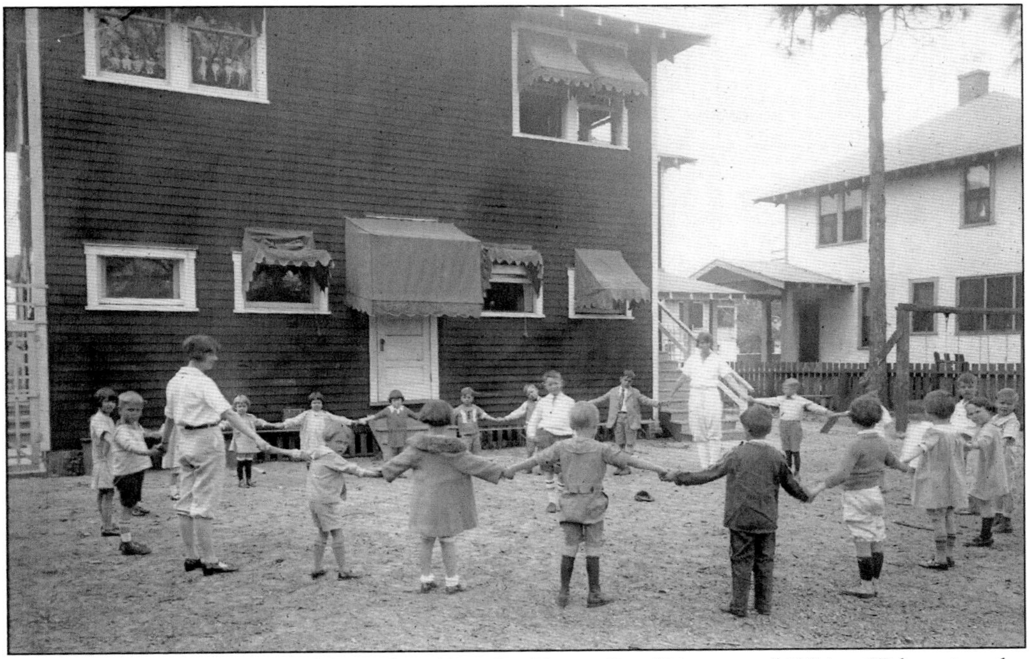

Helen Hill Private School publicized itself in the *Tampa City Directory* of 1934 as "Educating the child under ideal conditions." Individual instruction and art programs were also available at the school. When this photograph was taken behind the Dekle Avenue location, organized outdoor recreational activities were a new concept in education. (Tampa Bay History Center.)

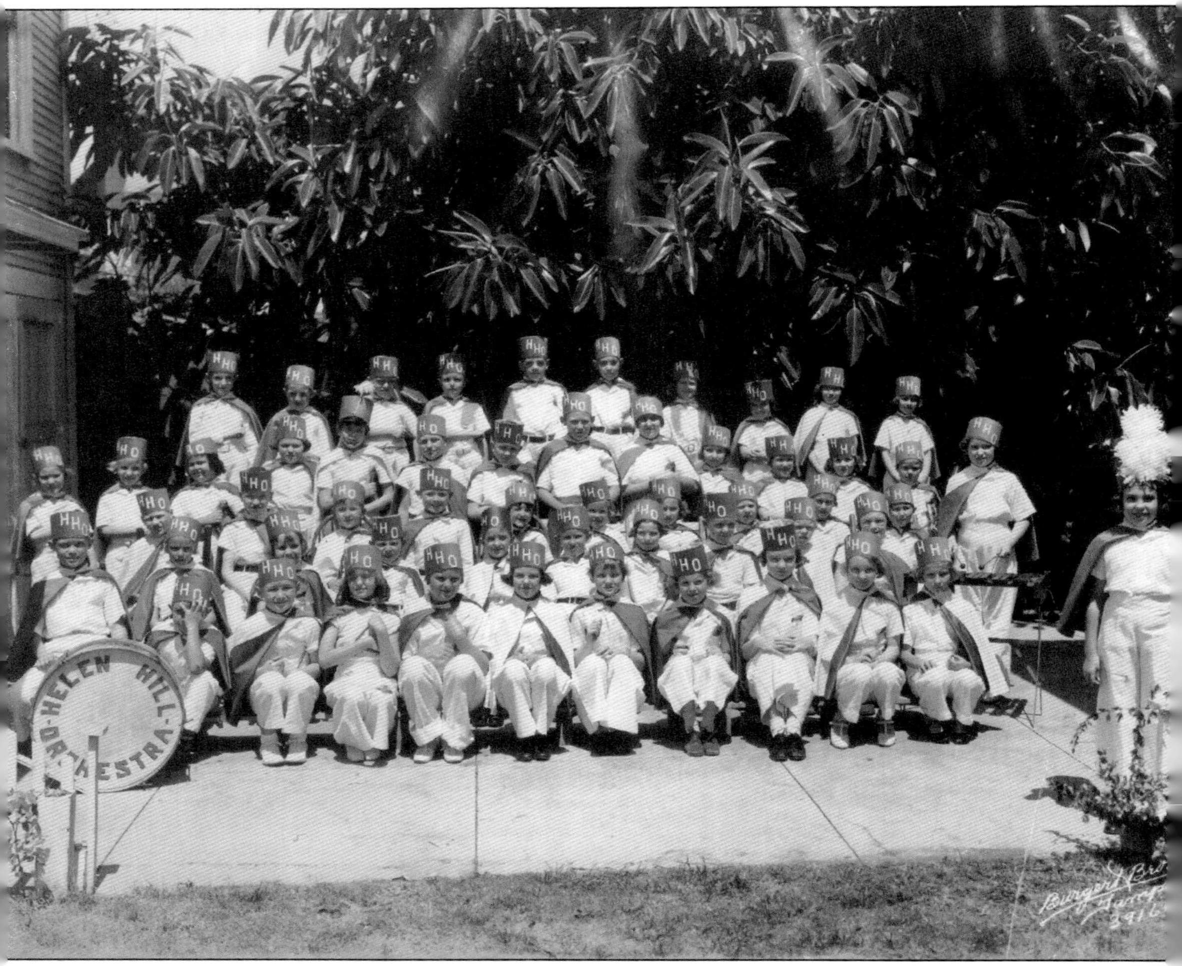

The arts were an important part of instruction at the Helen Hill Private School. In addition to the school orchestra shown here, the school regularly held plays, ballet recitals, dance presentations, and piano concerts. Each student in the school appeared at least once during each school year in a school production. (Tampa Bay History Center.)

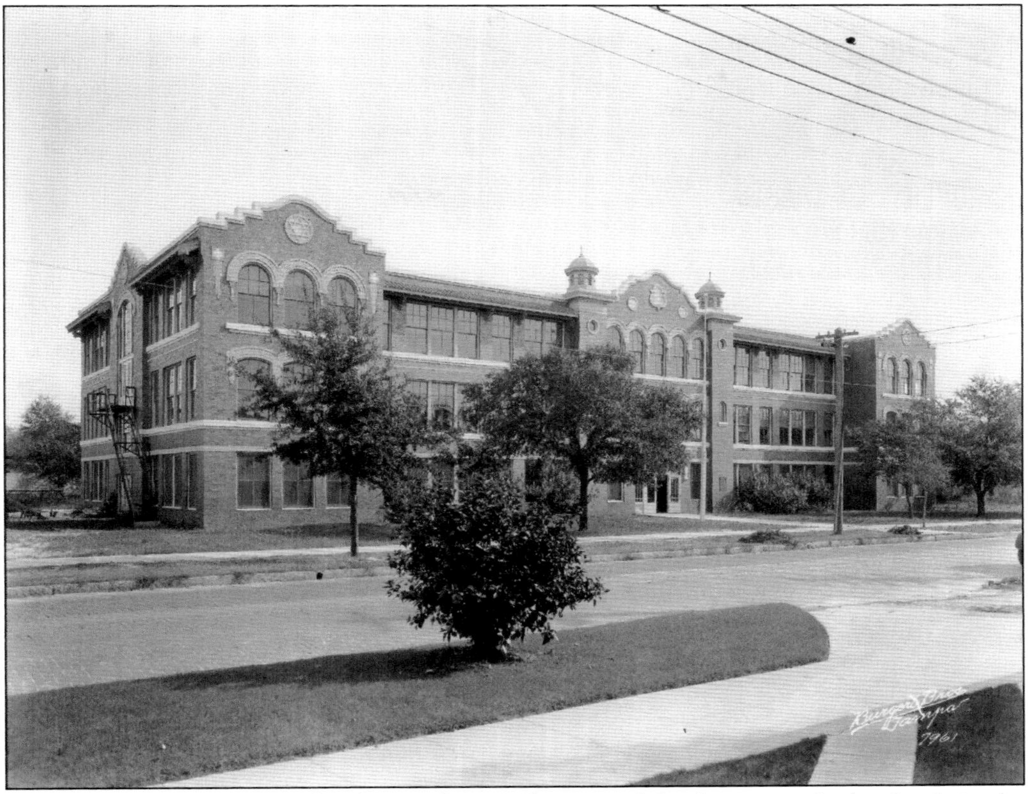

Woodrow Wilson Middle School opened in 1915 as one of the first junior high schools in the United States. Serving grades seven through nine was a major event; before the advent of junior high schools, students typically attended grades one through eight at an elementary school and went to high school starting in the ninth grade.

Pauline Busch began her career at Woodrow Wilson Middle School in 1918 as a teacher and retired as the school principal in 1960. She was responsible for starting the country's first student safety school patrol program in 1918, after several students were injured in an automobile accident in front of the school. (Wilson School Archives.)

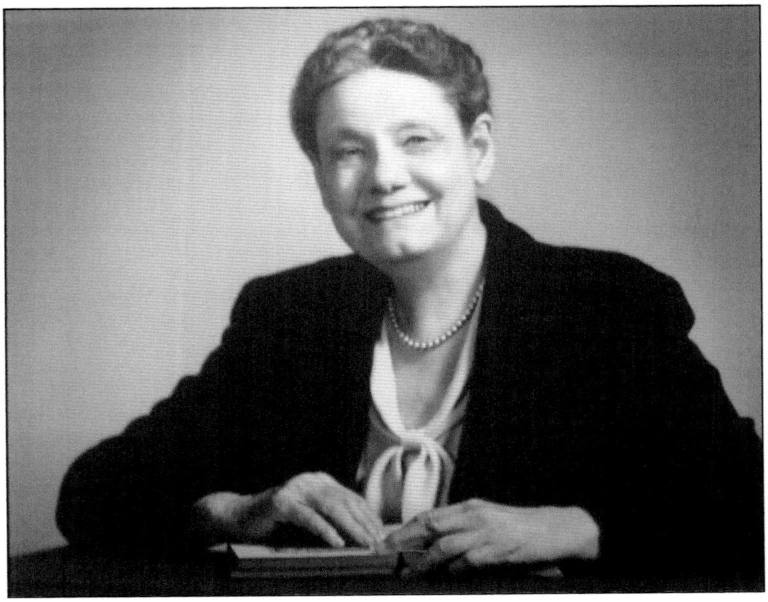

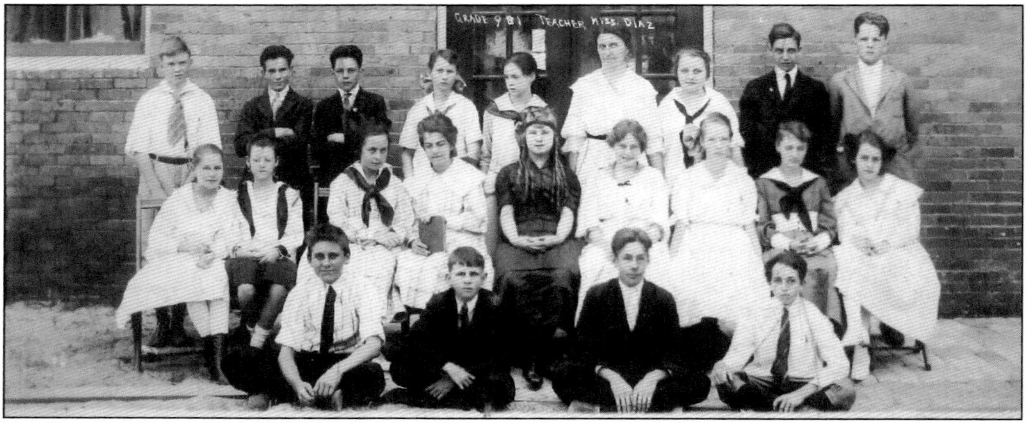

Miss Diaz's class was one of the three ninth-grade classes that graduated from Woodrow Wilson Middle School in 1922. Students who continued their education at a public school would have attended Hillsborough County High School, located north of downtown Tampa. It was not until 1926, when Henry B. Plant High School opened, that students in Hyde Park could attend elementary, middle, and high school west of the Hillsborough River. (Wilson School Archives.)

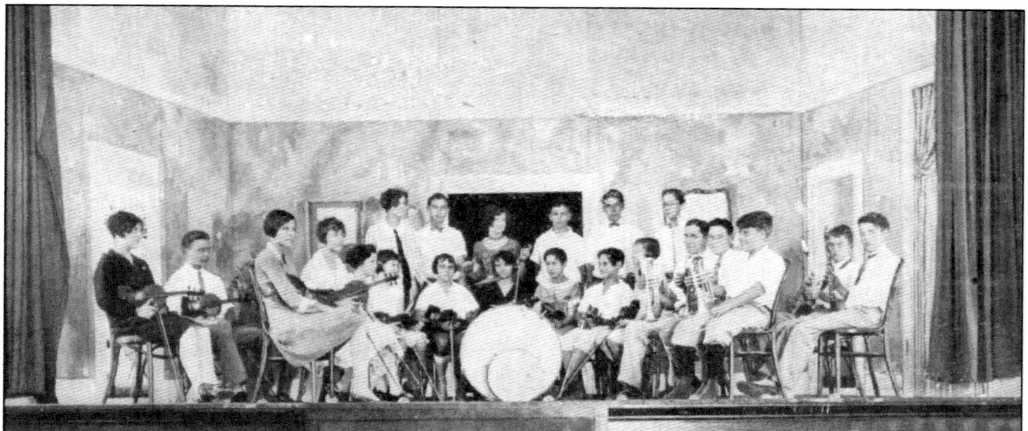

The Woodrow Wilson Middle School Orchestra was an important part of the cultural life of Hyde Park. This 1927 photograph was taken prior to an evening recital in the school auditorium. When the orchestra performed, it was common for every seat in the auditorium to be occupied. The orchestra also performed at community events throughout Tampa. (Wilson School Archives.)

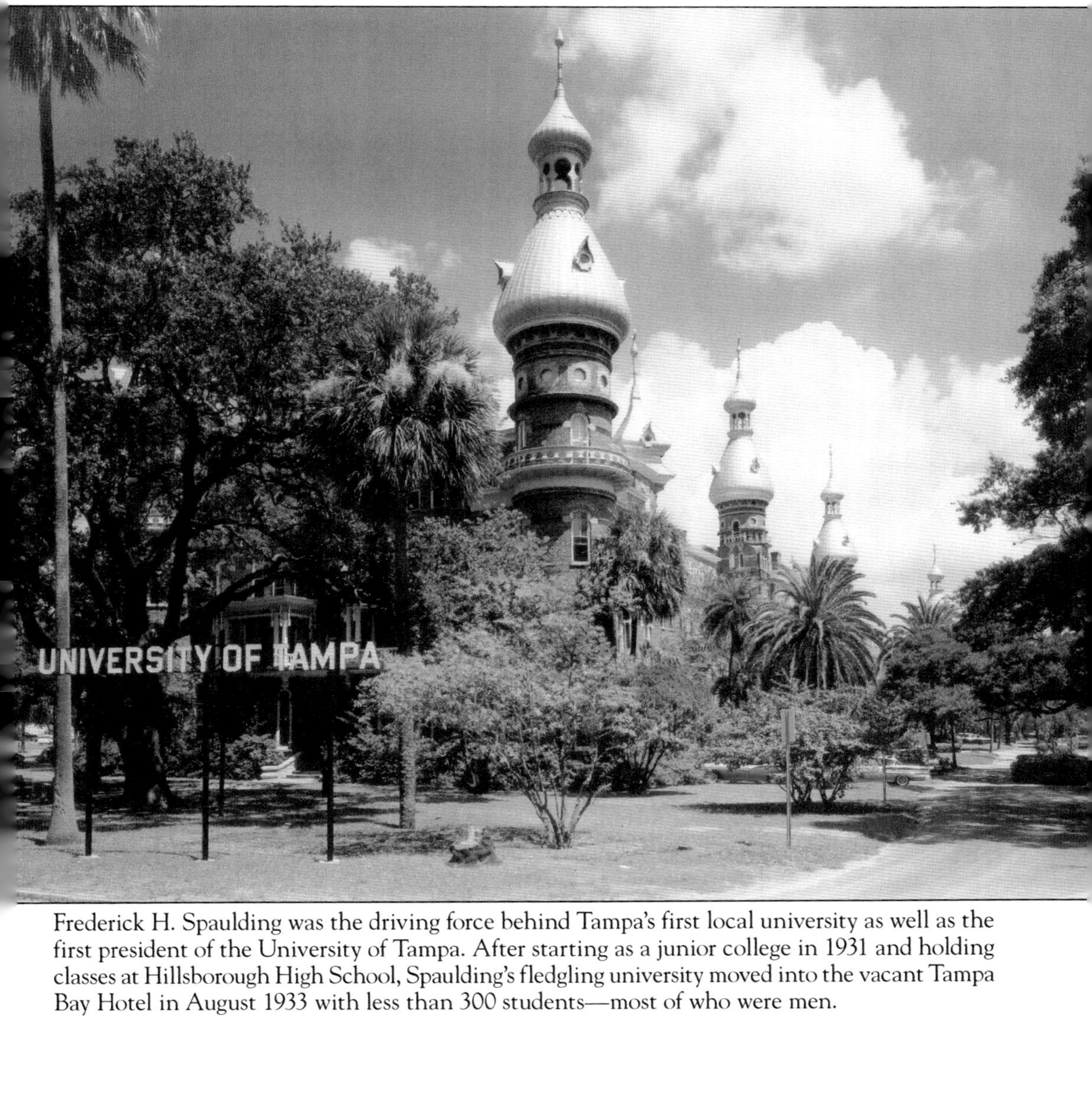

Frederick H. Spaulding was the driving force behind Tampa's first local university as well as the first president of the University of Tampa. After starting as a junior college in 1931 and holding classes at Hillsborough High School, Spaulding's fledgling university moved into the vacant Tampa Bay Hotel in August 1933 with less than 300 students—most of who were men.

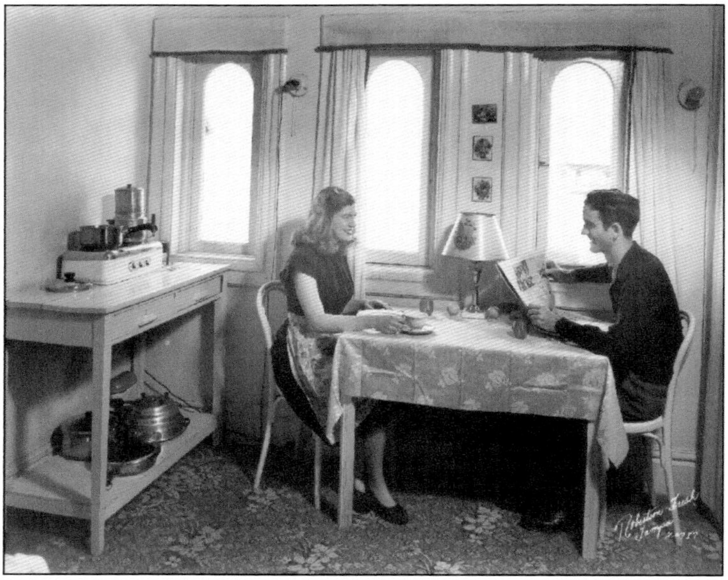

For many years, Henry B. Plant's opulent hotel provided the University of Tampa with classroom space, faculty offices, and student accommodations. Dormitory rooms were provided for single students, and efficiency apartments, like this one, were provided for married students. (University of Tampa, Macdonald-Kelce Library, Special Collection.)

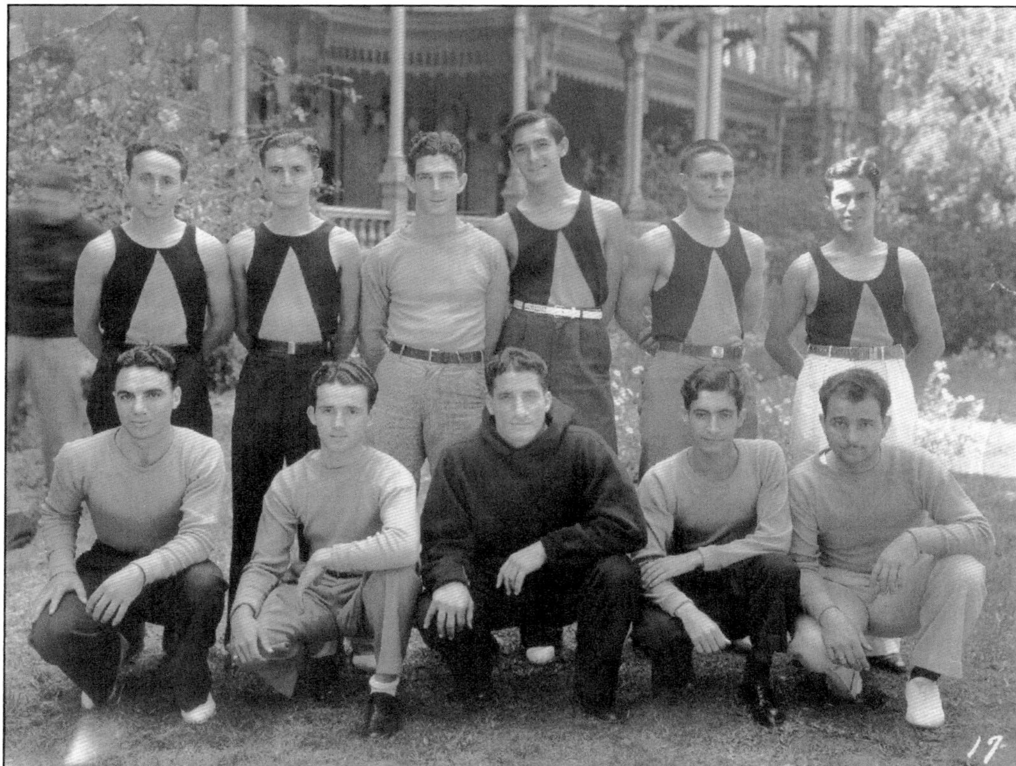

Intramural campus activities were an integral part of the University of Tampa from its inception. The Rho Nu Delta intramural sports team of June 1936 included, from left to right, (first row) Americus Spoto, Hugo Bonano, Bob Tramontana, Oswald Delgado, and J.R.S. Coniglio; (second row) Adolf Ramirez, Benigno Miyares, Ed Plumber, Aurelio Prado, Charles Sierra, and Manuel Ramirez. (University of Tampa, Macdonald-Kelce Library, Special Collection.)

Intercollegiate football was a popular part of the new university when classes began in the fall of 1933. The football program slowly developed during the early years and was interrupted during World War II. Games resumed in 1948 and continued with reputable seasons until 1974, when the university withdrew from intercollegiate football.

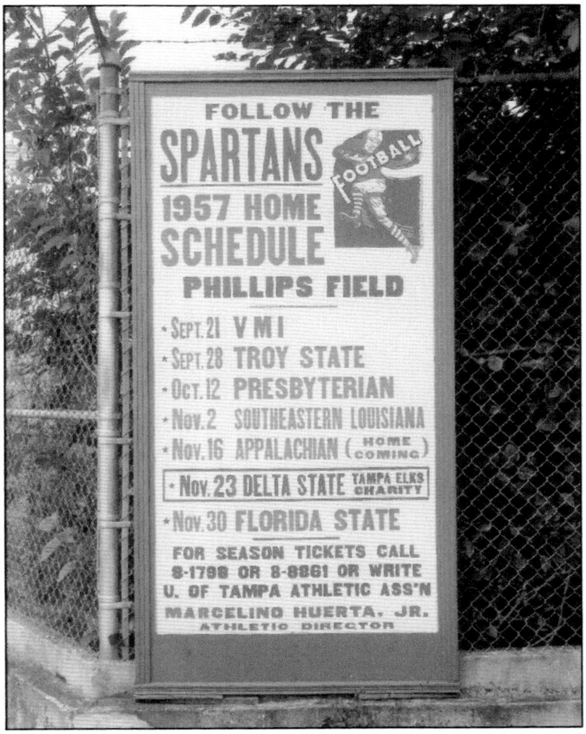

During World War II, the University of Tampa contracted with the federal government to provide Army Air Corps aviation cadets with classes to obtain a basic education degree. The 18th College Training Detachment is shown in this photograph from July 8, 1943. (University of Tampa, Macdonald-Kelce Library, Special Collection.)

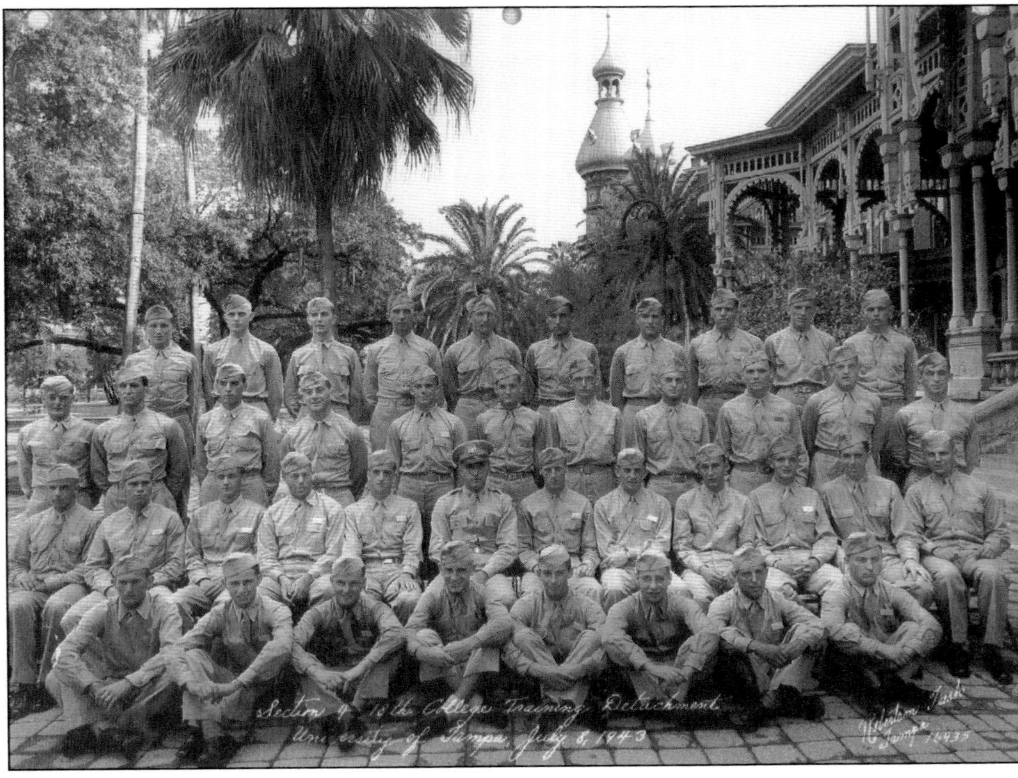

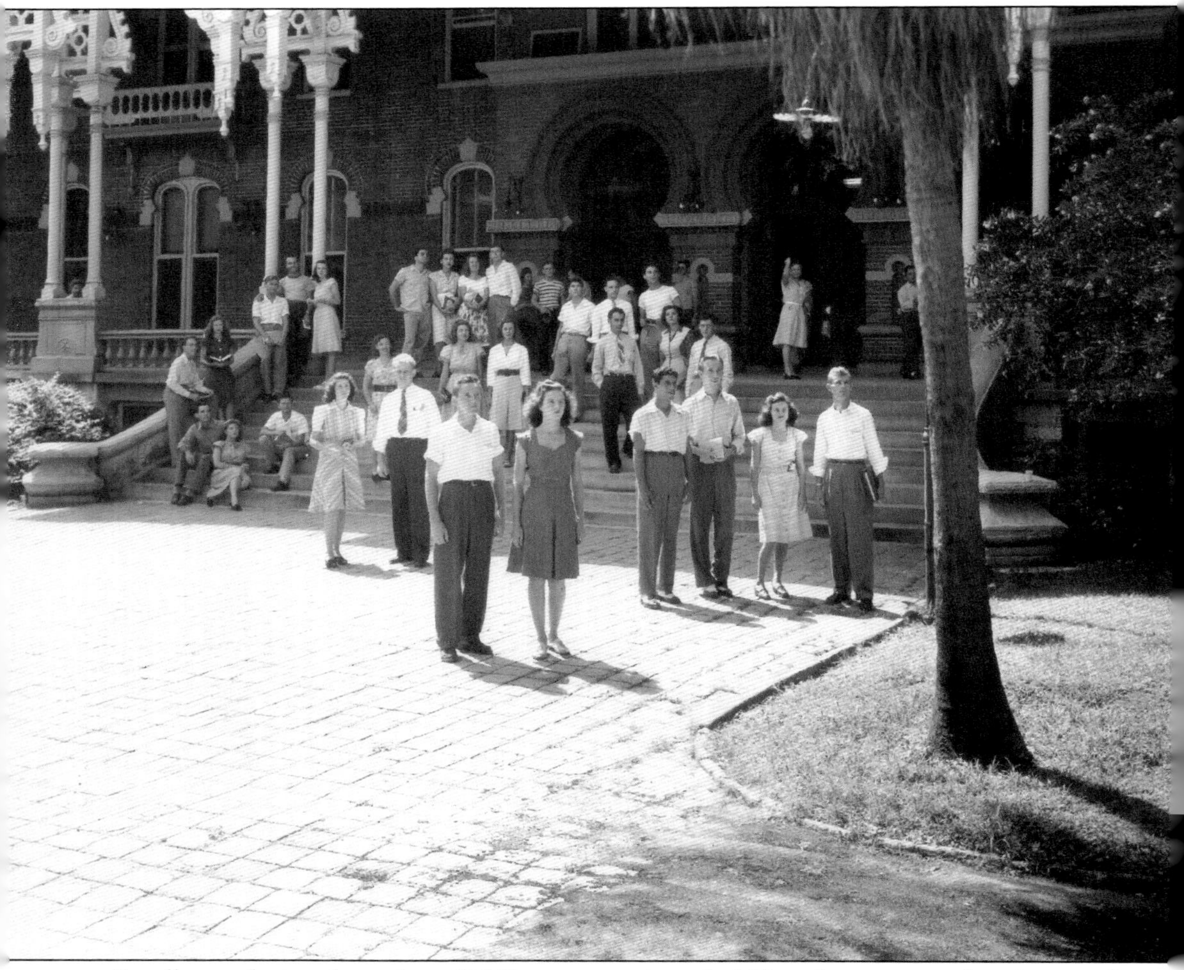

Enrollment during the spring of 1945 was approximately 200 students—a number that rapidly grew after World War II. The GI Bill allowed veterans to take advantage of the educational opportunities, females began to enroll in universities in greater numbers, and the University of Tampa became one of the first in the country to accommodate students with physical handicaps. This promotional photograph was taken in the late 1940s to encourage females to apply for admittance to the university. By the fall of 1949, approximately 1,100 students were enrolled.

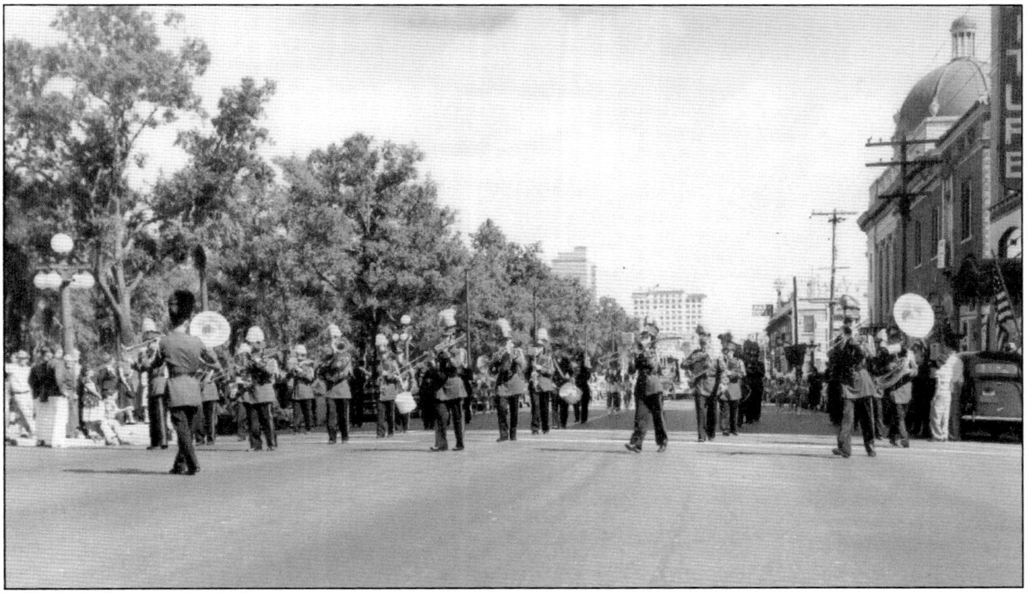

The University of Tampa marching band led the Homecoming Parade in the autumn of 1950. The band is turning into the main entrance of the university from Kennedy Boulevard. Behind the band was the decorated float of the Beta Chi fraternity. The university had a winning football team in the years after World War II.

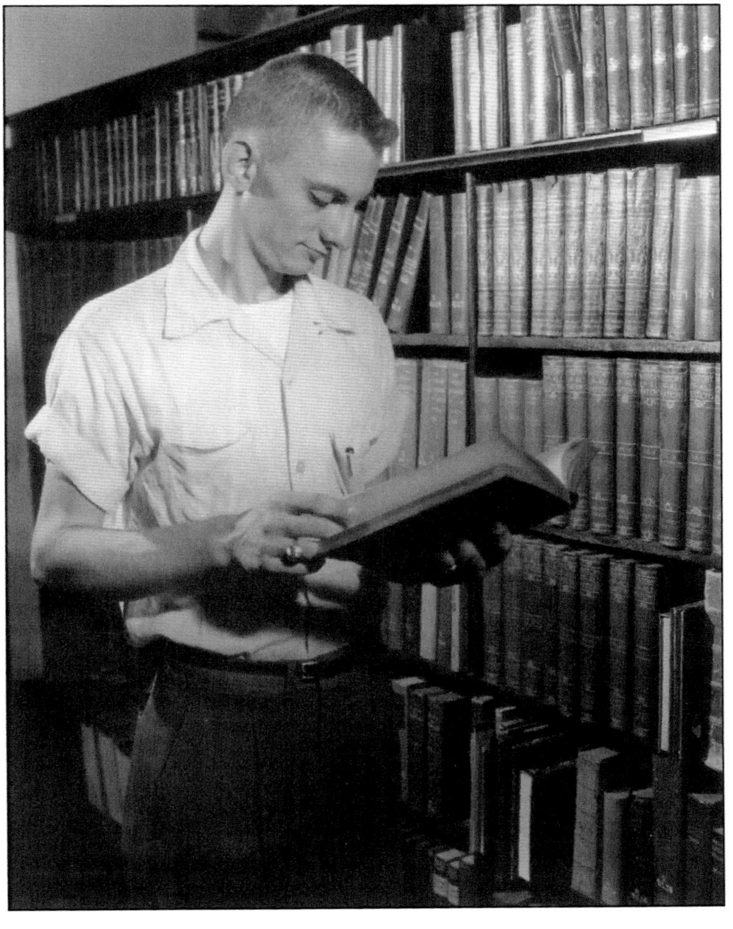

University of Tampa student Walter Carmody was photographed in 1957 researching in the rare book collection of the campus library. The library was housed in the main dining room of the former Tampa Bay Hotel until 1969, when a state-of-the-art library was built on campus.

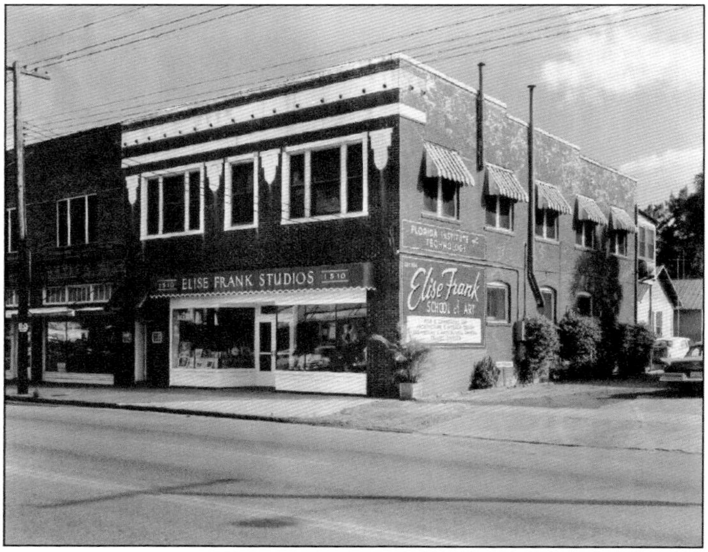

Elise Frank was a local artist who operated the Elise Frank School of Art on Grand Central Avenue (Kennedy Boulevard) from the late 1940s through the early 1960s. In addition to being a respected art school president, she was a successful ceramic potter. She and her brother operated Floramics Pottery in the early 1950s.

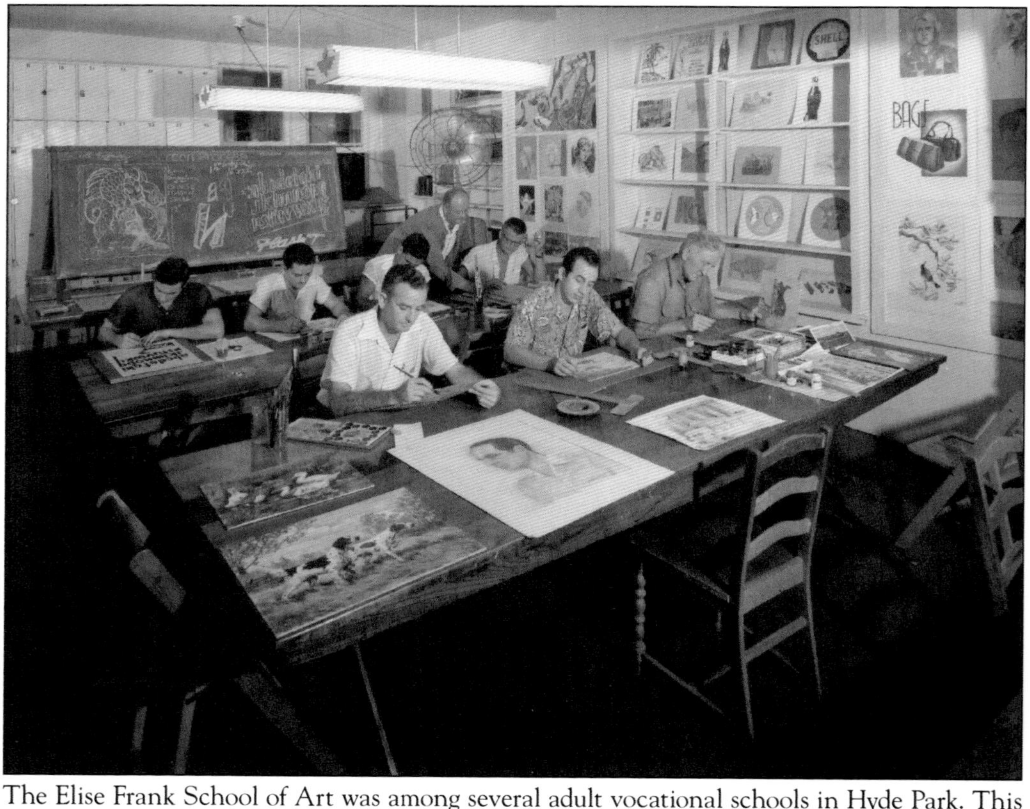

The Elise Frank School of Art was among several adult vocational schools in Hyde Park. This 1954 art class prepared students to take advantage of growing local demand for commercial art and printing. Most of the students were recent veterans attending school on the GI Bill, and several graduates became recognized portrait painters. Mechanical drawing classes were popular, primarily with males recently discharged from the military, and graduates were in demand at local engineering and architectural firms.

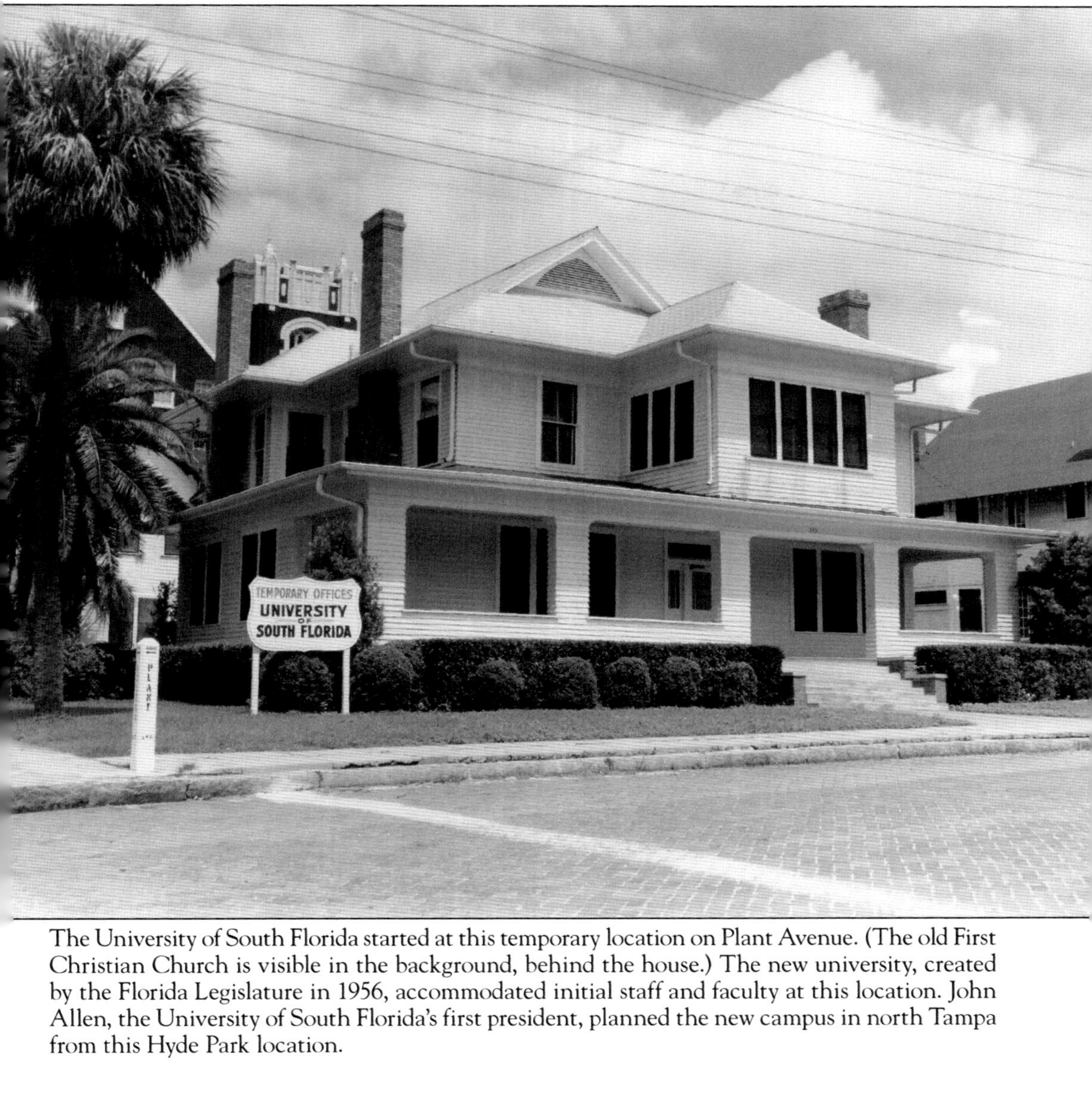

The University of South Florida started at this temporary location on Plant Avenue. (The old First Christian Church is visible in the background, behind the house.) The new university, created by the Florida Legislature in 1956, accommodated initial staff and faculty at this location. John Allen, the University of South Florida's first president, planned the new campus in north Tampa from this Hyde Park location.

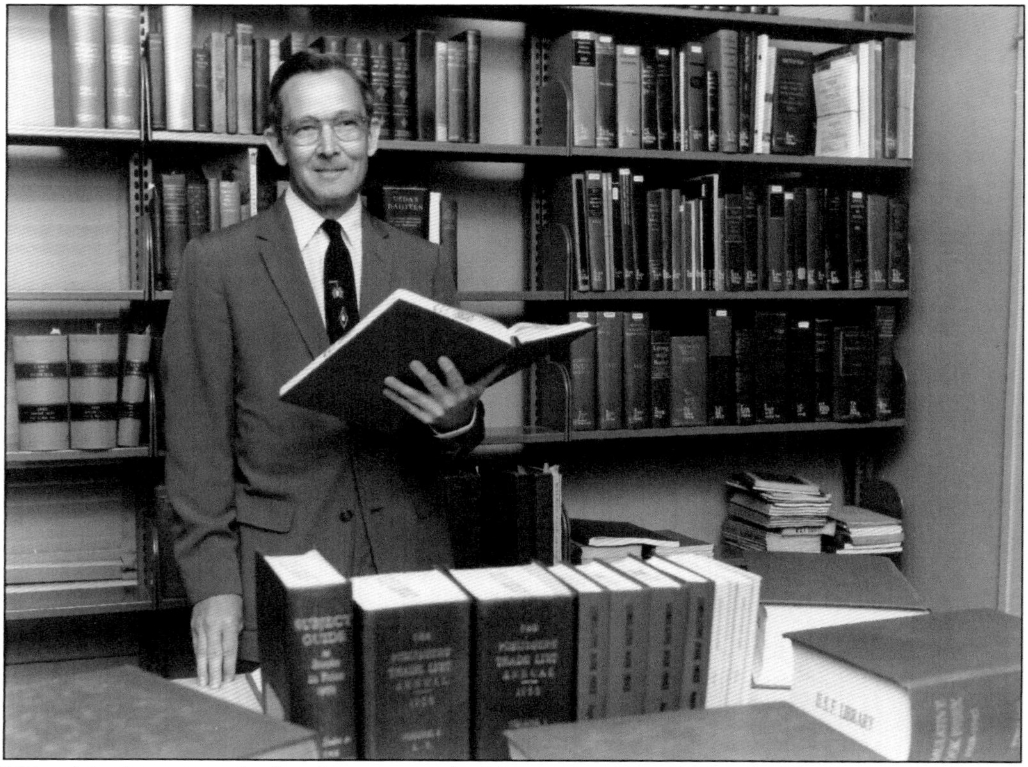

Elliott Hardaway was the first librarian at the University of South Florida. Hardaway was charged with establishing a major research library for the new university. Within 10 years, the library was one of the largest university research libraries in Florida.

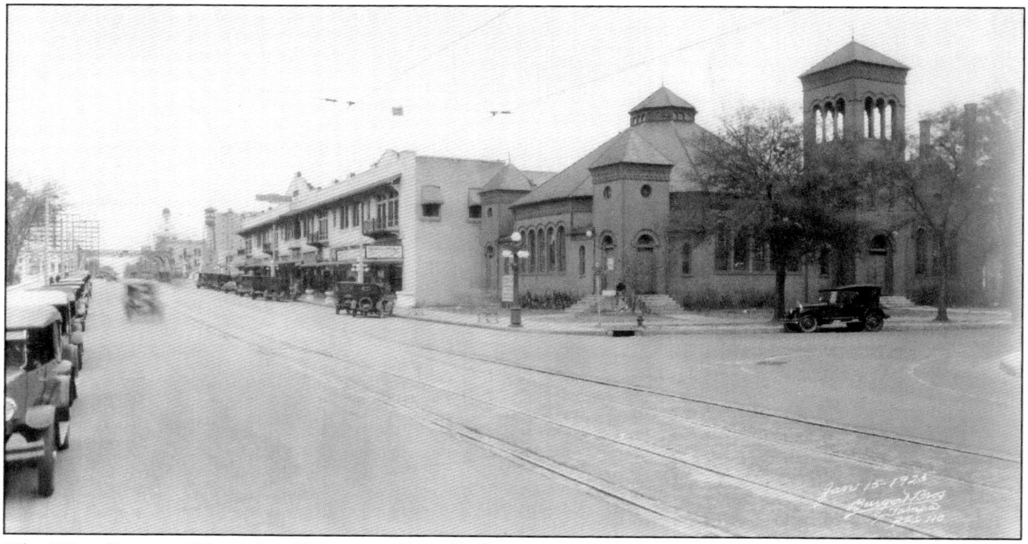

The First Baptist Church of Tampa officially began on July 23, 1859, in downtown Tampa. After the bridge was built across the Hillsborough River and church members began to construct homes in Hyde Park, the congregation relocated in 1896. The relocation was to the brick building at right, located at the intersection of Lafayette Street (Kennedy Boulevard) and Hyde Park Avenue.

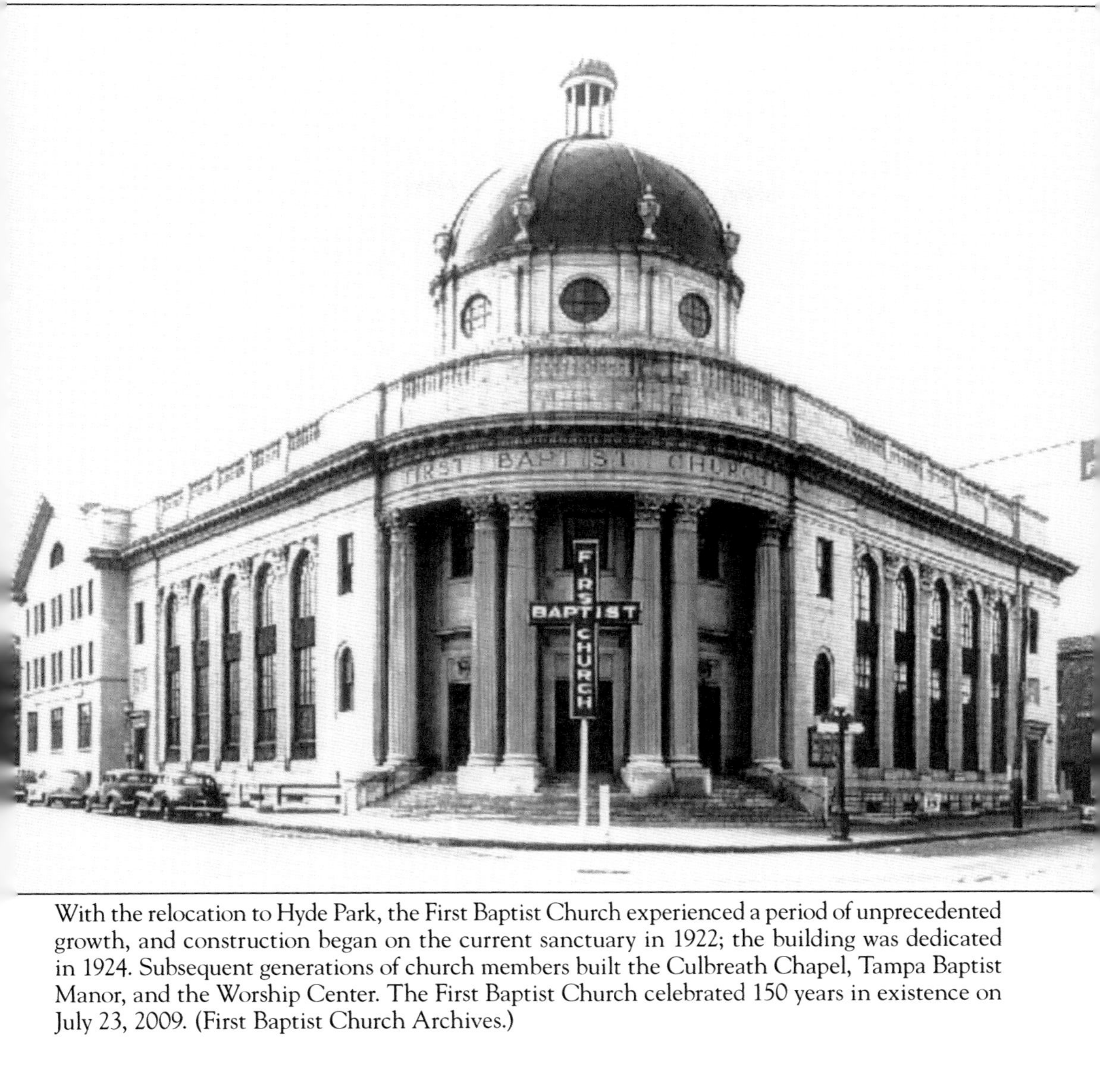

With the relocation to Hyde Park, the First Baptist Church experienced a period of unprecedented growth, and construction began on the current sanctuary in 1922; the building was dedicated in 1924. Subsequent generations of church members built the Culbreath Chapel, Tampa Baptist Manor, and the Worship Center. The First Baptist Church celebrated 150 years in existence on July 23, 2009. (First Baptist Church Archives.)

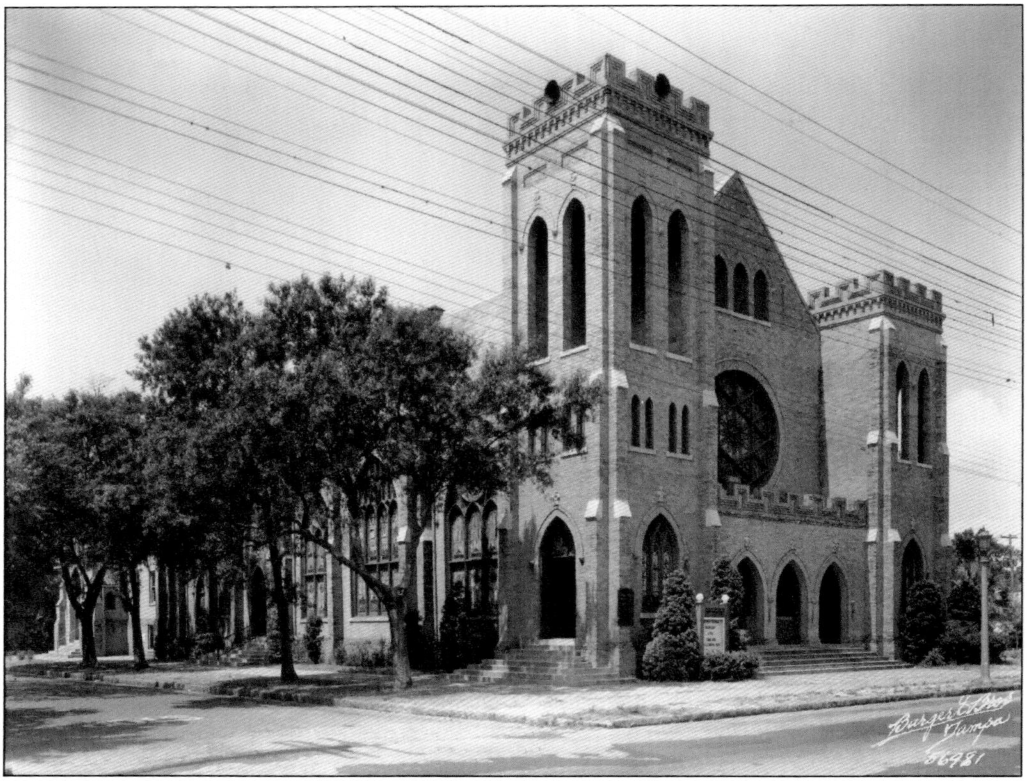

The Hyde Park United Methodist Church has maintained a significant presence in Hyde Park since its inception in 1899. The first 30 members met at the two-room Hyde Park Grammar School, which was then located at Platt Street and Magnolia Avenue. The church was officially organized in 1900 with 29 members. This photograph was taken in 1945.

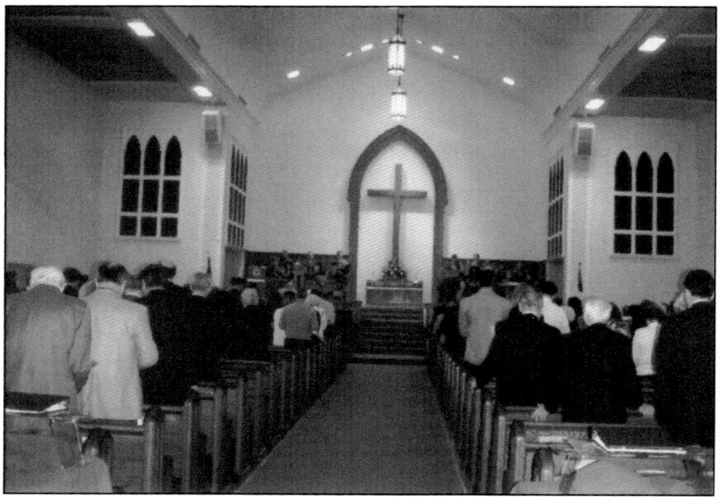

The main sanctuary of the church was constructed in 1907, and the first education building was completed in 1921. This photograph was taken of the interior of the main sanctuary before the building was expanded. Hyde Park United Methodist Church has undertaken several expansions adjacent to the initial Platt Street location. (Hyde Park United Methodist Church Archives.)

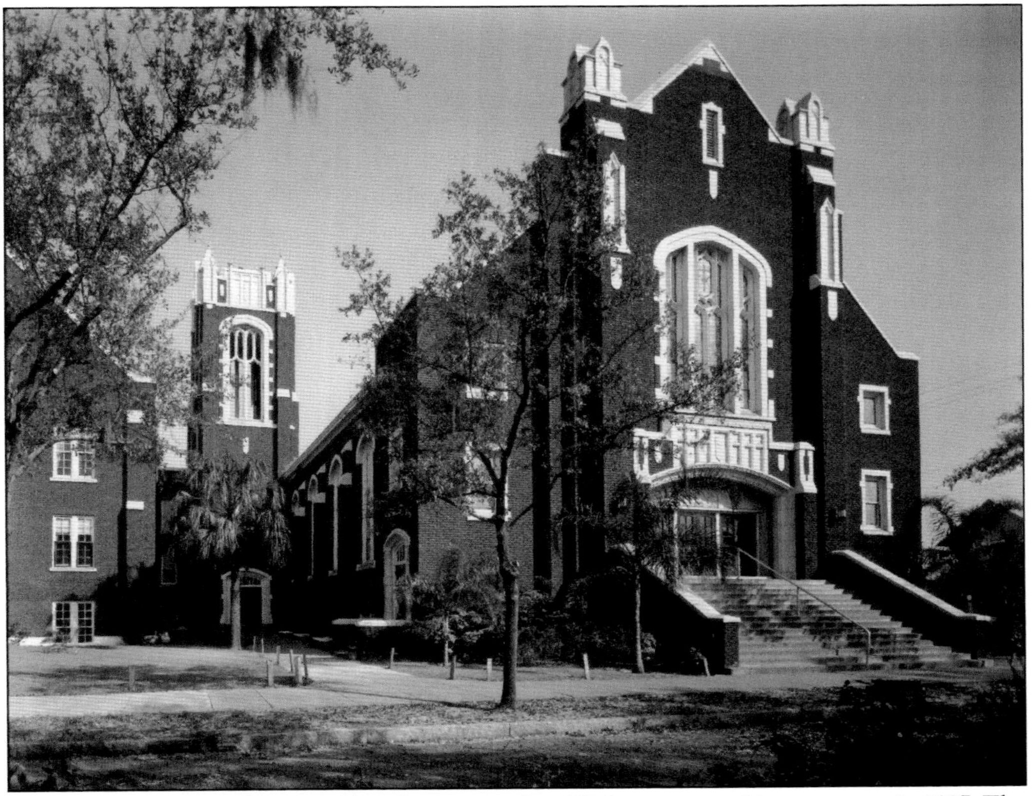

The Hyde Park First Christian Church, organized in 1900, constructed its sanctuary in 1927. The church maintained a prominent presence until the spring of 2009, when the congregation held its last service. In October 2009, the Holy Trinity Presbyterian Church, the current occupant of the building, held its first service in the sanctuary.

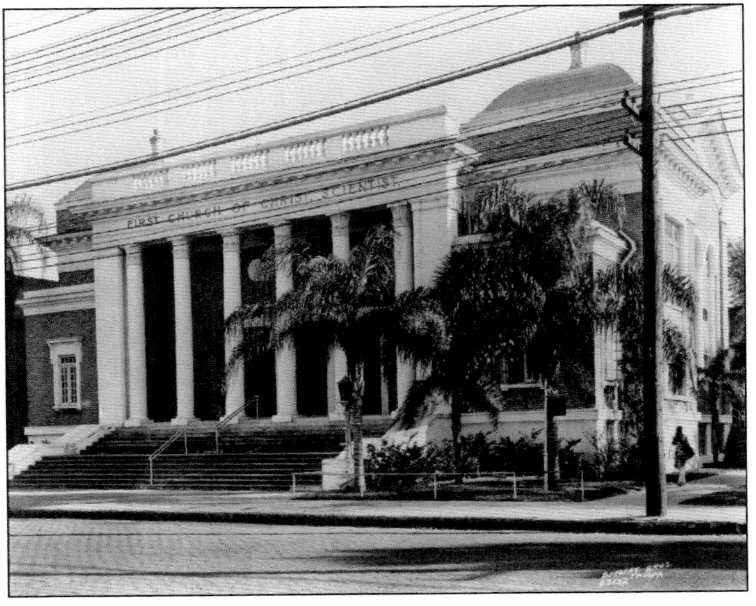

In 1908, the First Church of Christ, Scientist was organized in Tampa. Seeking an appropriate location, in 1920 the congregation acquired its present Hyde Park site for construction of a new building. On January 24, 1926, the first service was held at the Grand Central Avenue location pictured here. Dedication services were held on March 5, 1944, after the building mortgage was satisfied.

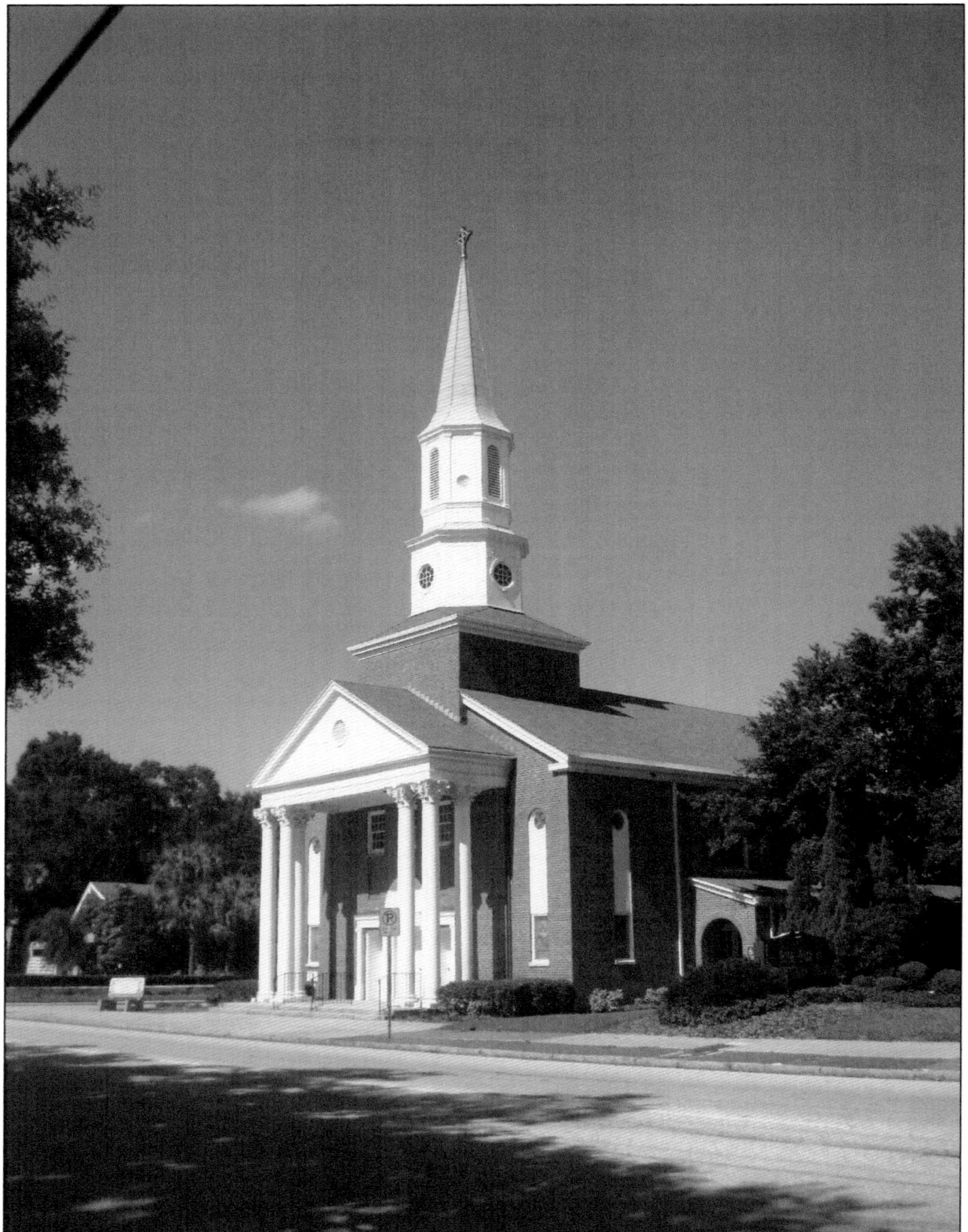

The Hyde Park Presbyterian Church began as an outpost Sunday school chapel in 1910 on the corner of Oregon and Inman Avenues. The success of the outpost enabled the congregation to begin construction of a masonry church building, which opened in 1917. The building served the church until 1953, when the brick Georgian sanctuary in the photograph was completed. (JRSPhotos.com.)

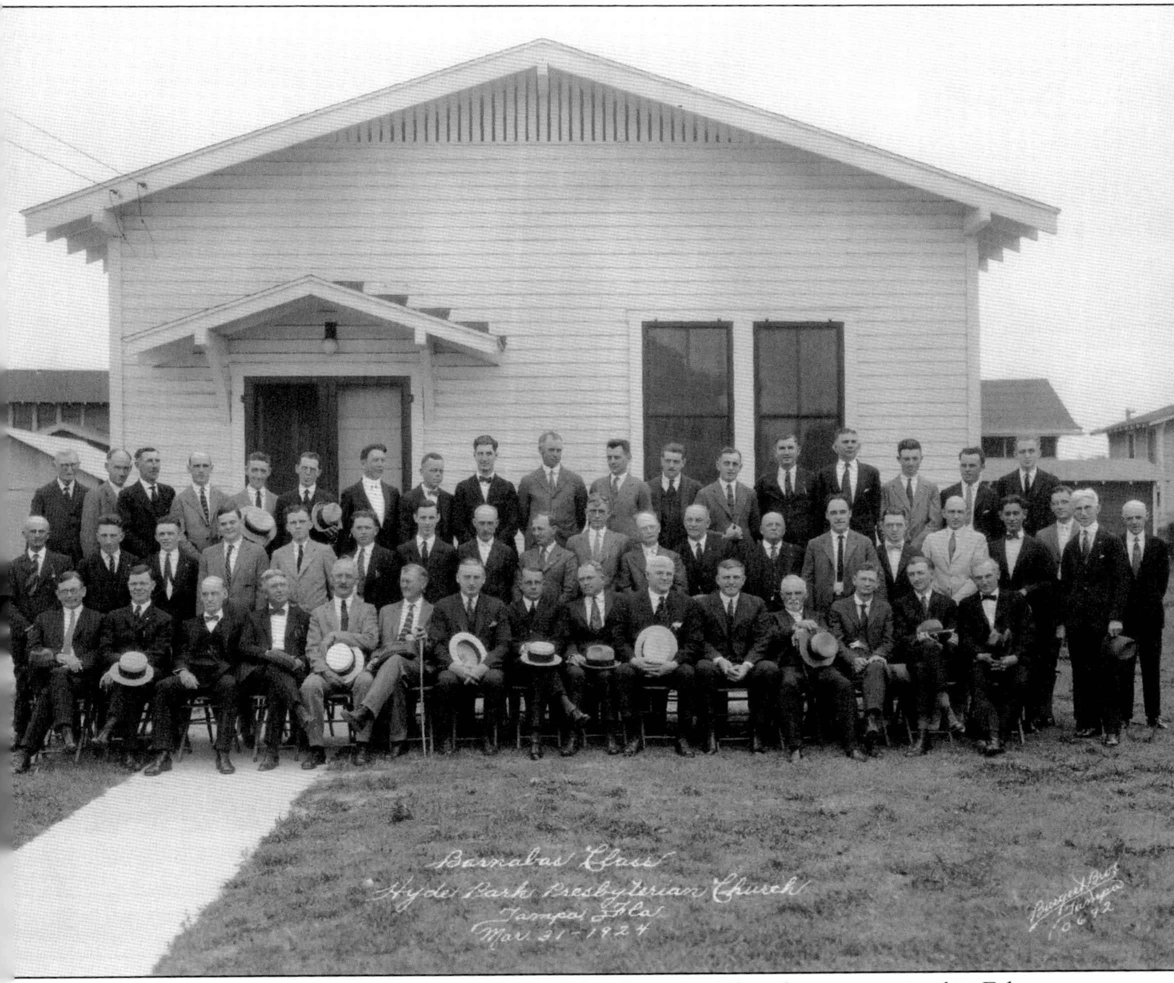

The Barnabas Men's Bible Class of the Hyde Park Presbyterian Church was organized in February 1923. This photograph from March 31, 1924, depicts a class of 53 men. For many years, attendance averaged 50 men, but during the Florida land boom years, it spiked to approximately 75.

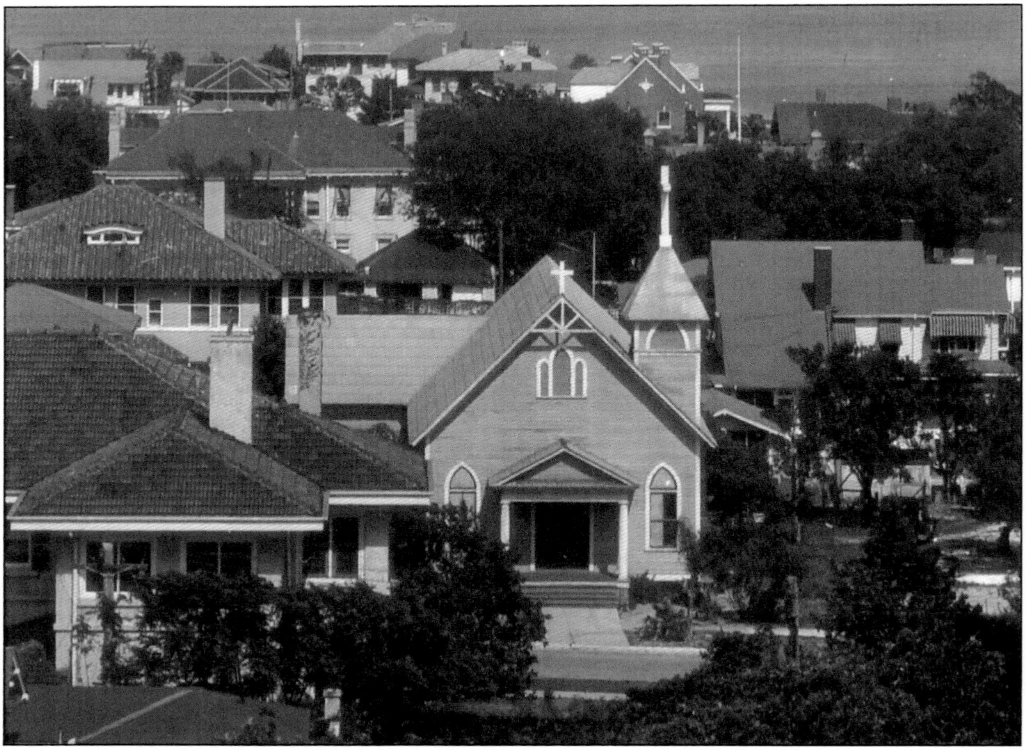

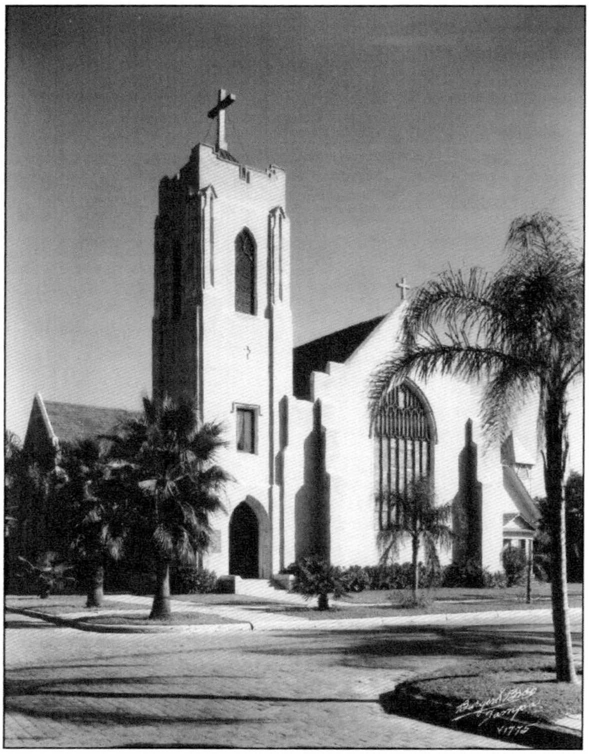

St. John's by the Sea Episcopal Mission was established in Hyde Park in 1912. After the first building was lost in a fire, the wooden structure shown here was constructed. In 1917, the mission became a parish with 108 communicants. Construction began on the current building in 1924, and the wooden church was moved adjacent to the construction and became the parish hall.

The current St. John's Episcopal Church and a new pipe organ were dedicated in 1928. F.J. Kennard designed the Mediterranean Revival–inspired church. By 1944, the mortgage on the church was completely satisfied, and the building was consecrated.

St. John's Episcopal Church continued to expand its presence, establishing St. John's Parish Day School in 1951 with a kindergarten class. Today, St. John's Parish Day School offers pre-kindergarten through eighth grade on several campuses in Hyde Park. This c. 1953 photograph was taken after a First Communion ceremony at the church. (St. John's Episcopal Archives.)

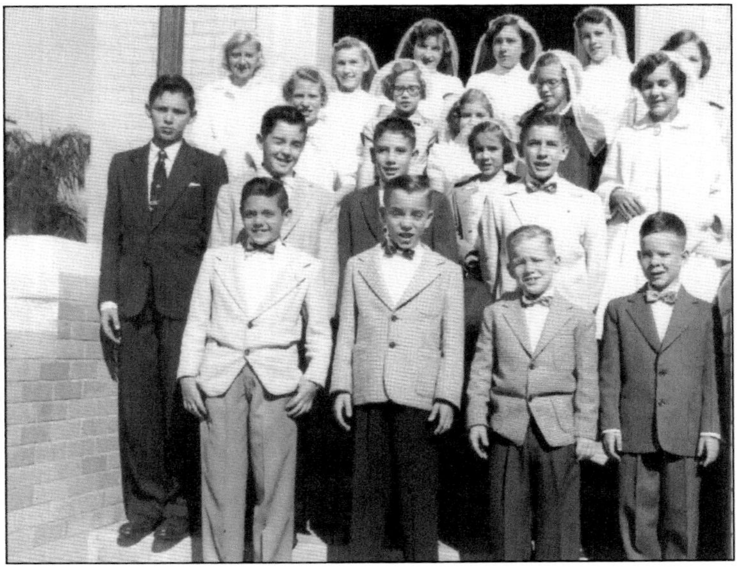

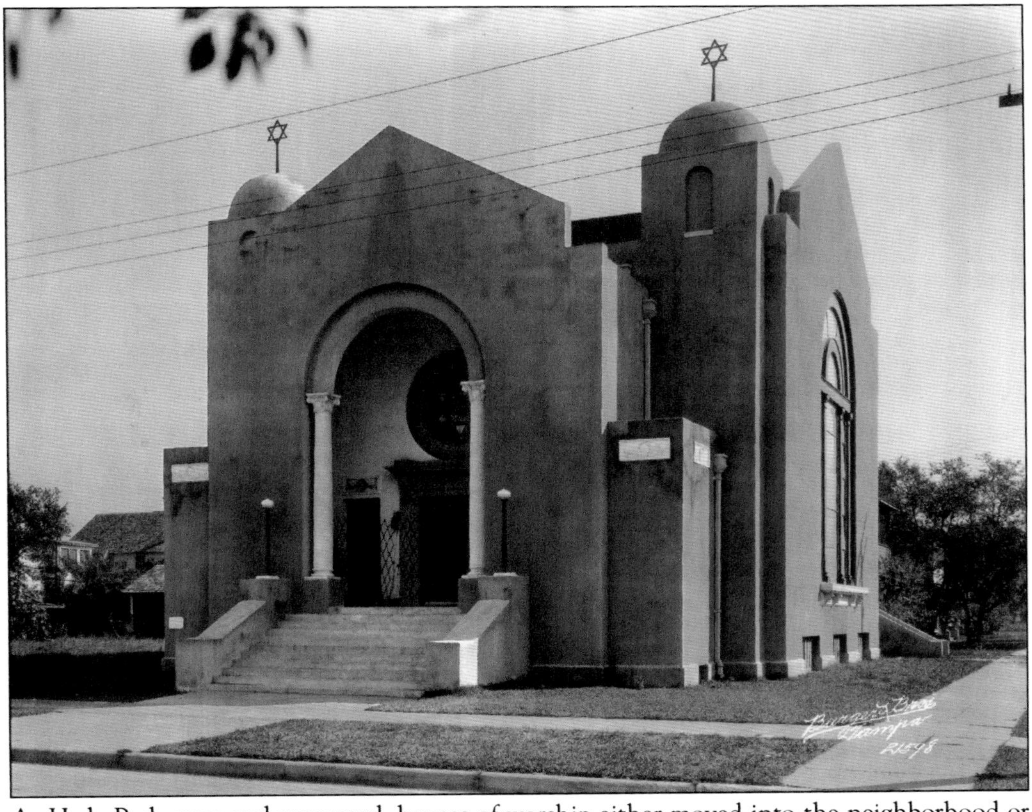

As Hyde Park grew and prospered, houses of worship either moved into the neighborhood or started new congregations. In 1924, Congregation Schaarai Zedek moved from downtown Tampa to Hyde Park following construction of the temple at De Leon Street and Delaware Avenue. The congregation remained in Hyde Park until 1957, when a new campus was built several miles west of Hyde Park. This building was demolished after the congregation moved.

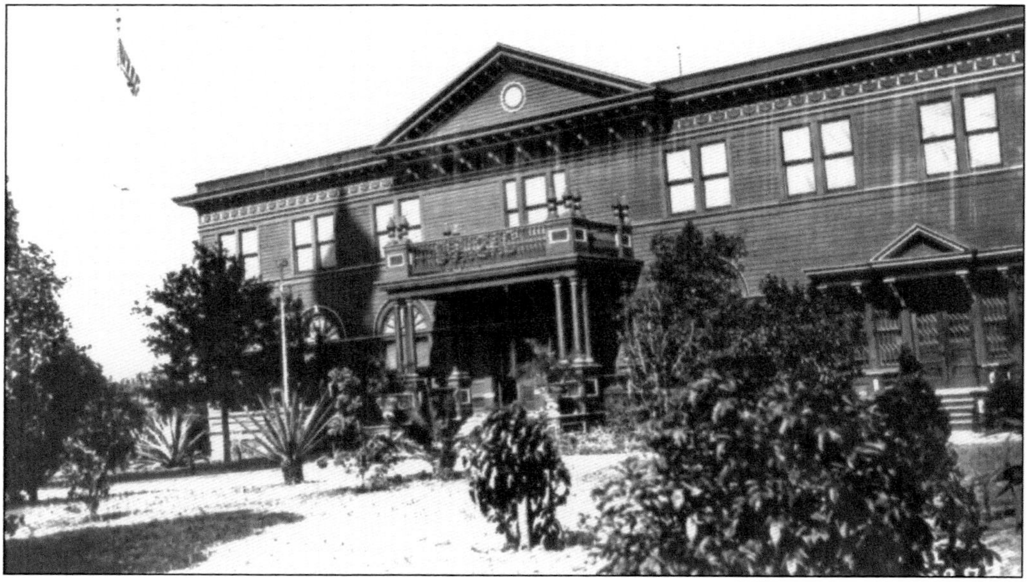

The Casino on the grounds of the Tampa Bay Hotel became Tampa's first performing arts venue. In 1902, Mrs. W.H. Ferris and Louise F. Dodge founded the Friday Morning Musicale, which used the Casino for all its performances. The group met every other week on Friday mornings. They became affiliated with the Federation of Women's Clubs in April 1921. Soon after the alliance, Mrs. Frank Jackson donated the current site on De Leon Avenue, and prominent Tampa architect Frank Durham was retained to design the building, which had a 385-seat theater and two meeting rooms. The building was dedicated in 1926 and has been in use since it opened in 1927. The new space became the first home of the Tampa Little Theater, launched Tampa's first opera company, and the in-house orchestra became the forerunner of the present-day Florida Orchestra. (Above, Florida State Archives; below, Florida Bureau of Historic Preservation.)

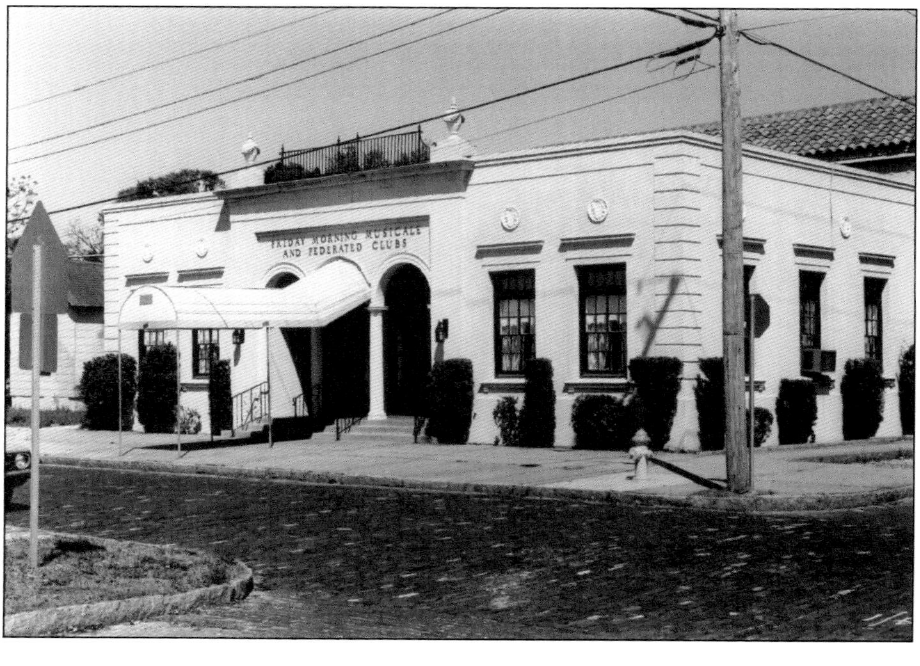

Frances Friedman Williams had completed her performance at the Friday Morning Musicale and Federation of Women's Clubs theater when this photograph was taken in May 1961. The organization continues to sponsor a season of musical performances each year from October to May and provides amateur and professional musicians throughout the Tampa Bay area with opportunities to perform. (Friedman Family Collection.)

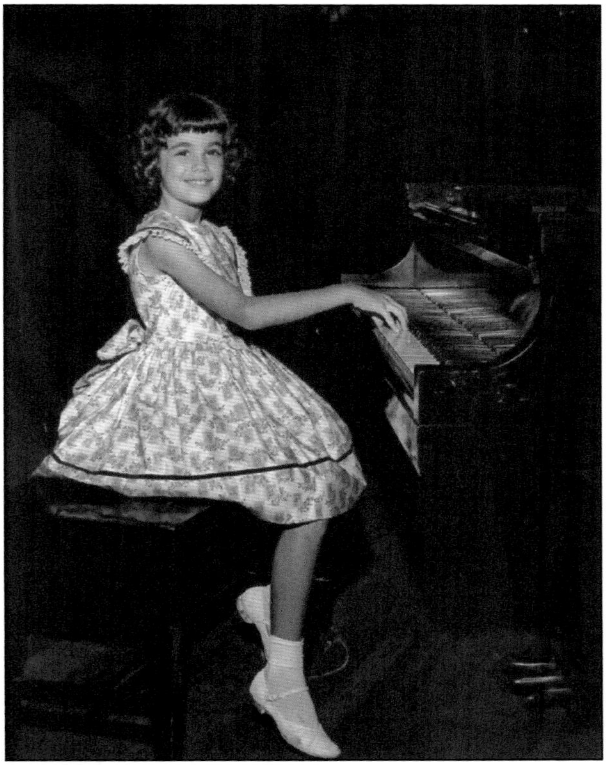

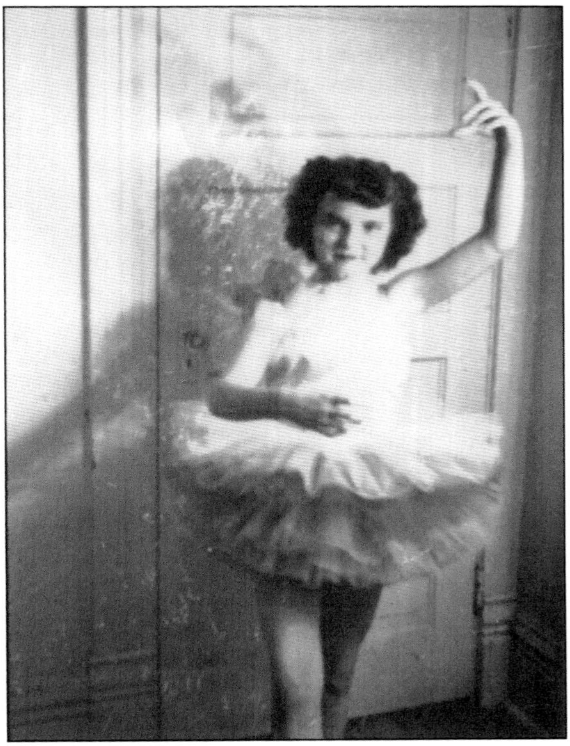

The stages of Hyde Park provided appropriate venues for not only professional talent, but also for young, local performers. This photograph of Irene Morales was taken in 1953 before a ballet recital at the Tampa Municipal Auditorium. Performances of dance, music, and theater could be enjoyed year-round at various performing arts locations. (Carmen Morales.)

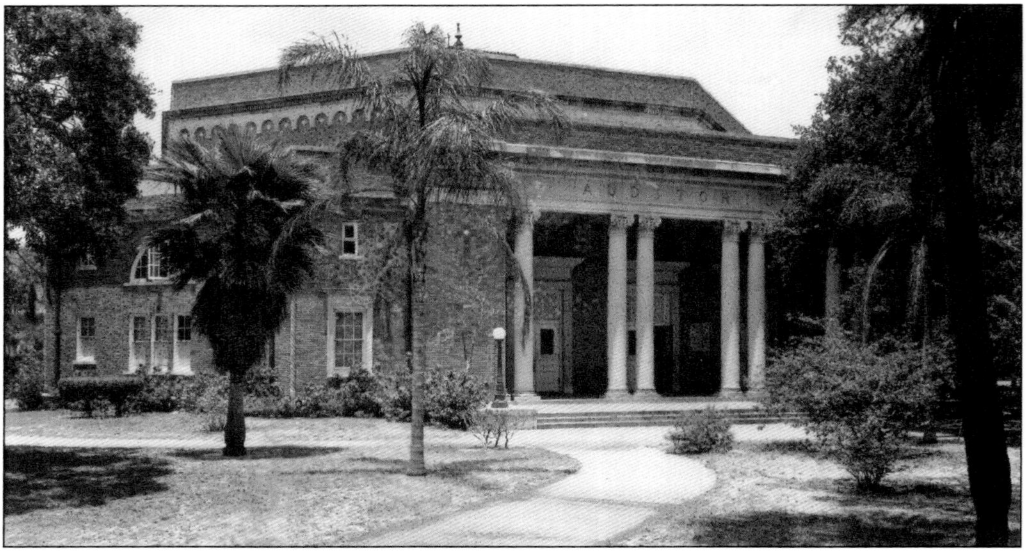

The rapid growth of Tampa necessitated the opening of the Tampa Municipal Auditorium west of the Tampa Bay Hotel. The Neoclassical building was designed as a multipurpose facility and could accommodate concerts, Gasparilla festivities, and even trade shows. The building, now part of the University of Tampa campus, currently houses the John H. Sykes College of Business. Each year, local civic groups staged seasonal holiday shows, such as the 1946 production of *Toyland* pictured below. The productions were intended to encourage children to perform in public as part of Tampa's cultural programming. Parents and tourists visiting Hyde Park for the winter season anticipated the events, and students were involved in every aspect of the productions.

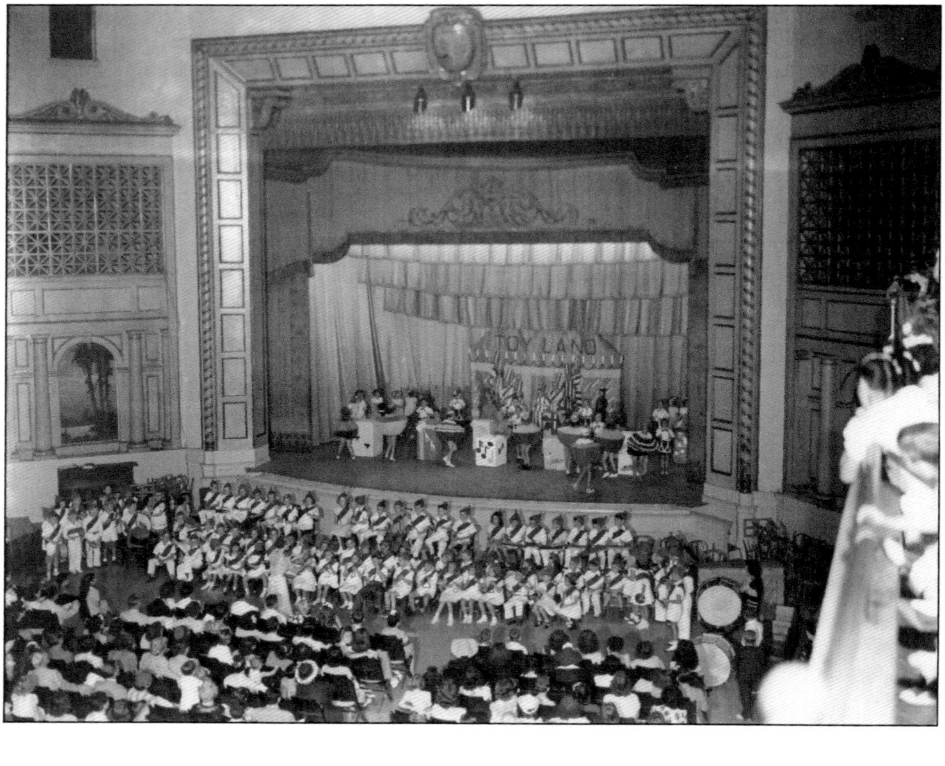

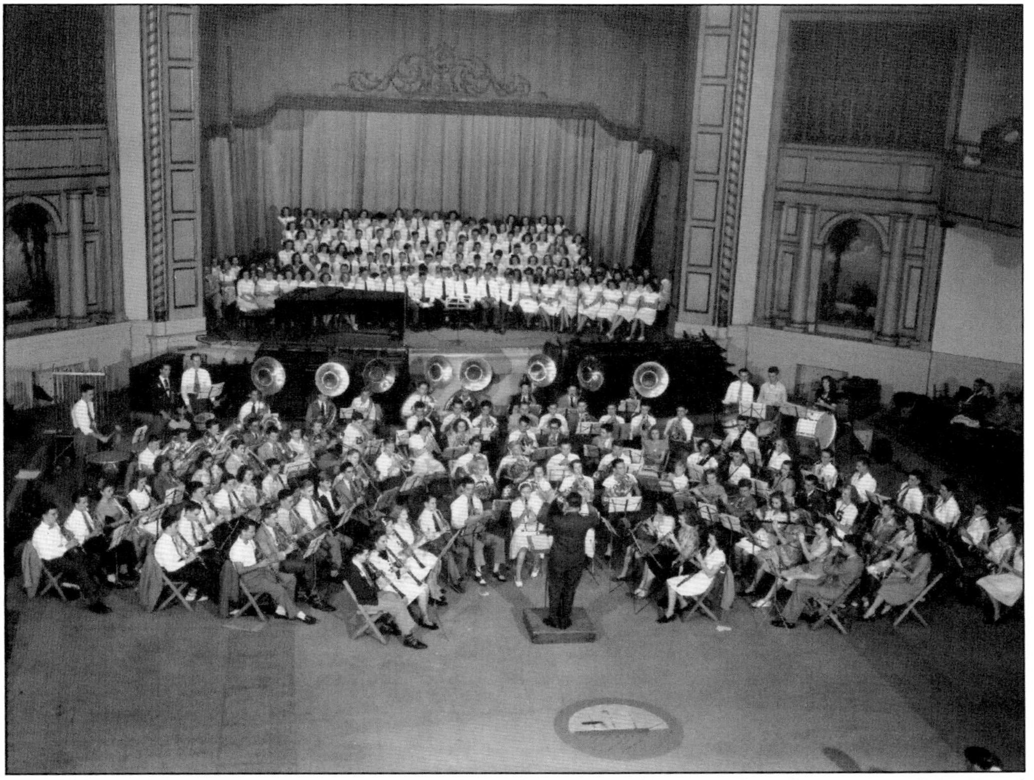

Children throughout Hillsborough County participated in the annual performances of the Band and Youth Chorus at the Tampa Municipal Auditorium, as shown in the 1946 photograph above. They would often spend the day in Hyde Park after the concert, exploring the museum at Plant Hall or enjoying the various amenities along Bayshore Boulevard. In the years after World War II, consumer goods became widely available after years of wartime rationing. The 1946 fashion show below was produced by Maas Brothers Department Store and was intended for high school students. Similar events were presented to showcase new consumer products, such as kitchen appliances and home furnishings.

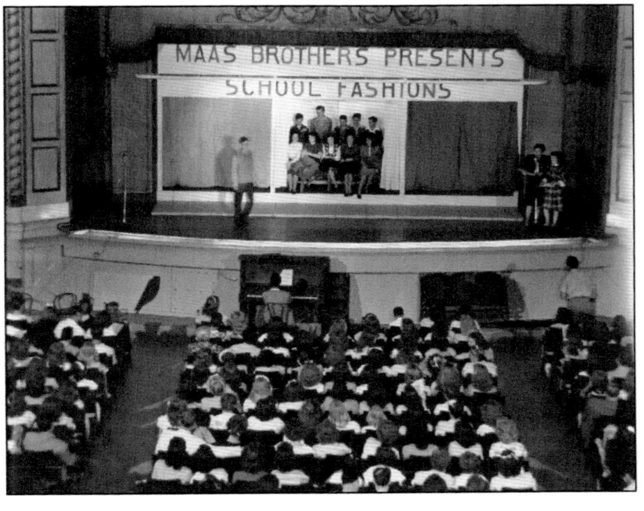

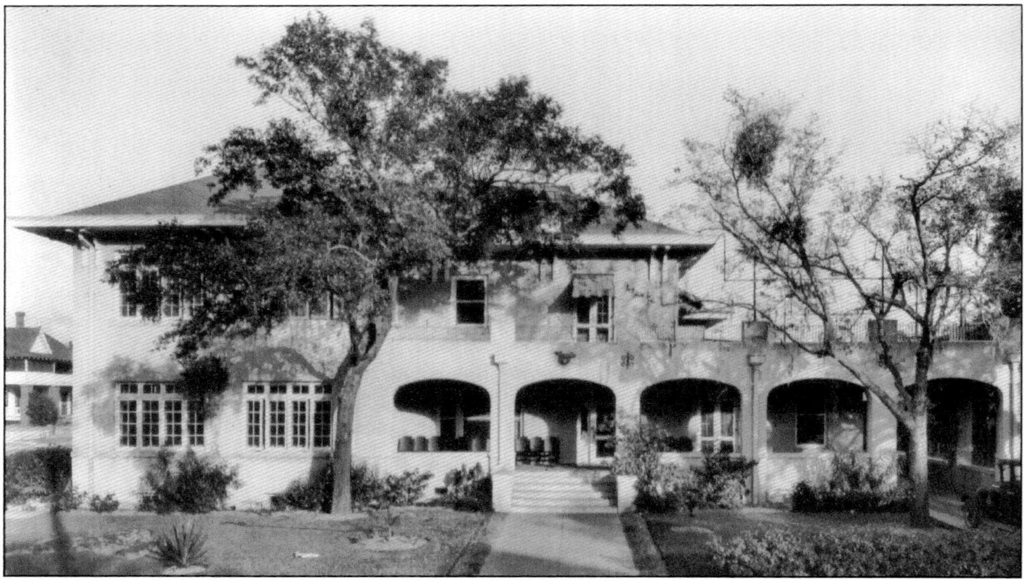

The Tampa Egypt Shrine was founded in 1918 with 175 chapter members. Initial meetings were conducted in a secondhand circus tent at various Hyde Park locations. In 1924, this house on South Boulevard Avenue was purchased and renovated to serve the needs of the shrine. A second building later erected behind the house was known as the "Barn." (Tampa Egypt Shrine Archives.)

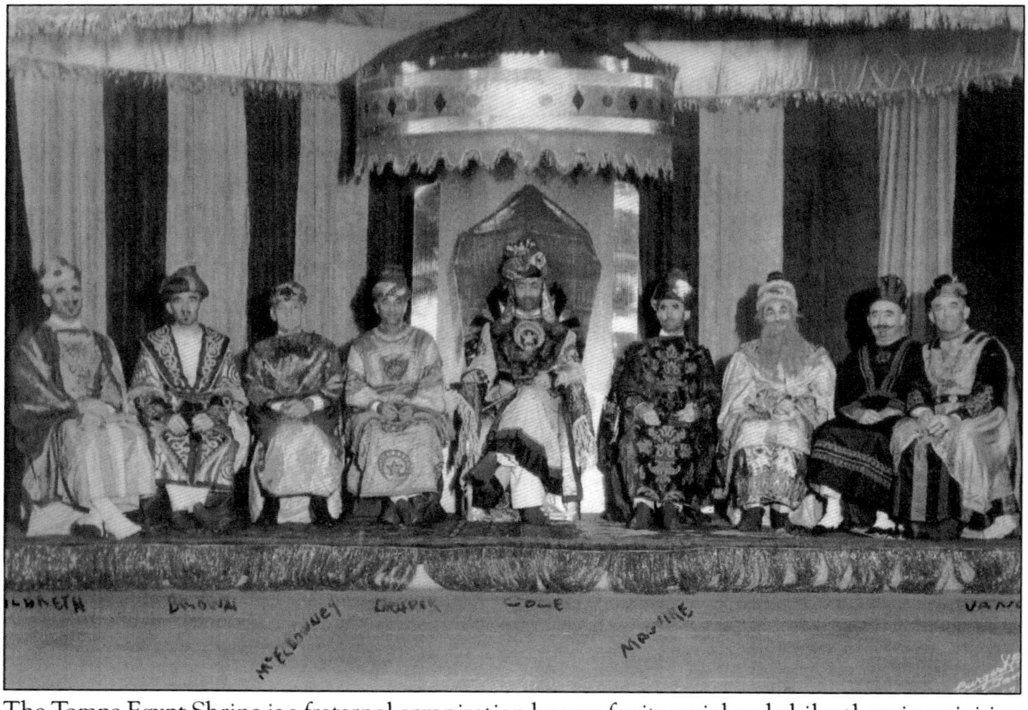

The Tampa Egypt Shrine is a fraternal organization known for its social and philanthropic activities. The organization provides the opportunity to develop lasting friendships with people from all walks of life. This 1939 photograph was taken during an officers' Thanksgiving ceremonial at the organization's former building on South Boulevard Avenue. (Tampa Egypt Shrine Archives.)

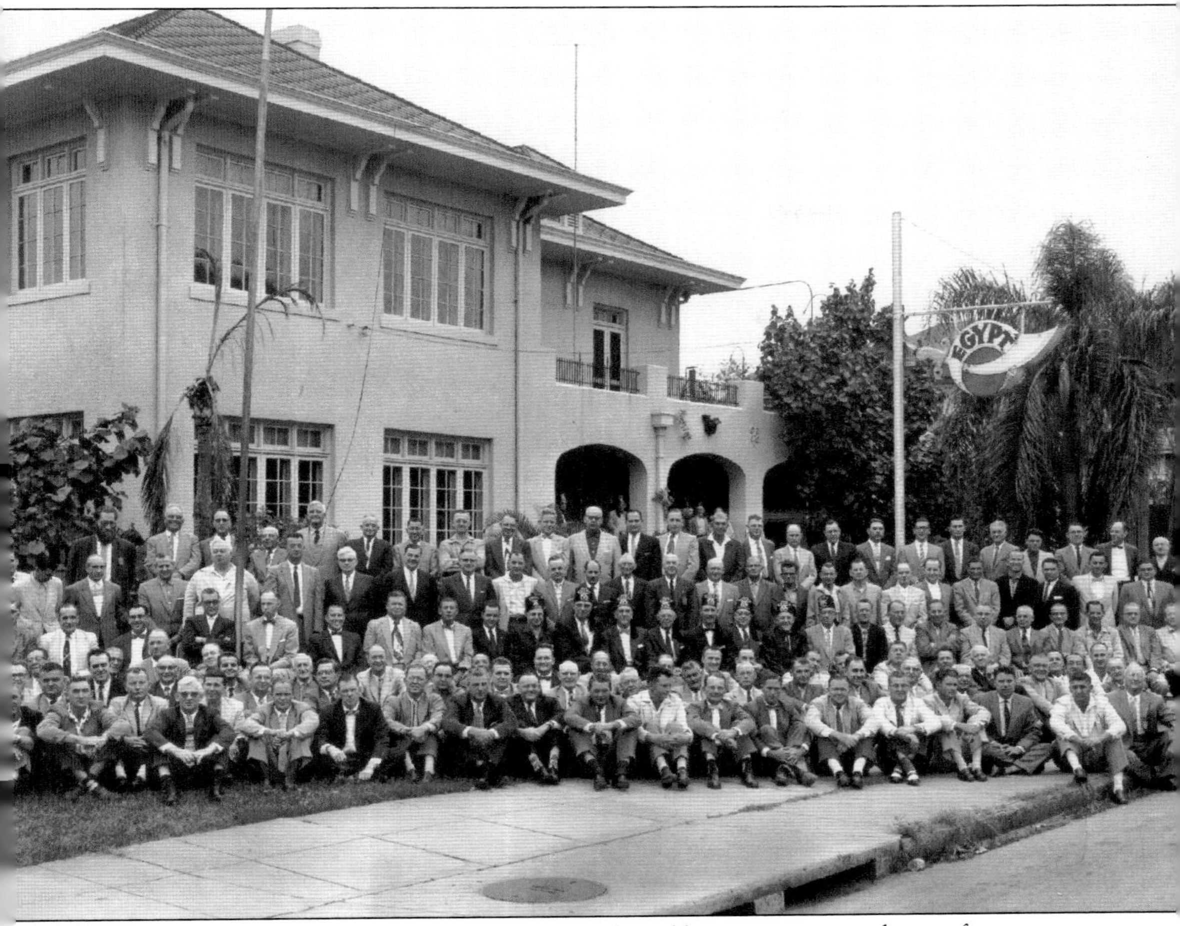

The Tampa Egypt Shrine enjoyed continuous growth and became an integral part of numerous community projects. This 1955 photograph includes numerous new members. The shrine remained in Hyde Park until 1967, when the organization moved to the Town and Country area of Tampa. The building was demolished after the shrine relocated. (Tampa Egypt Shrine Archives.)

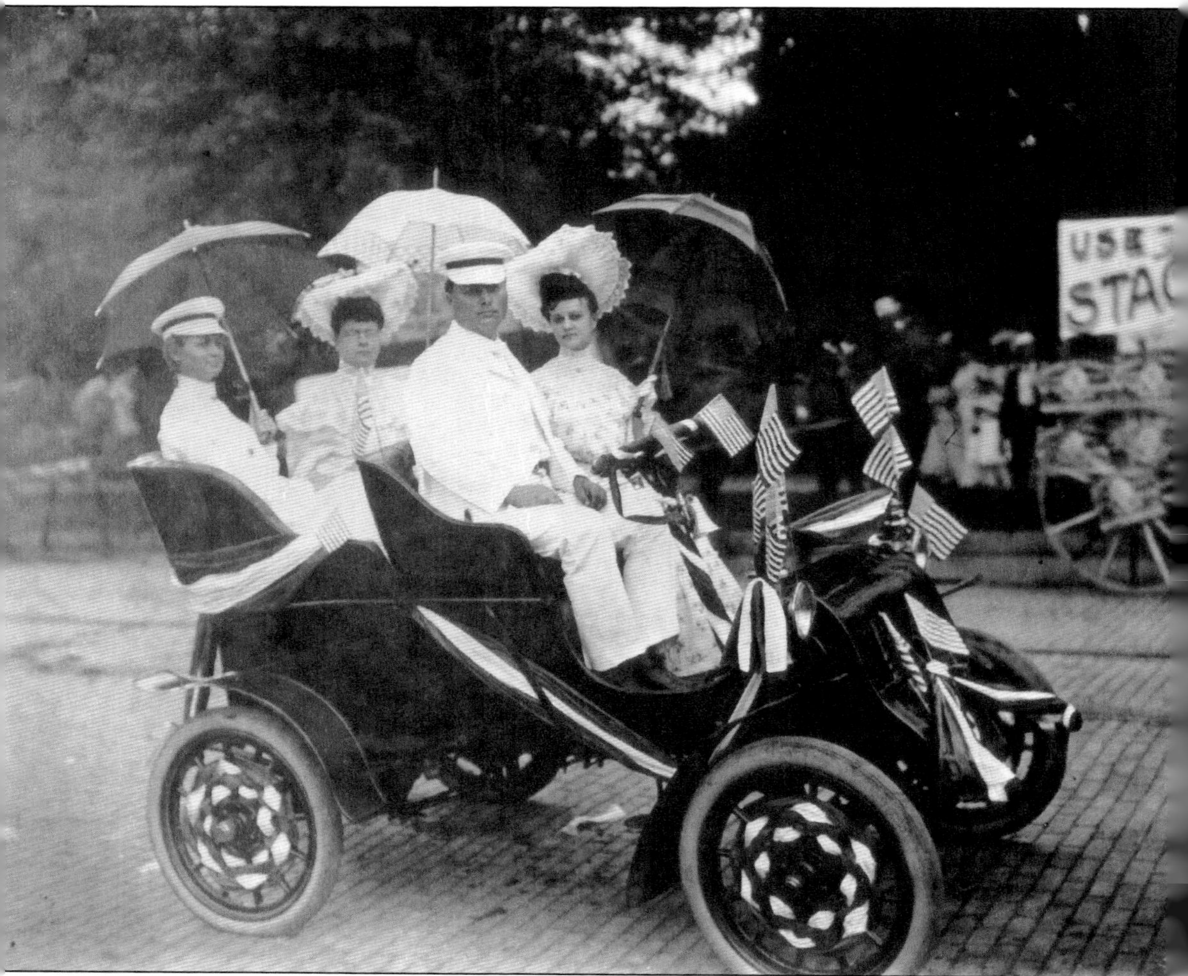

As the growing city matured, Tampa was ready to start having fun. The Tampa Bay Hotel provided a setting for both indoor and outdoor activities, and in 1904, Tampa's community leaders started the forerunner to the present-day Gasparilla festivities—the May Day Festival. The first parade, held on May 4, 1904, started in front of the east veranda of the hotel and traveled four blocks east to the old Courthouse Square in downtown Tampa. Tampa's leading male citizens, dressed as pirates, led the parade; half of the pirates rode on horseback. This family participated by riding along the parade route in their 1903 Cadillac.

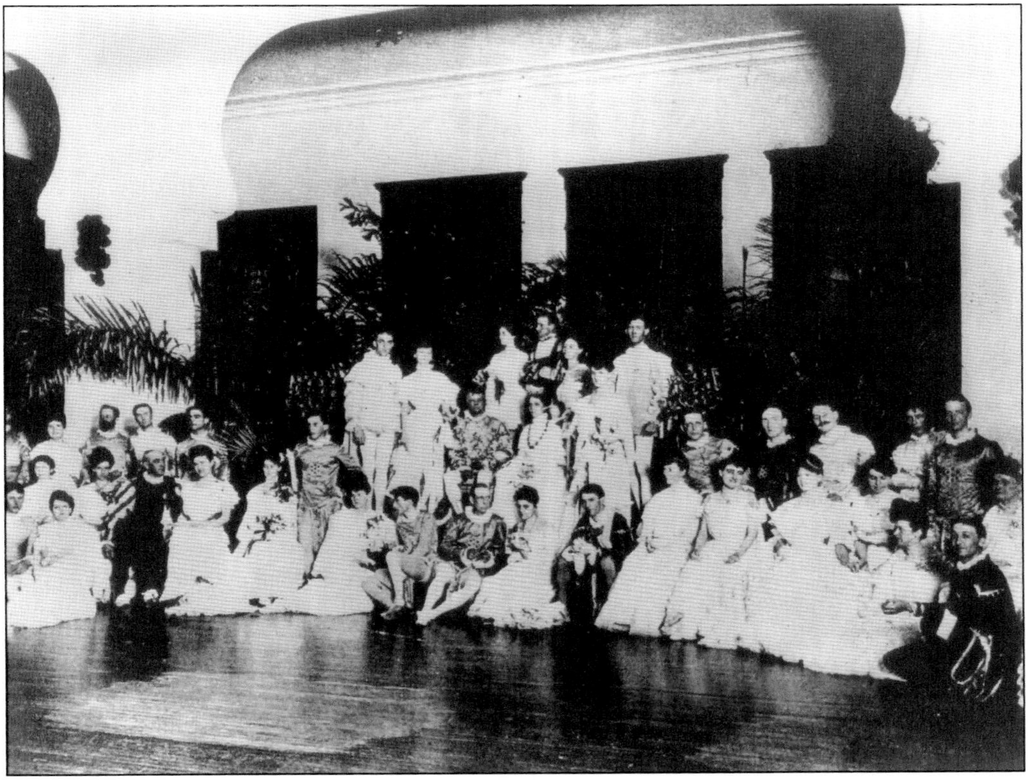

The first Coronation Ball (above) was held on May 6, 1904, with Edward R. Gunby and Mary Lee Douglas Ligat reigning as the first king and queen of Gasparilla. The ball was held at the Tampa Bay Hotel in what is now the University of Tampa's Fletcher Lounge. Ye Mystic Krewe of Gasparilla was born from this early event, along with the annual festivities that continue today. At right is a photograph of the 1960 Royal Court of Gasparilla, including King XLVII James L. Ferman Sr.; his queen, Pamela Logan Smiley; and attendants W.F. McLane (left) and Joe L. Reed III. The traditions established in 1904 continue in Hyde Park and Tampa today. (Right, Ferman family archives.)

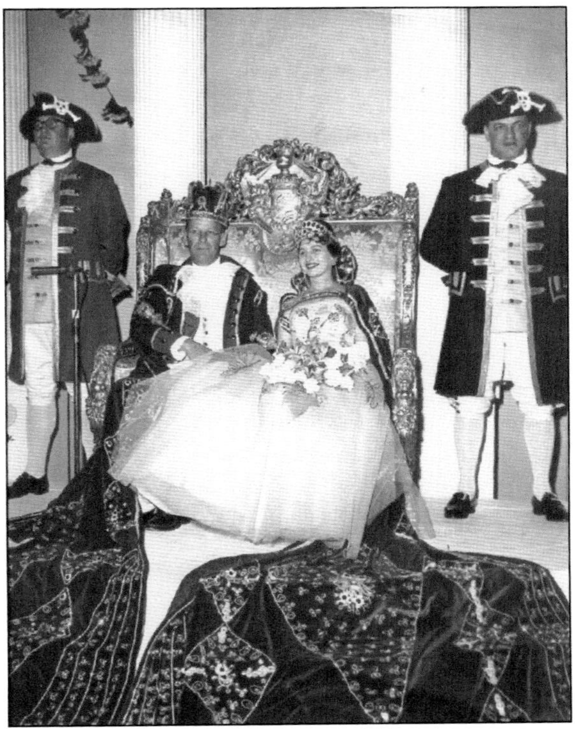

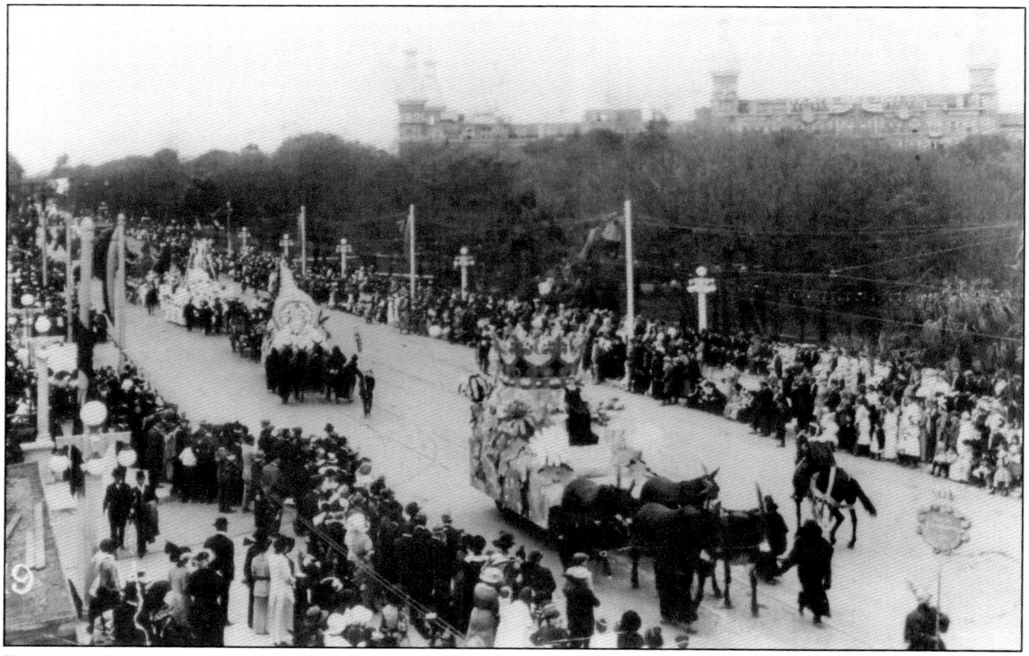

By 1914, the Gasparilla Parade (above) had become an exciting carnival with activities spanning several weeks. Tampa's leading businesses entered elaborate floats in the friendly competition. The 1914 parade also celebrated the opening of the then new Lafayette Street Bridge (now known as the Kennedy Boulevard Bridge). The parade route began at the Florida State Fair, on the former stable grounds for the Tampa Bay Hotel, and ended north of downtown. Tampa Egypt Shrine (below) participated in the 1920 Gasparilla Parade and Florida State Fair festivities that had been eagerly awaited after a three-year hiatus because of World War I. The parade route now began in downtown Tampa, flanked by thousands of citizens and tourists, traveled through Hyde Park, and terminated at the Florida State Fair grounds. At the time, the organizers of the 1920 parade and state fair did not know that the event would mark the beginning of the 1920s Florida land boom. (Below, Tampa Egypt Shrine Archives.)

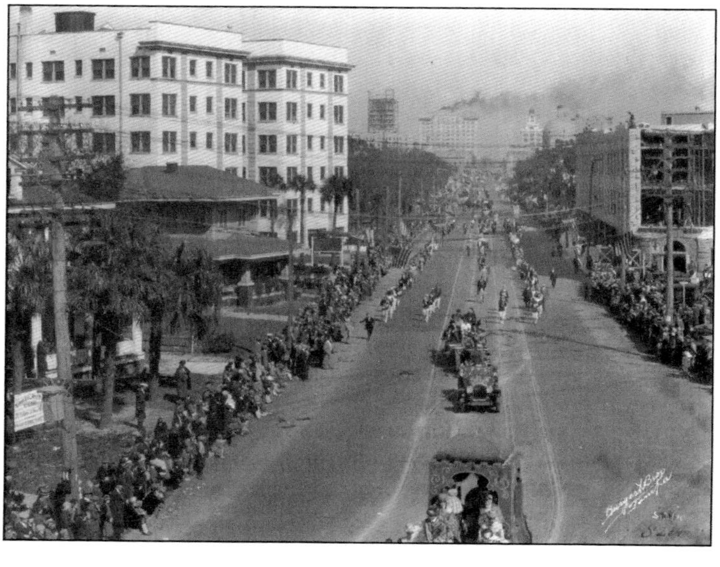

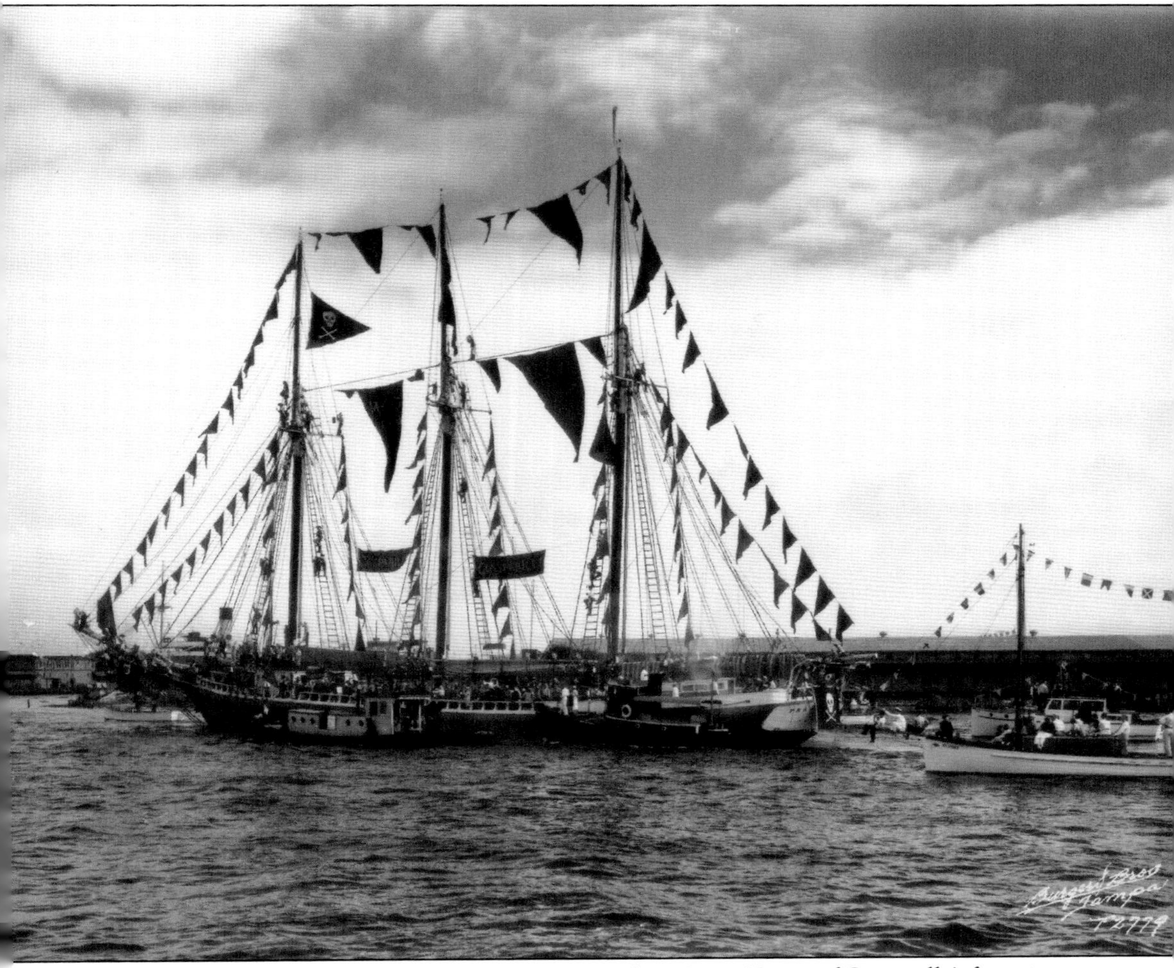

The 1937 Gasparilla Parade heralded the christening of Ye Mystic Krewe of Gasparilla's first pirate ship, which meant that the Krewe no longer had to borrow or rent a ship for the event. Tampa's tourists were captivated by the sight of the pirate ship from Bayshore Boulevard and along the shores of the Hillsborough River. Decked out with brightly colored flags and colorfully dressed pirates, the ship attracted media outlets from throughout the United States.

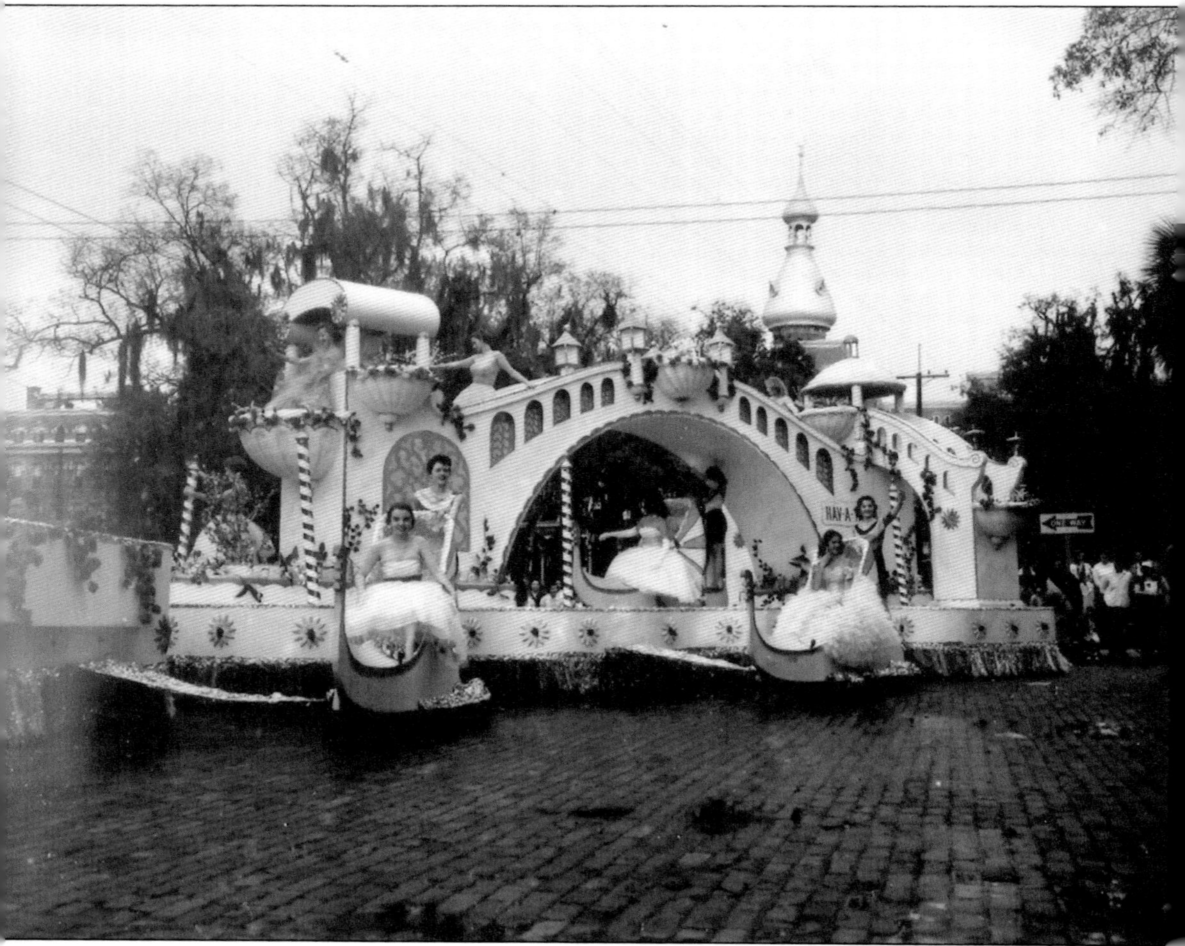

As the Depression years began to wane, the 1939 Gasparilla Parade became a more extravagant event. The elaborate Hav-a-Tampa Cigar Company float pictured here was joined by 53 floats, numerous marching bands from area high schools, social organizations, and the University of Tampa. The governor and local politicians often participate in the parade.

Four

The Great Depression, World War II, and Suburban Growth

The economic boom that Tampa and Florida enjoyed during the early 1920s started to go downhill in 1927. Two severe hurricanes hit South Florida in 1926, and a ruthless outbreak of the Mediterranean fruit fly killed most of the citrus crops in central Florida. These two hurricanes, crop destruction, and the weak national economy were devastating to Hyde Park. By 1929, Hyde Park—along with the entire United States—was in an economic depression. Construction came to a standstill, and few tourists were able to visit the area.

In 1932, the Tampa Bay Hotel went bankrupt and the hotel closed. Families and private investors were also affected by the economic situation, and residences and commercial buildings in Hyde Park faced foreclosure. After several decades of rapid population growth, Tampa's growth slowed to a trickle. Yet, during this period of economic hardship, two significant occurrences brought change to Hyde Park—the opening of the University of Tampa on the former site of the Tampa Bay Hotel and the redevelopment and expansion of Bayshore Boulevard as a New Deal project.

By the end of the 1930s, Hyde Park and Tampa were coming out of the Depression as the United States entered World War II. Suddenly, the area saw an influx of military personnel looking for housing. Apartments and hotels suddenly filled up, and large homes were subdivided into rental units. After years of economic drought, property owners eagerly enjoyed increased income from real estate.

Public policy and a new, relaxed lifestyle saw young families shy away from older neighborhoods, such as Hyde Park, and toward newly developing suburbs. Large homes and former mansions were converted into rooming houses and low-rent office buildings or razed for parking lots. The construction of the Tampa Crosstown Expressway bifurcated Hyde Park and resulted in the demolition of a significant number of the Victorian buildings that were constructed by the pioneer families. Expressway construction resulted in an almost total loss of Dobyville, Hyde Park's African American community.

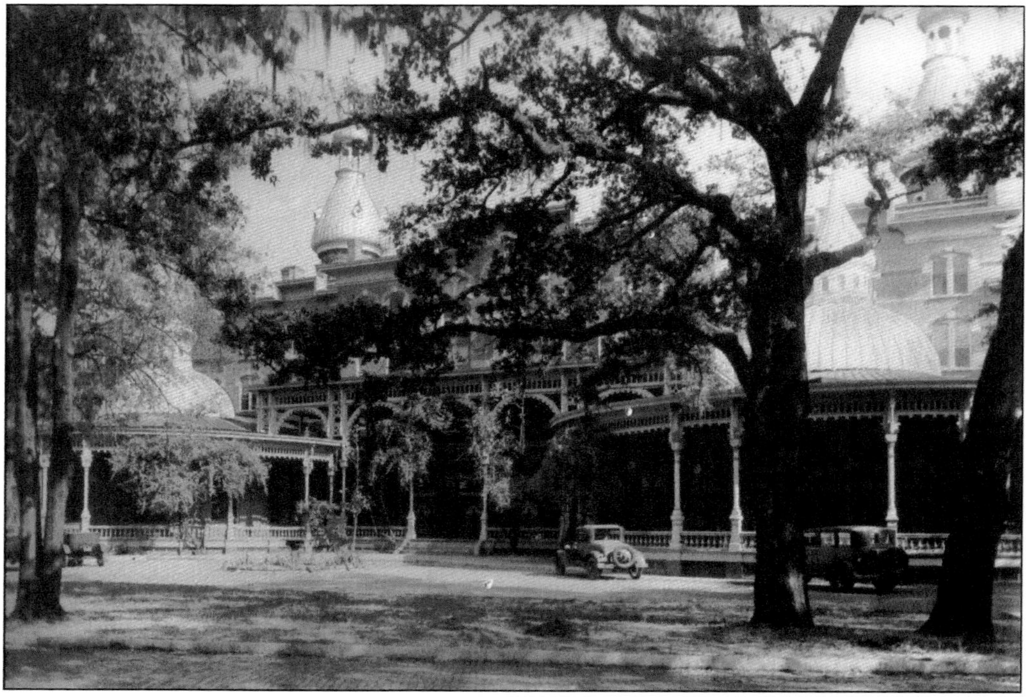

The lavish Tampa Bay Hotel opened in 1891 and welcomed its last guest during the winter of 1932. The lingering Depression contributed to the closing of the hotel and dramatically affected Hyde Park's status as a tourist destination. The building stood vacant for a little more than a year before becoming the permanent home of the fledgling University of Tampa in August 1933. The grandeur of Henry B. Plant's historic hotel continues to inspire generations of students, as shown in the 2011 photograph below, who choose to explore the possibilities of their futures in this historic setting. (Above, Henry B. Plant Museum Archives, Tampa, Florida; below, JRSPhotos.com.)

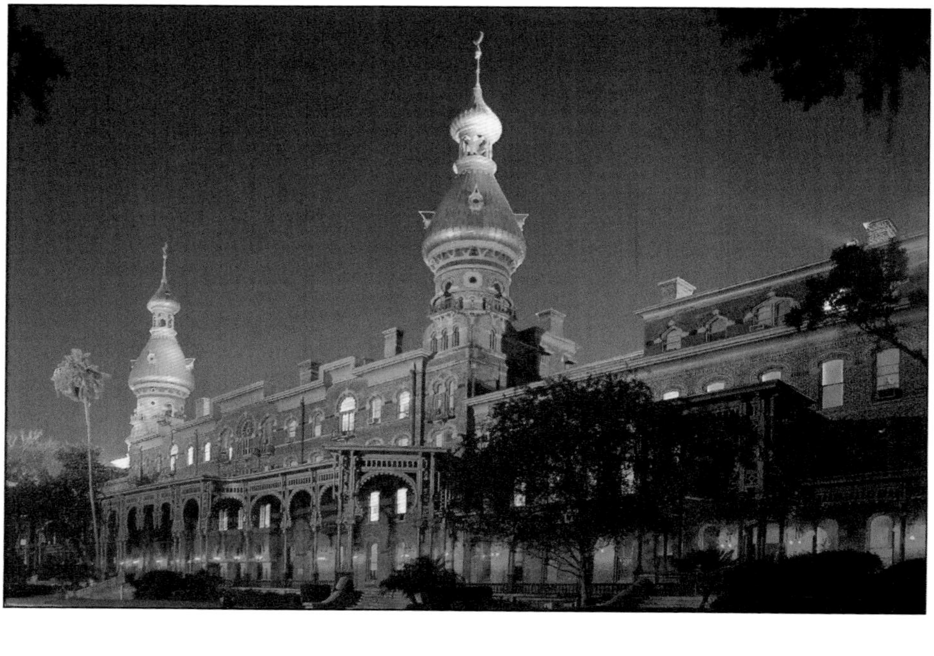

This tourist information building was constructed in the 1930s on the edge of Plant Park to provide information and assistance to tourists. The building was constructed as a Works Progress Administration (WPA) project to help the local economy maintain the tourist industry, and it was staffed by volunteers from local civic organizations. Hyde Park gradually lost its tourist base as the hotels closed or were converted to permanent residential buildings.

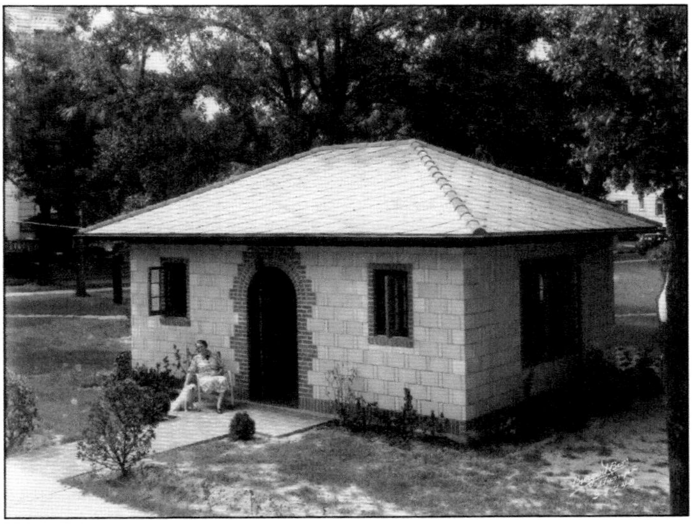

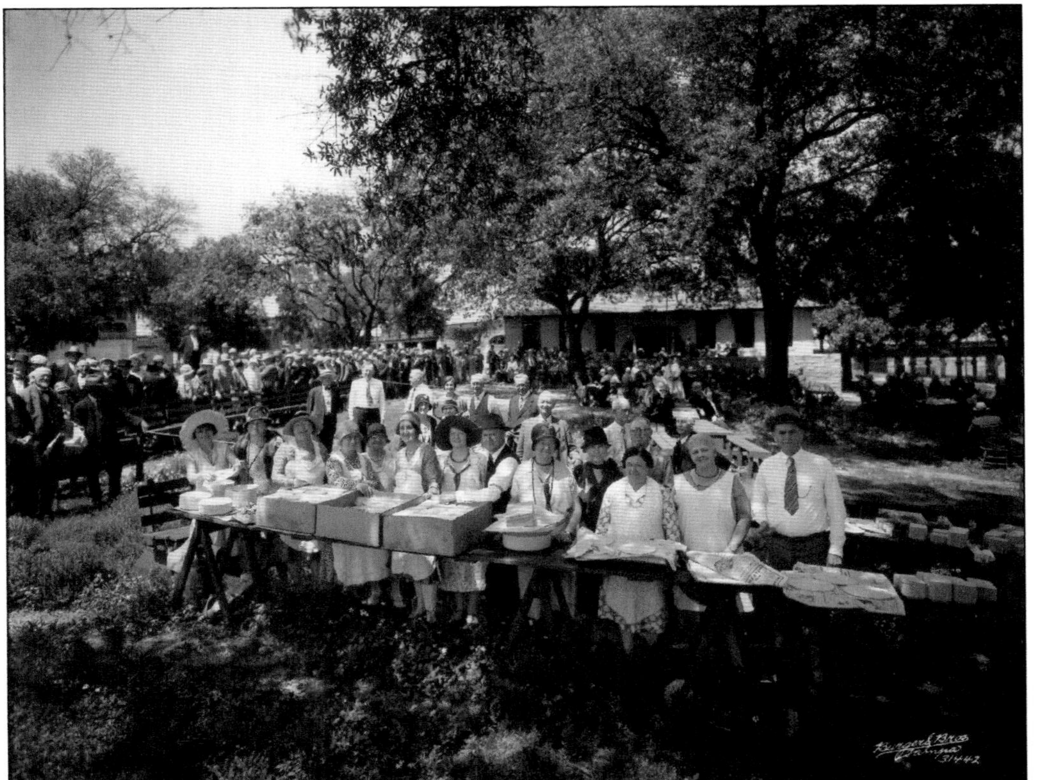

Various activities were planned for visitors to the resort areas of Hyde Park. This 1936 photograph was taken at a picnic in Plant Park. Several local restaurants closed during the Depression, and picnics were staged to maintain a festive atmosphere. Events like this proved popular and were held until the start of World War II.

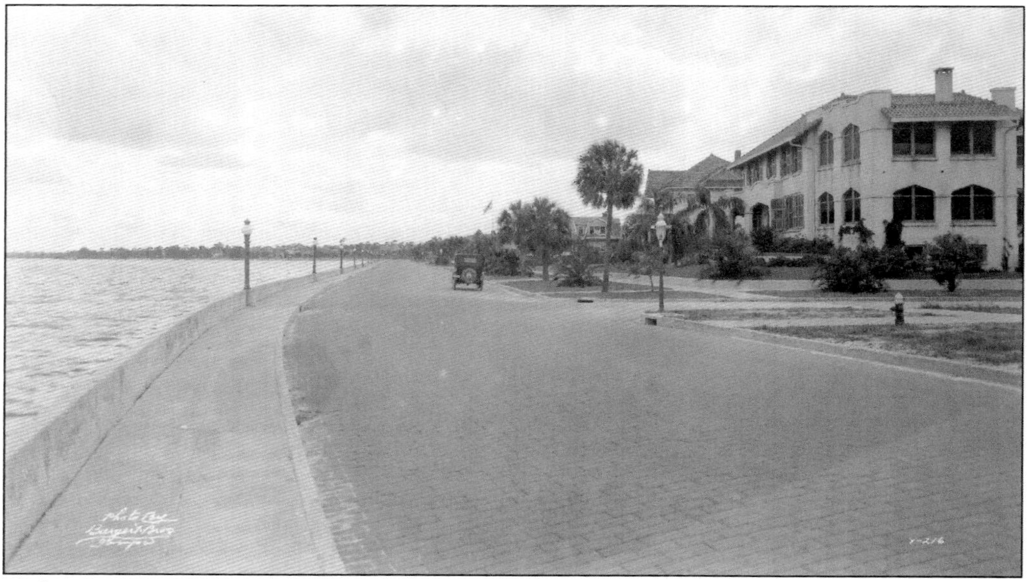

In the 1920s, Bayshore Boulevard became an elegant promenade along Hillsborough Bay, as shown in this photograph. The entire length had a restrained seawall, electric lighting was in place, the roadway was covered with pavers, and the famous sidewalk—said to be the longest continuous sidewalk in the world—accommodated leisurely pedestrian travel. Bayshore Boulevard was the link between downtown Tampa and the residential neighborhoods along Hillsborough Bay, including the eastern boundaries of Hyde Park.

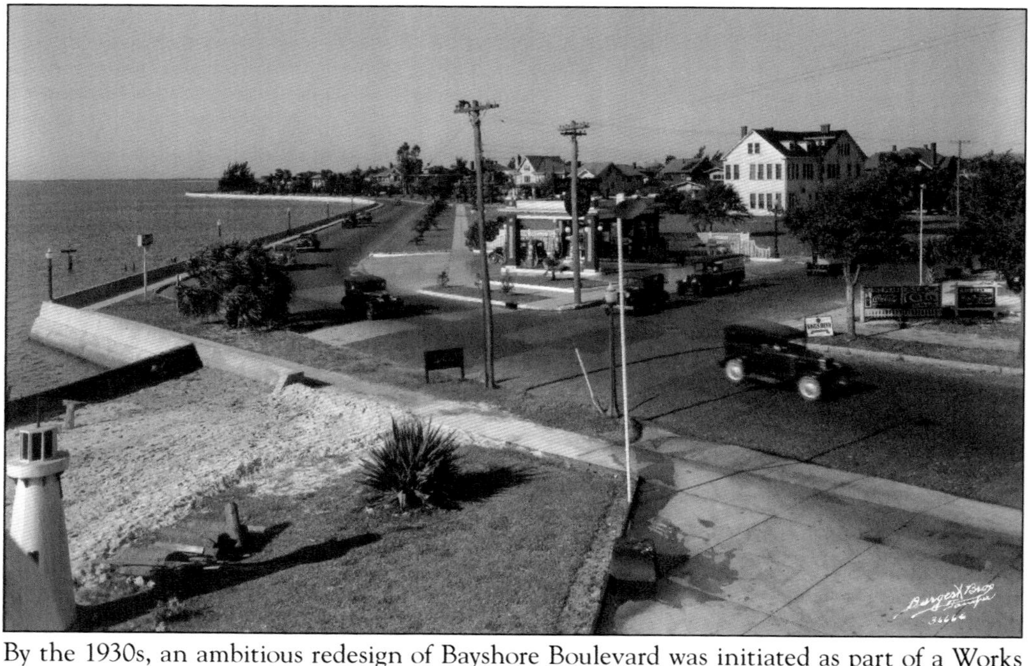

By the 1930s, an ambitious redesign of Bayshore Boulevard was initiated as part of a Works Progress Administration project. The boulevard would be widened and paved with concrete, and landscaping would be introduced along with improvements to the seawall. This 1934 photograph shows a New Deal project under way at lower left.

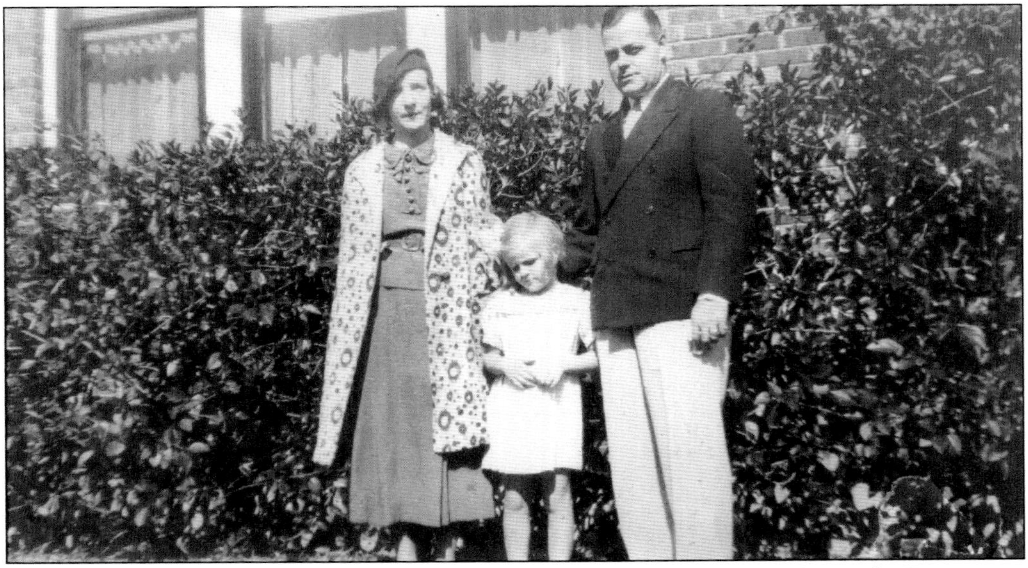

Holidays and special events were a time to dress up in Sunday clothing, even during the Depression. Dr. James and Gladys Holdstock and their daughter Jacqueline stand in the side yard of their house on Edison Street during the spring of 1934. Dr. Holdstock was a prominent local dentist, and he spent the World War II years in field hospitals in Italy and North Africa. (Holdstock family archives.)

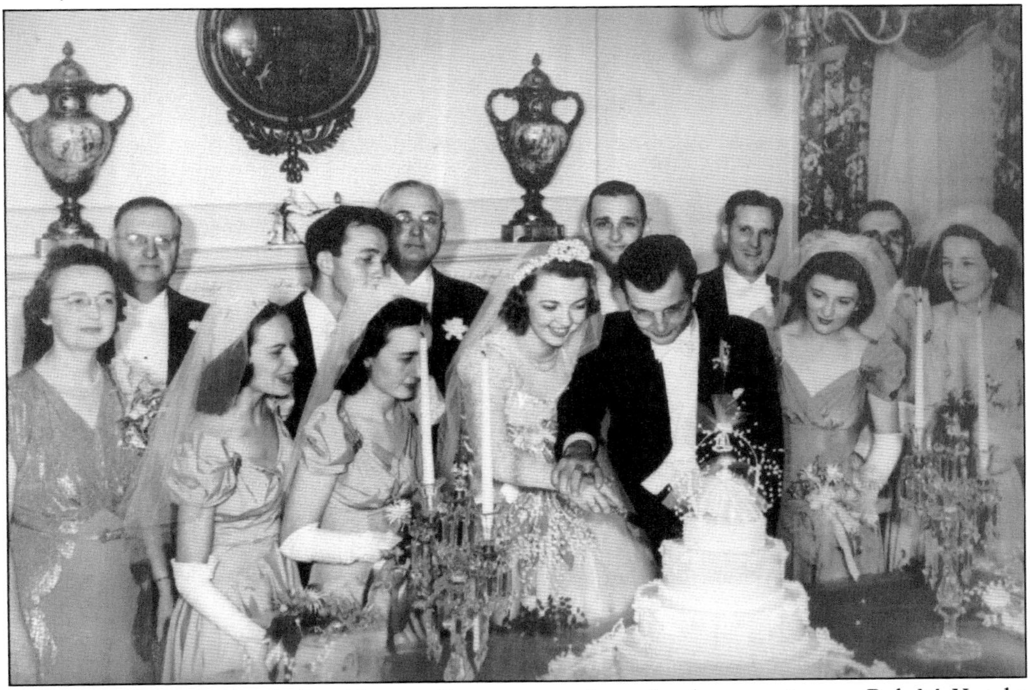

This 1939 photograph of Mary Frances Swann was taken after her marriage to Bob McKnight in the dining room of the Swann house, located on Bayshore Boulevard. Swann was queen of Gasparilla in 1938, as was her mother, Mary Cotter Lucas, in 1914. Jim Swann, father of the bride, was a prominent local real estate developer. (Ferman family archives.)

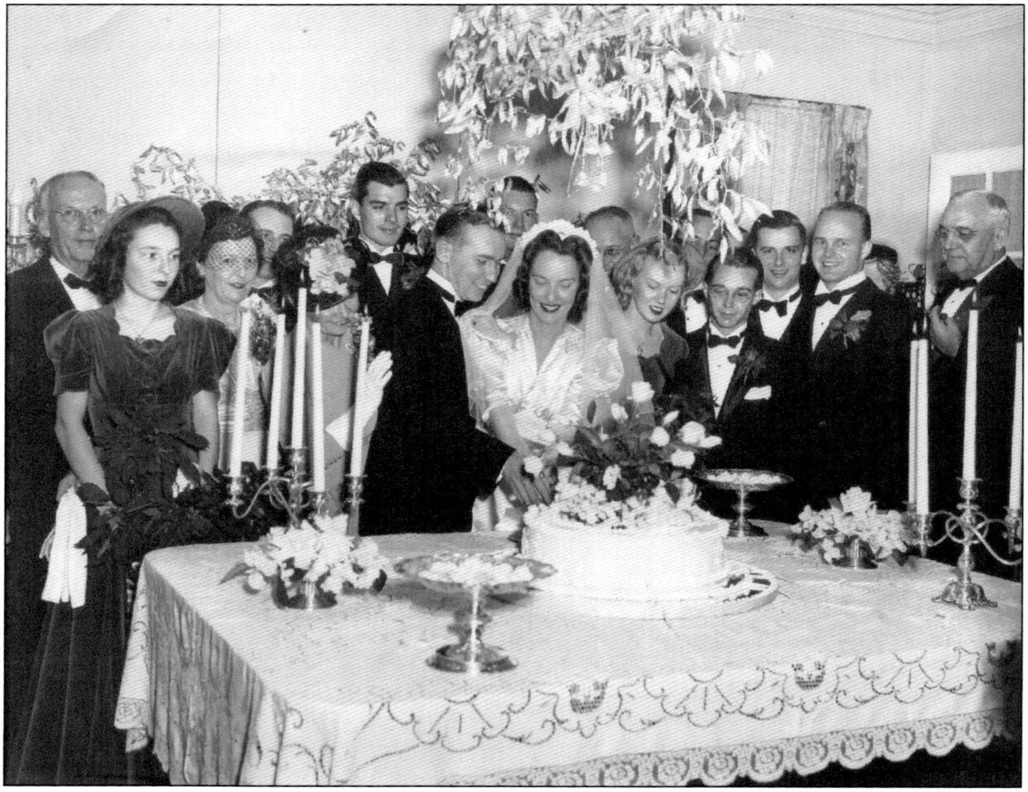

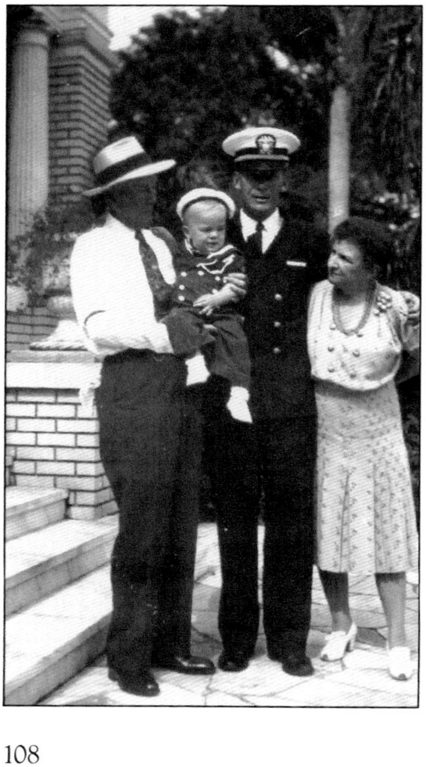

The wedding of Mary Shackleford and Norman Brown took place on January 2, 1941, at a candlelight service at St. John's Episcopal Church. Following the ceremony, the reception was held at the Hyde Park home of the bride's parents. The United States would enter World War II by the end of 1941, and formal weddings were held less often during the war as the nation focused on the military. (Ferman family archives.)

Three generations of the Ferman family—from left to right, Fred, James Jr., Lieutenant James, and Bess—posed in front of the family home for this 1944 photograph. (Ferman family archives.)

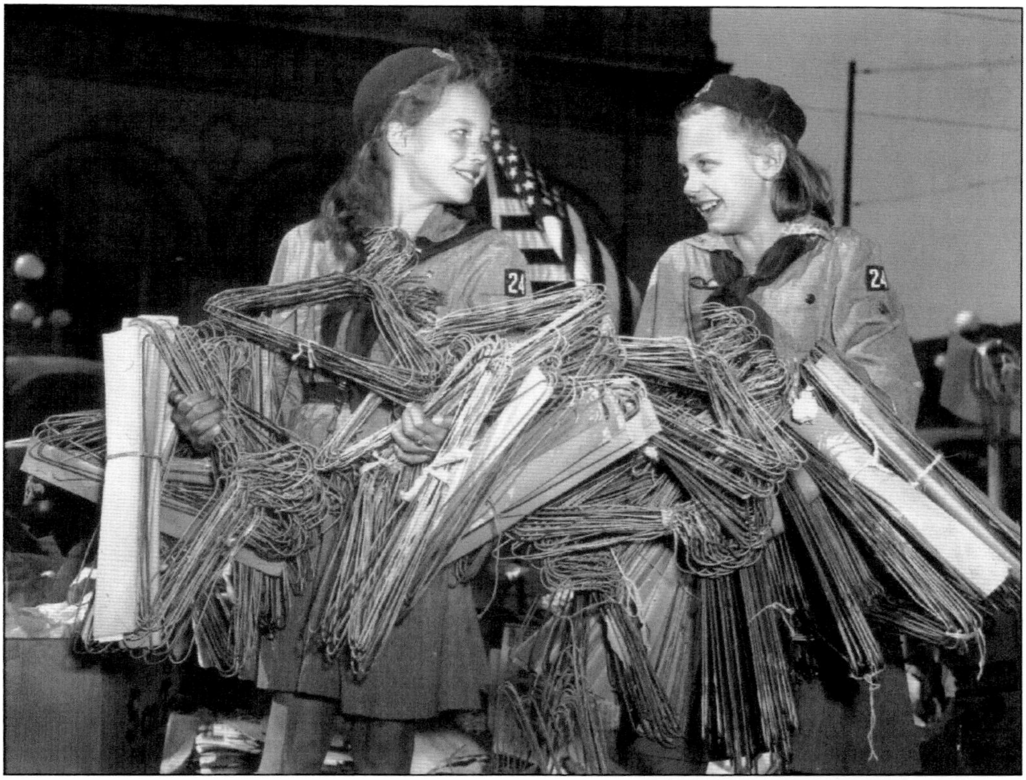

World War II gathered the efforts of the entire country, including the Girl Scouts of Tampa. This January 1942 photograph shows one of several drives they held as part of the war effort, as Delta Mae Holley and Betty Gurney collect wire hangers for recycling. (Girl Scouts of West Central Florida Archives.)

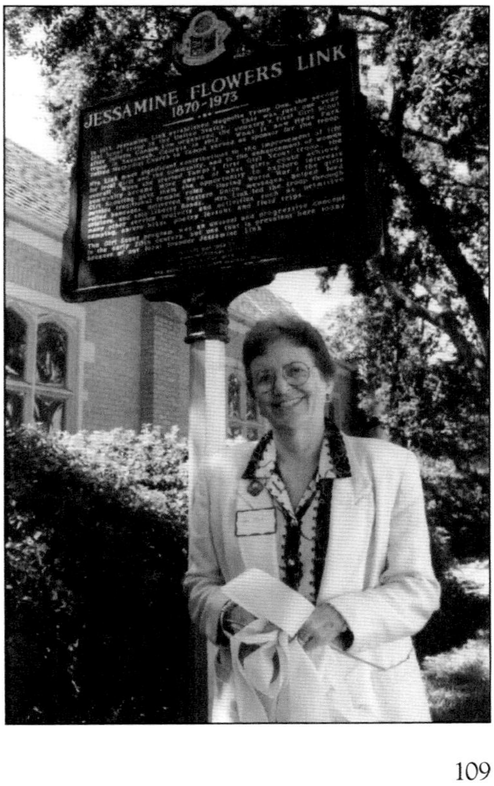

Tampa civic leader Jan Platt, a longtime advocate of historic preservation and a driving force behind local Girl Scout programs, stands in front of the Jessamine Flowers Link marker adjacent to the Hyde Park Methodist Church in 1998. In 1913, Link established Magnolia Troop One, the second Girl Scout Troup in the United States, just one year after Juliette Gordon Low established the first troop in Savannah, Georgia, in 1912. (Girl Scouts of West Central Florida Archives.)

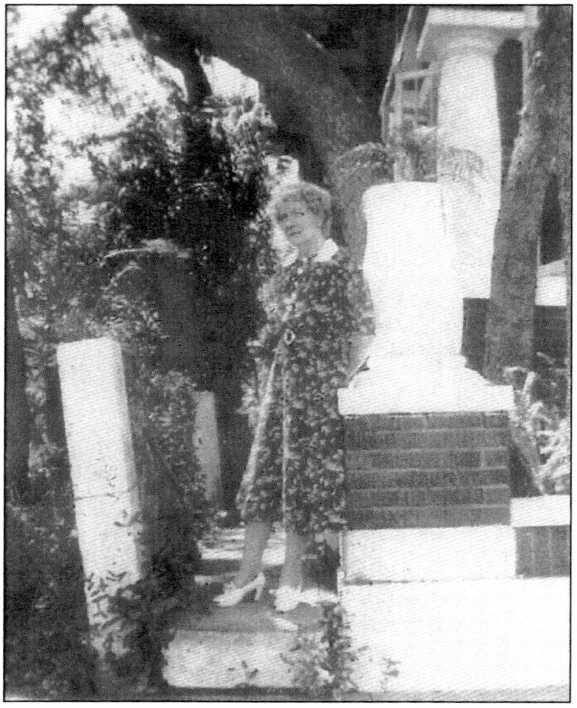

The era after World War II was a time of transition in Hyde Park. Mabel Bean (left), who was a published author when this 1940 photograph was taken in front of her Hyde Park apartment, spent her early years in Port Tampa City and, as a child, was a reconnoiterer during the Spanish-American War, traveling from Port Tampa on her bicycle to deliver messages to military officers camped in the vicinity. The November 1952 photograph below shows Bessie L. Zimmer sitting in the drawing room of her home, located at 345 Hyde Park Avenue. Zimmer was an important hostess, and this formal portrait was taken in anticipation of a charity event planned to take place in her home. (Left, Holdstock family archives.)

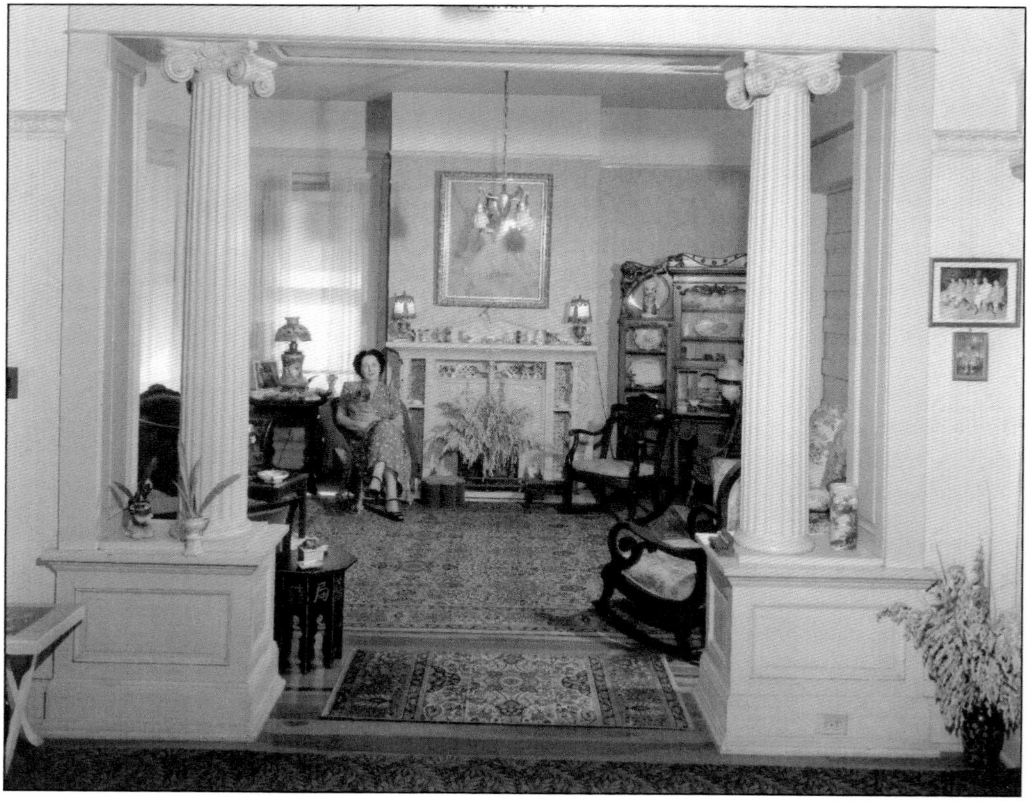

Five

The Renaissance of Hyde Park

The generation that followed the Great Depression and World War II—the baby boomers—went on an unprecedented spree after years of economic hardship and rationing. After the war, what was bought was rarely fine—just new and often fun to own. Policy makers wanted to discard or tear down the old and replace with all things new. The national interstate system, conceived as the ideal way to travel between cities, accelerated the deterioration of older neighborhoods. Fashion promoted the "new look," and a "dream home" was new, physically separated from established neighborhoods, and frequently located in a sandy, unfinished landscape.

Postwar Hyde Park was populated by the elderly, those left behind amidst the renewed economic prosperity, or those fortunate enough to weather the difficult years. The stately buildings, beautiful Bayshore Boulevard, and pedestrian-friendly, tree-shaded streets lingered, too.

Even as the nation became obsessed with futurism, historic preservation had begun a slow but steady rebirth in Hyde Park. In 1959, Sunny Delo, whose husband, David, was the president of the University of Tampa, gathered some of Tampa's prominent women and initiated a restoration of the original fireplaces in the once-splendid Tampa Bay Hotel. Their efforts paralleled a quiet renewal effort under way by another wife living in Georgetown with her husband, who was a rising political star. Jacqueline Kennedy would soon share her passion for historic preservation, garnering a record-breaking television audience for her tour of the newly restored White House in 1963. The resulting passage of the Historic Preservation Act of 1964 proved to be a springboard for preservation efforts across the country.

Suddenly, Hyde Park was "rediscovered" by young, creative professionals seeking an alternative to the suburbs. Hyde Park's public schools were rehabilitated, encouraging young families to purchase historic homes. Public facilities and parks were expanded and improved. The new generation relocating to Hyde Park often over invested in their optimism about Hyde Park's future. One structure at a time and one street at a time, Hyde Park has evolved into one of the most beautifully restored single-family neighborhoods of early-20th-century Craftsman, Prairie, and Mediterranean Revival buildings in the United States.

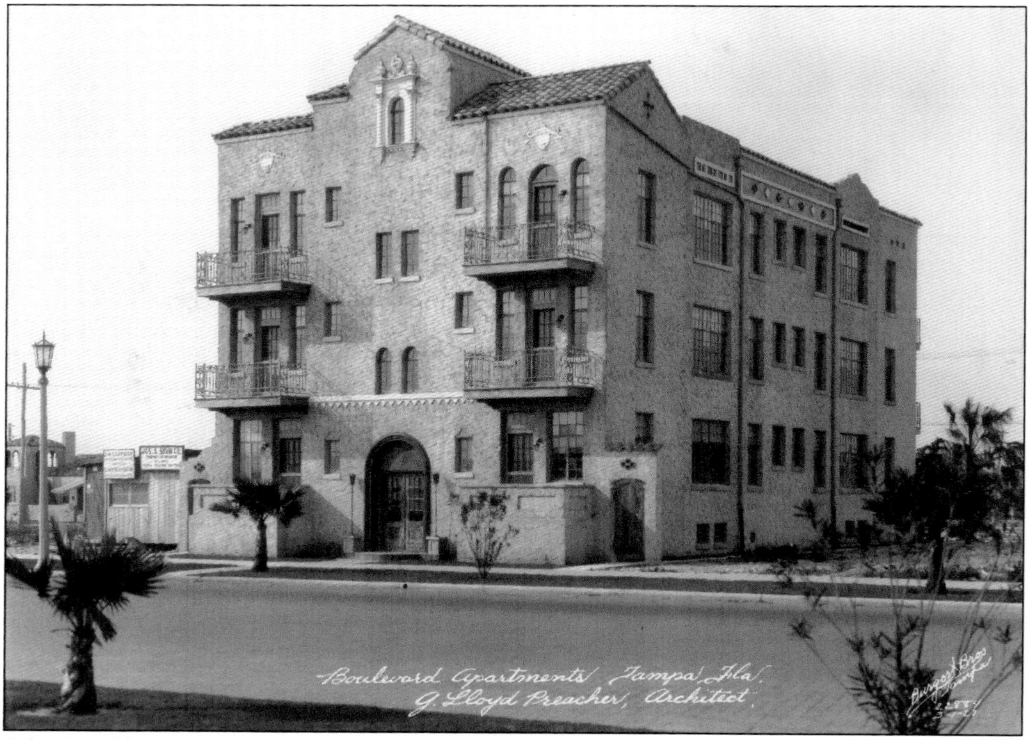

After World War II, Hyde Park experienced a steady decline—the result of young families moving to the newly developed suburbs, downtown's expansion, and lax building maintenance that led to deterioration. While Hyde Park was not directly impacted by the national interstate system, the rapid growth of Hillsborough County accelerated the need for highway construction. In the early 1970s, land was purchased for the Crosstown Expressway, which would slice through a section of Hyde Park that was built in the late 19th and early 20th centuries. The Boulevard Apartments (above), located on South Boulevard, were razed for construction of the freeway overpass bridge in the photograph below. The impact was not only felt in terms of destroyed buildings, but also in the loss of continuity. The bifurcation of the Hyde Park Historic District and the construction of the freeway bridge significantly altered the street grid and resulted in most of the Dobyville community being displaced, along with a loss of many Victorian and eclectic homes. (Below, JRSPhotos.com.)

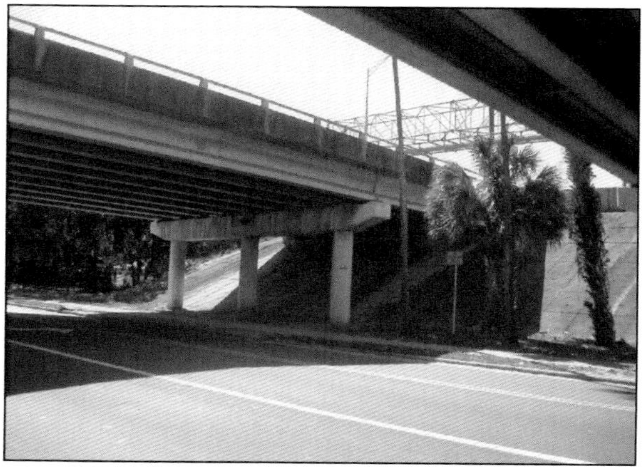

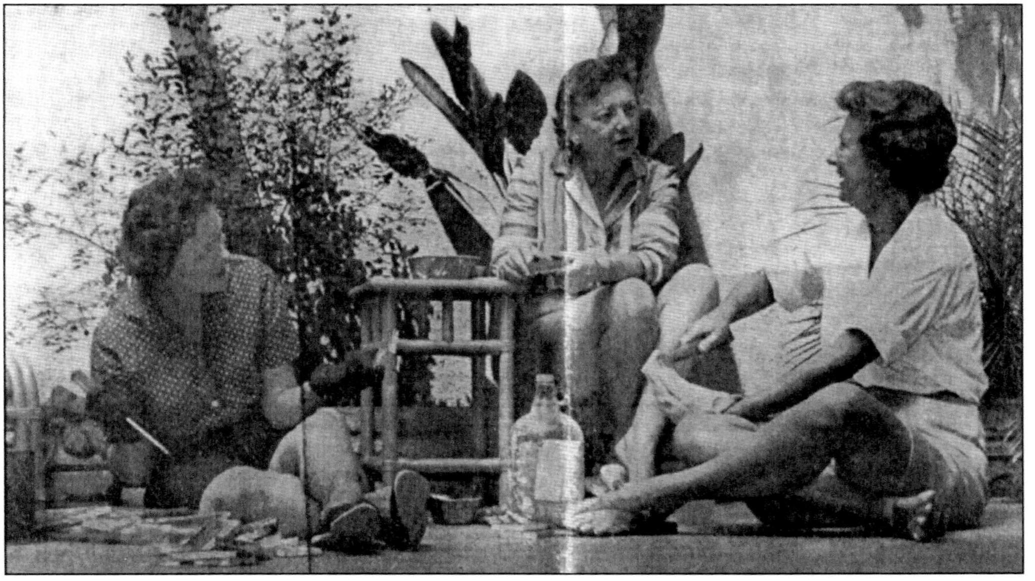

Restoration of Henry B. Plant's Tampa Bay Hotel began in 1959 when a small group of women decided to restore an original fireplace in the Grand Parlor of the historic hotel. The initial task involved the arduous removal of paint and masonry from historic tiles using chisels. After a successful summer of tile restoration, the group of 27 women incorporated, calling themselves the Chiselers. (The Chiselers, Inc.)

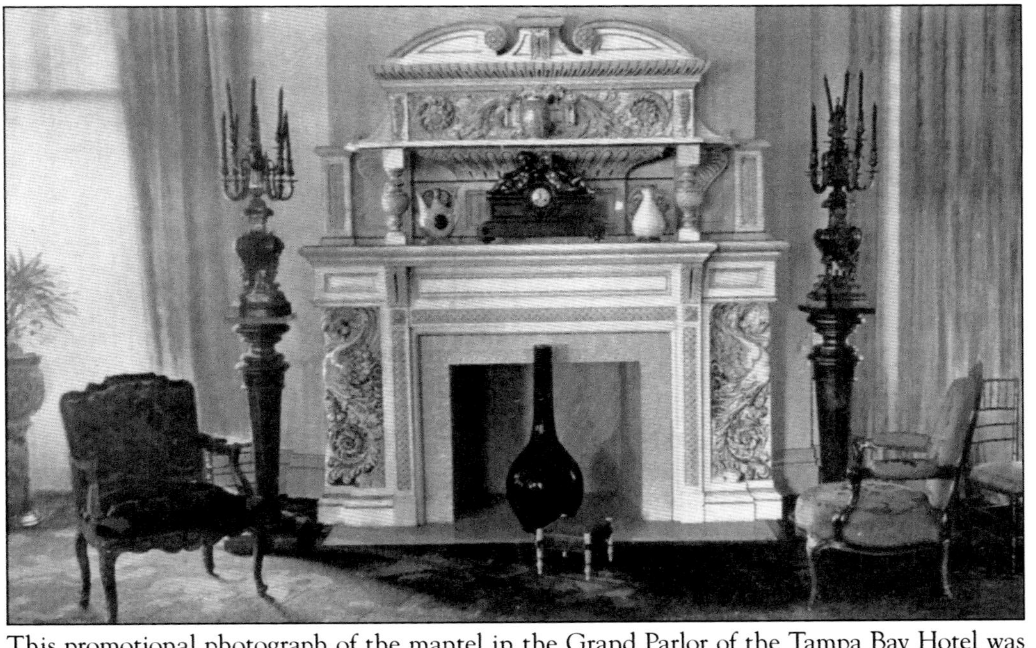

This promotional photograph of the mantel in the Grand Parlor of the Tampa Bay Hotel was an inspiration for the restoration efforts of the Chiselers. In 1959, Tampa's most recognizable building was in a state of neglect and disrepair when the Chiselers began efforts to restore Plant Hall. (Henry B. Plant Museum Archives, Tampa, Florida.)

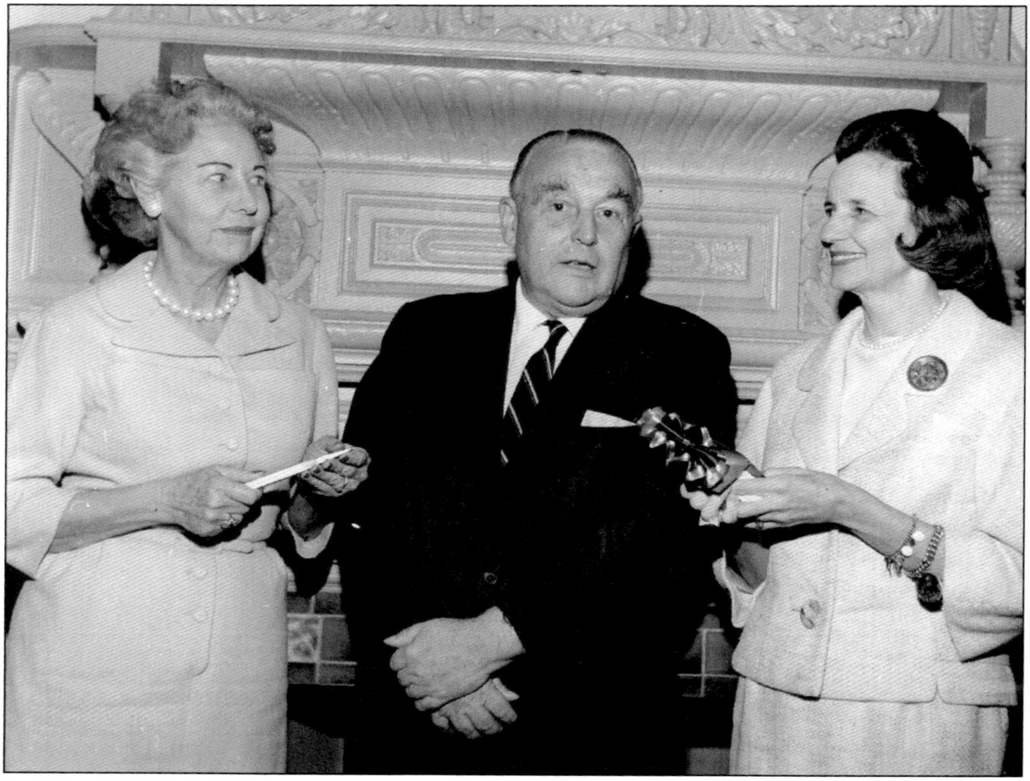

The work of the Chiselers has evolved from the unassuming job of cleaning fireplace tiles to become the primary support organization for the preservation of Plant Hall. This 1964 photograph was taken in the Grand Parlor in front of the first fireplace that was restored. Pictured here are, from left to right, Chiseler Mildred Hill, University of Tampa president Dr. David Delo, and charter Chiseler Louise Lykes Ferguson. (The Chiselers, Inc.)

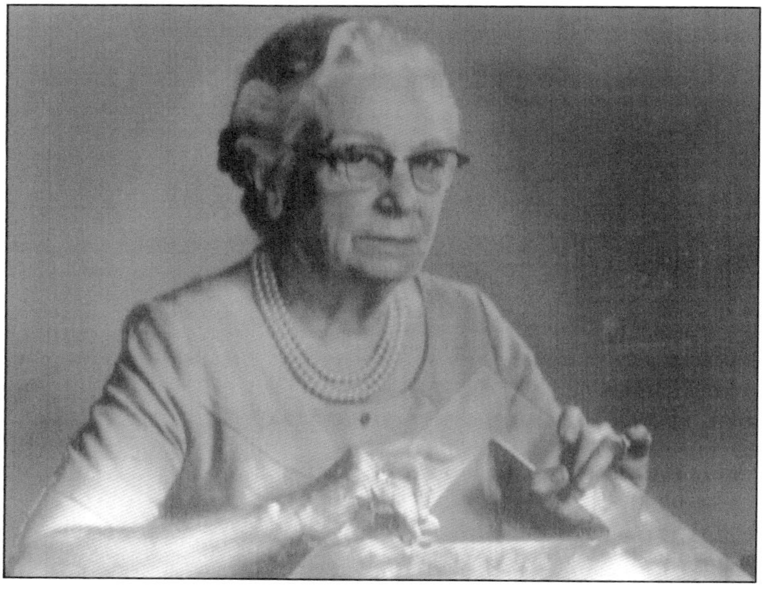

Hazel Lee Ward was one of the first professionally trained interior designers in Florida. A graduate of a Chicago art school, she was associated with her husband, Paul T. Ward, in their interior design business. In addition to being a successful businesswoman, she was an early advocate for the preservation of the Tampa Bay Hotel and a founding member of the Chiselers. (The Chiselers, Inc.)

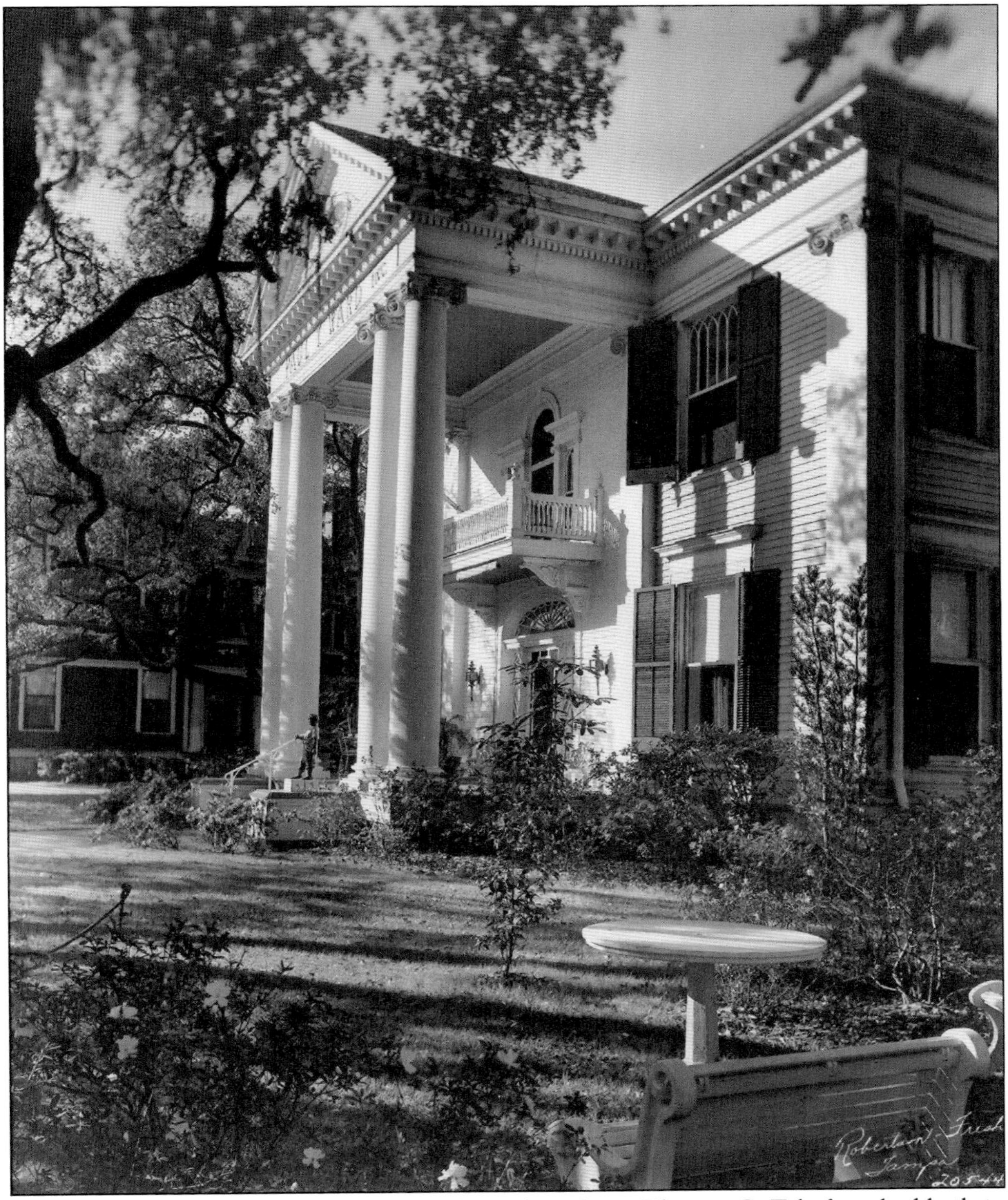

Hazel and Paul Ward purchased the Neoclassical residence Thomas C. Taliaferro had built in 1893 for his family. The Wards operated their successful interior design business in the historic home from 1941 until they closed up shop in 1977. (Tampa Bay History Center.)

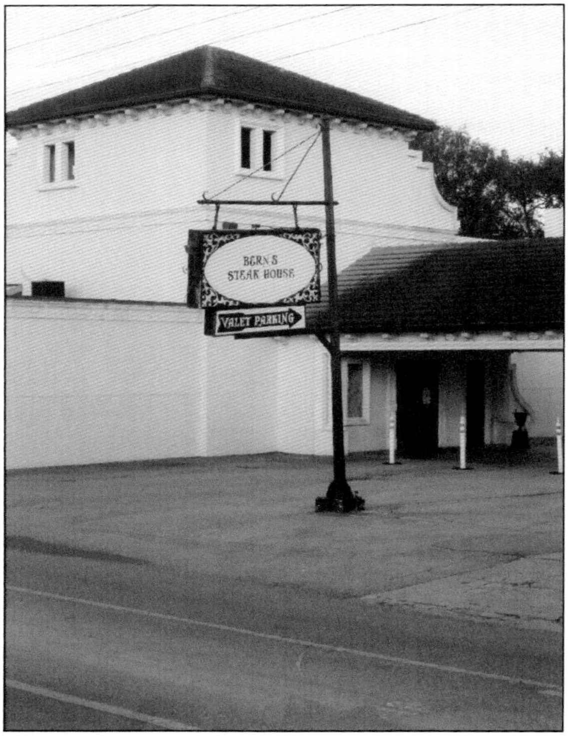

Hyde Park's culinary roots can be traced back to the Tampa Bay Hotel, and they have grown with each generation. The area continues to be a gastronomic destination with an extensive variety of restaurants of all types and price ranges. Bern's Steak House, located at 1208 South Howard Avenue, opened in 1956 and evolved into an internationally famous steak house, contributing to the rehabilitation of Hyde Park. (JRSPhotos.com.)

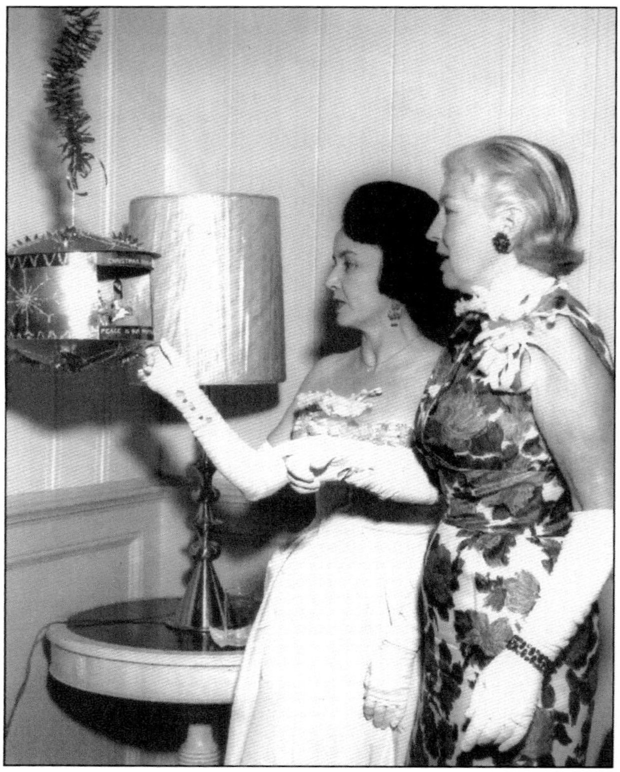

Martha Ferman (left) and Sunny Delo (right) were committed supporters of the preservation of Hyde Park and the University of Tampa's Plant Hall. Ferman was also active in numerous civic activities, and Delo was the founder of the Chiselers. This 1965 photograph was taken during a holiday event supporting the University of Tampa. (Ferman family archives.)

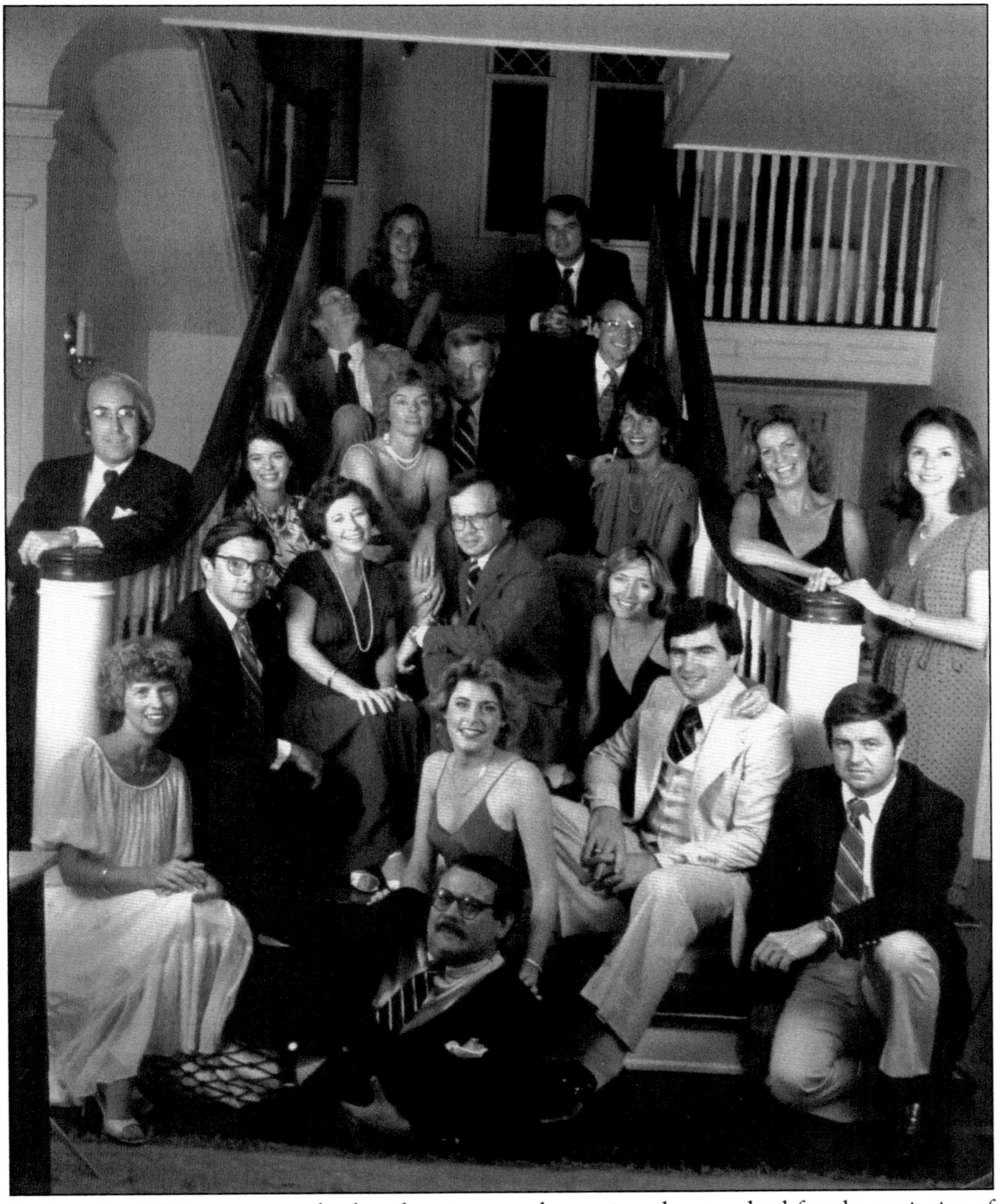

During the 1970s, as new, suburban housing was becoming the standard for the majority of Americans, discerning young professionals rediscovered the old residences of their grandparents, as evidenced in this 1975 photograph. Years of neglect and abandonment had taken a toll on Hyde Park. Nevertheless, the sturdy homes, pedestrian-friendly streets, and gracious tree canopies waited to be reconsidered by a new generation. Whether as a formal setting for the end of an evening gala or an informal gathering of friends, the homes of Hyde Park had a new generation willing to restore and renew the historic neighborhood. (Henderson archives.)

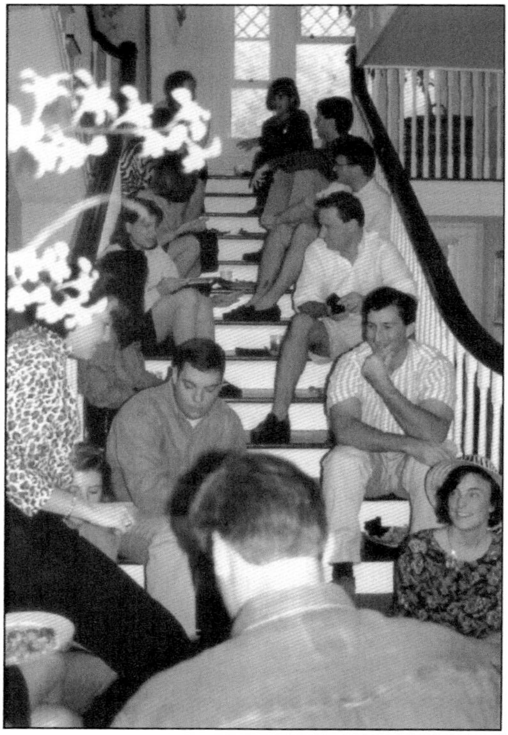

This 1992 photograph shows a pre-wedding party, demonstrating how Hyde Park's historic homes easily adapt to the needs of each new generation. (Ward family archives.)

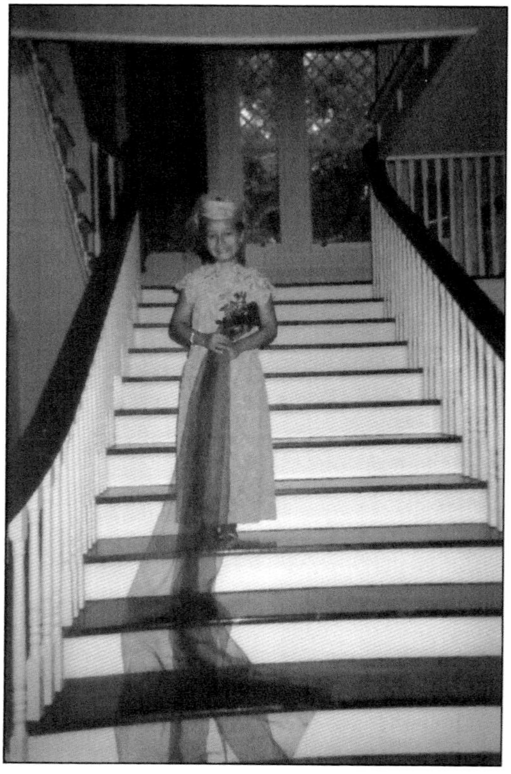

Several generations of the descendants of Paul D. Cochran family have explored the endless possibilities of the stairway in the family home. Here, Cochran's great-great-granddaughter is participating in a fantasy celebration. The preservation of Hyde Park's historic buildings has helped to maintain the cultural heritage of Hyde Park. (Ward family archives.)

Bayshore Boulevard, established trees, and subtropical foliage have served as a backdrop for generations of Hyde Park family celebrations and important events. This century-old live oak tree is an appropriate and symbolic background in this 1994 photograph of the just-married Leigh Ann Charles and Doug King. (Ward family archives.)

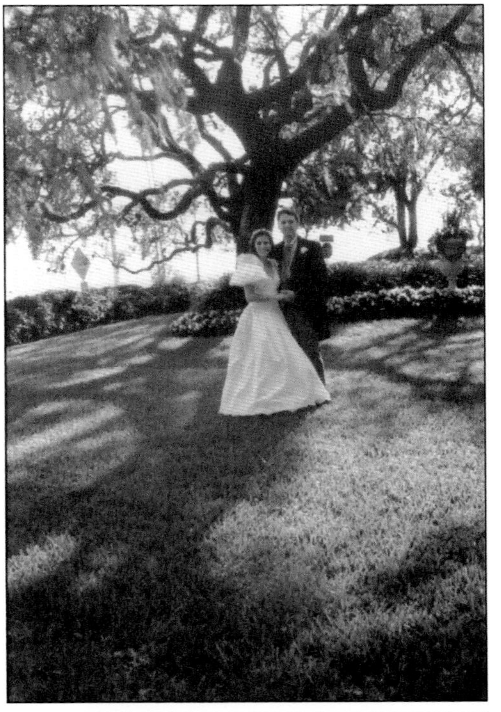

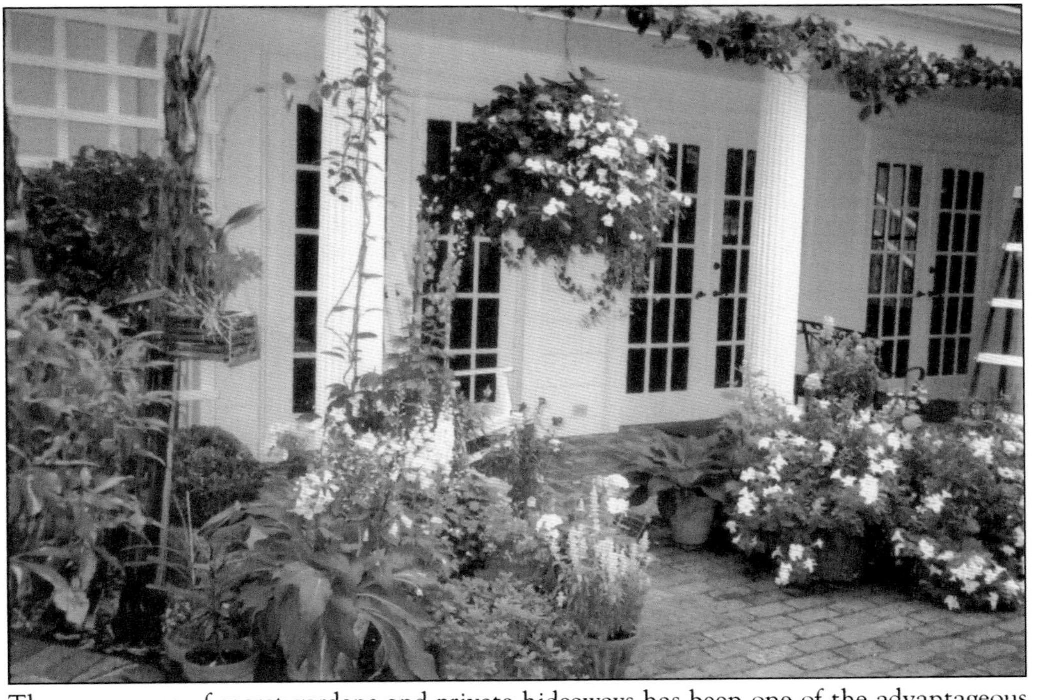

The emergence of secret gardens and private hideaways has been one of the advantageous consequences of the rehabilitation of Hyde Park. The rear lots of historic homes no longer need outdoor service yards, so whether connected to a large estate or a tiny bungalow, many formerly service-oriented backyards have been transformed into private retreats. (Ward family archives.)

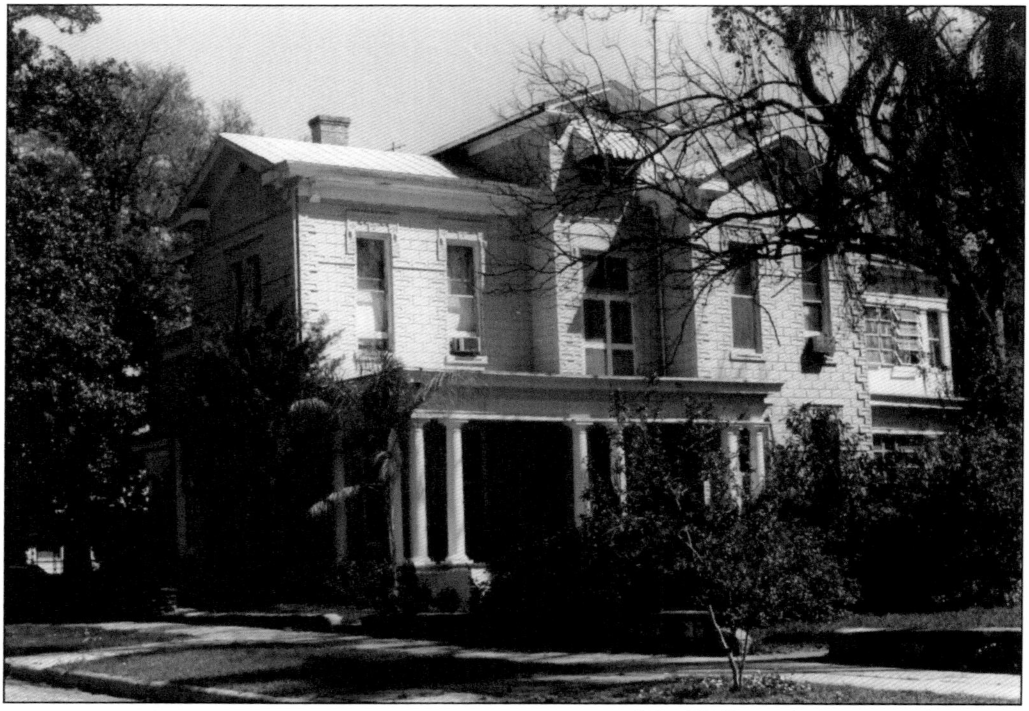

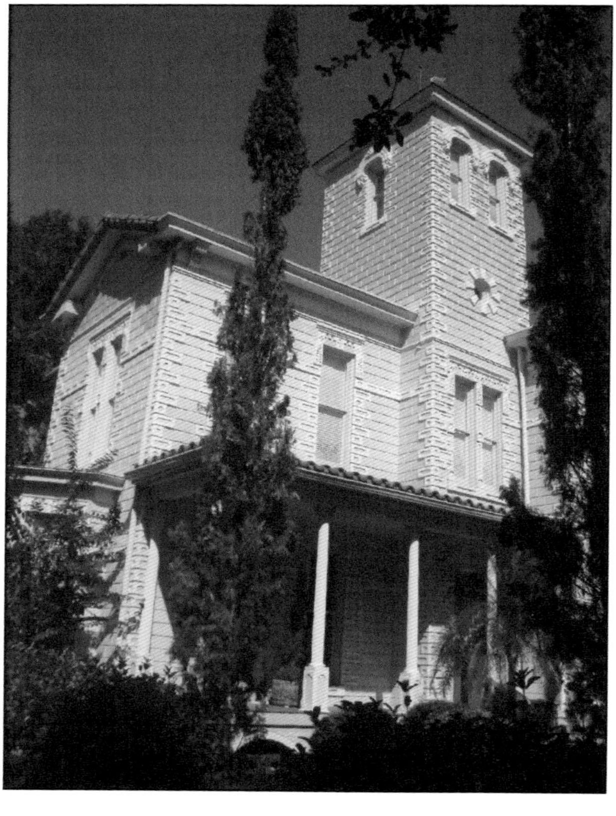

The William A. Morrison house, one of Hyde Park's oldest homes, endured serious neglect and inappropriate additions over the years. The home once stood in the middle of a citrus grove and, fortunately, remained intact as the surrounding land tracts were subdivided into urban lots. The house lost its distinctive tower during a severe windstorm, but the distinctive Italianate building maintained its presence. The tower has since been reconstructed and the home restored and expanded. The Morrison house, pictured at left in its current state, remains an important link in the evolutionary chain of Hyde Park's architectural heritage. (Above, Florida Bureau of Historic Preservation; left, JRSPhotos.com.)

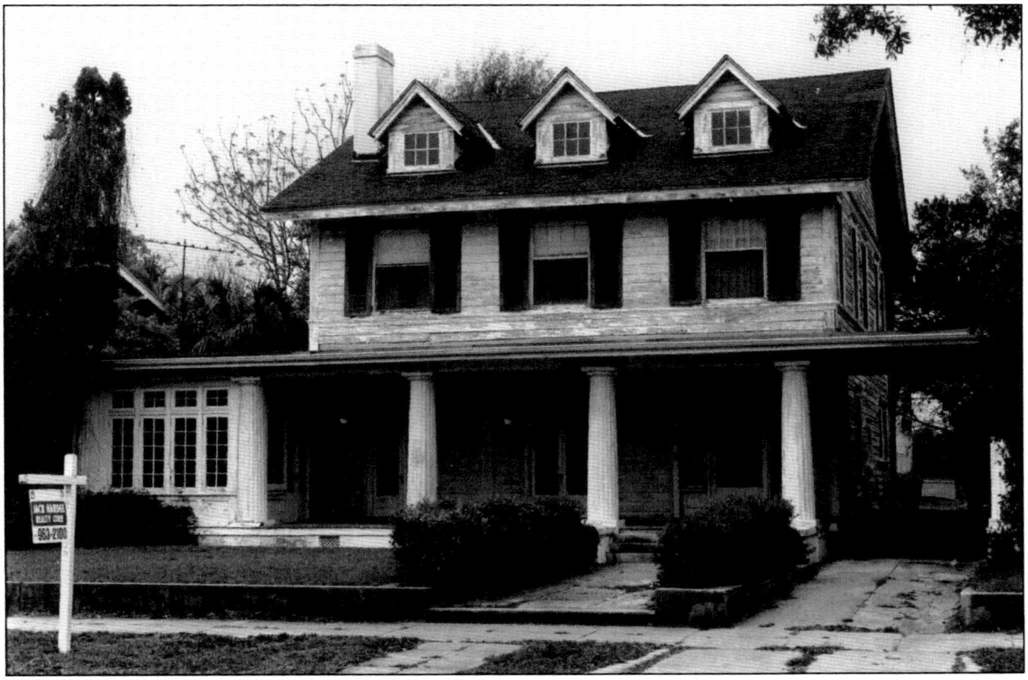

The rehabilitation of Hyde Park has been a continuous and slowly increasing process of recycling family homes. While still solid and stately, by the 1980s this Colonial Revival house was a victim of neglect and the addition of inappropriate decorative details. Changes in public policy, a unique architectural inventory, and community stabilization encouraged long-term investments in the area, and several years after the above photograph was taken, the home was carefully restored—as shown in the photograph below—in the course of Hyde Park's renewal. Improvements extended to the public right-of-way, with landscaped parkways, historic street lighting, and improved paving. (Above, Florida Bureau of Historic Preservation; below, JRSPhotos.com.)

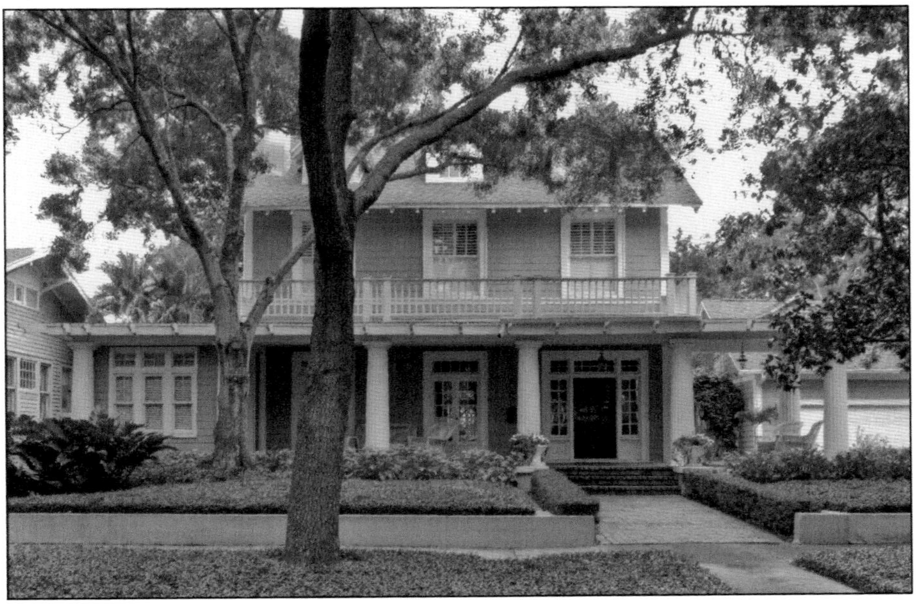

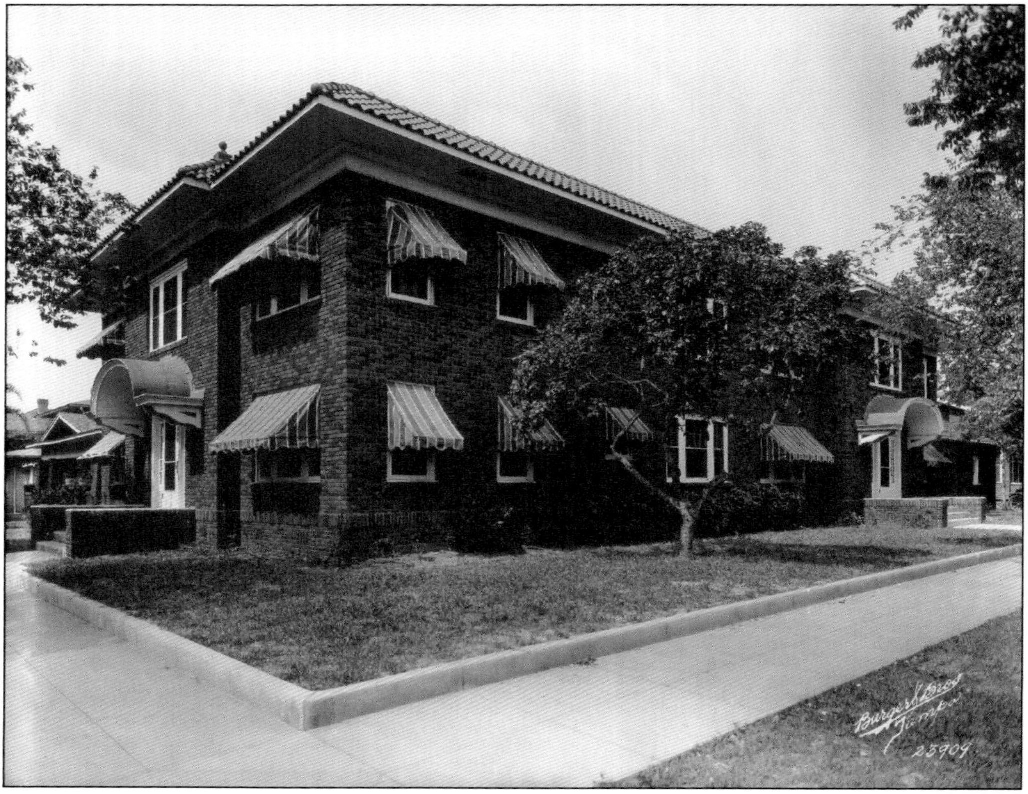

The Thompson Apartments have adapted to the diverse lifestyles of area residents. The redbrick building originally offered fully furnished rooms and provided housing for seasonal residents. More recently, the building has been rehabilitated, and each residential unit has become more personalized to the tenant.

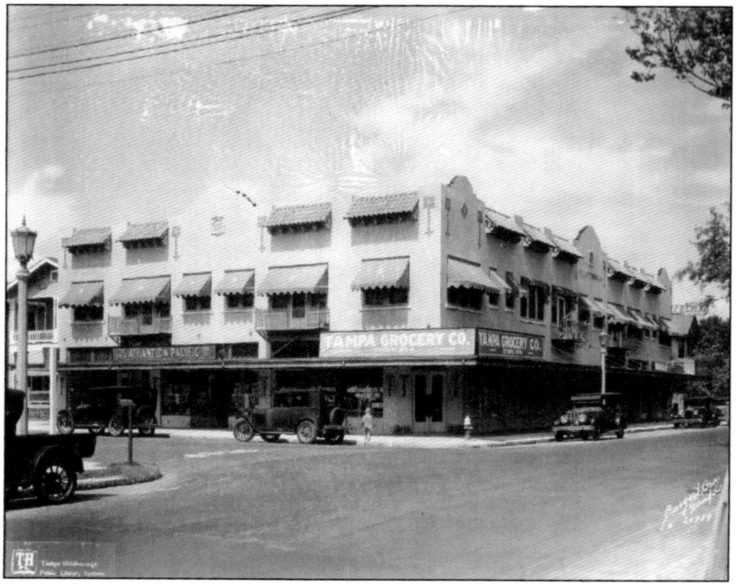

The Plattonian Building, located at Platt Street and South Boulevard, has been a prominent presence since its completion in the early 1920s. It has always been a mixed-use building, with commercial and office spaces on the first floor and residential apartments on the second floor. The Mediterranean Revival building has been a continuous landmark in the historic district.

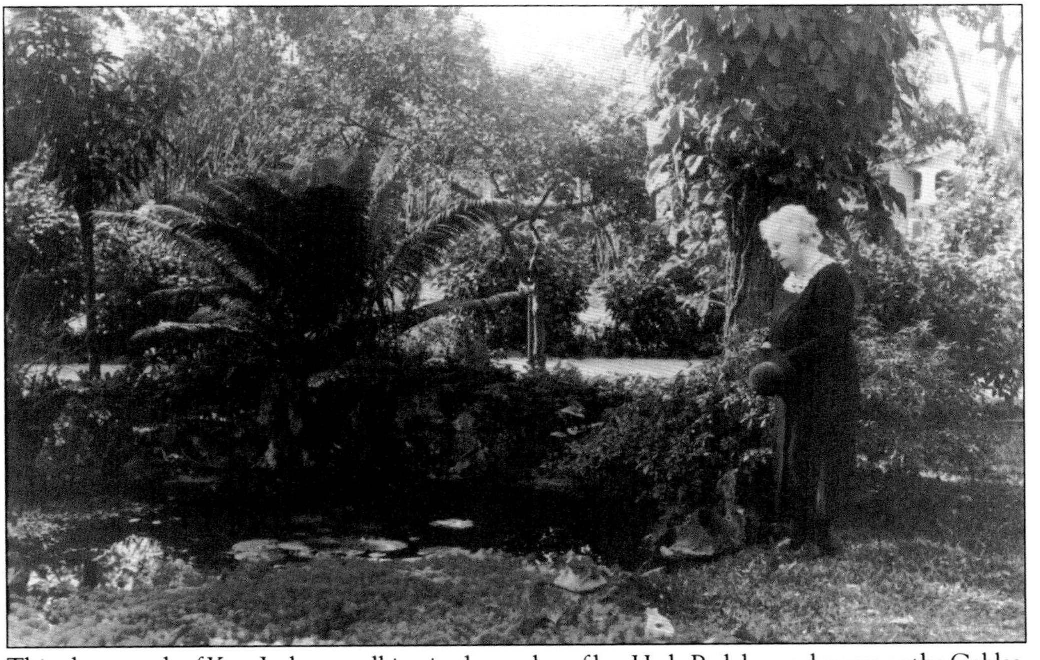

This photograph of Kate Jackson walking in the garden of her Hyde Park home, known as the Gables, was taken in the 1930s. Jackson was a member of an early Tampa family and a local philanthropist. She was a devout Catholic and supported programs that benefited neighborhood children.

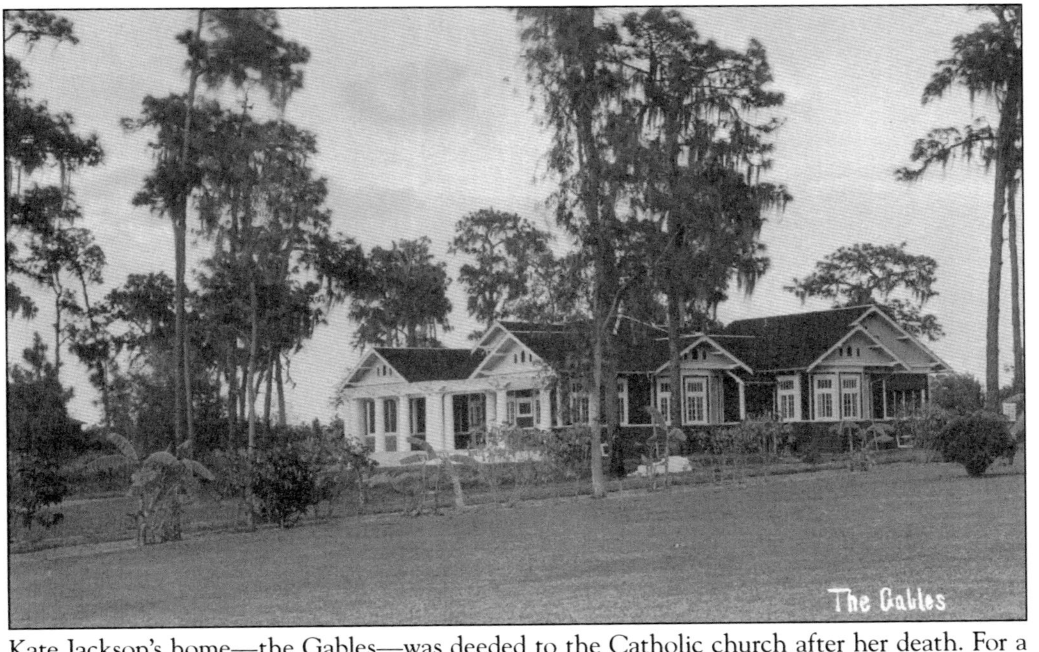

Kate Jackson's home—the Gables—was deeded to the Catholic church after her death. For a short time, the building served as a Catholic kindergarten. The property was eventually sold to the City of Tampa and the home was demolished. The city established a recreation center on the property, naming it the Kate Jackson Community Center in recognition of her efforts to support a public playground. (Tampa Historical Society.)

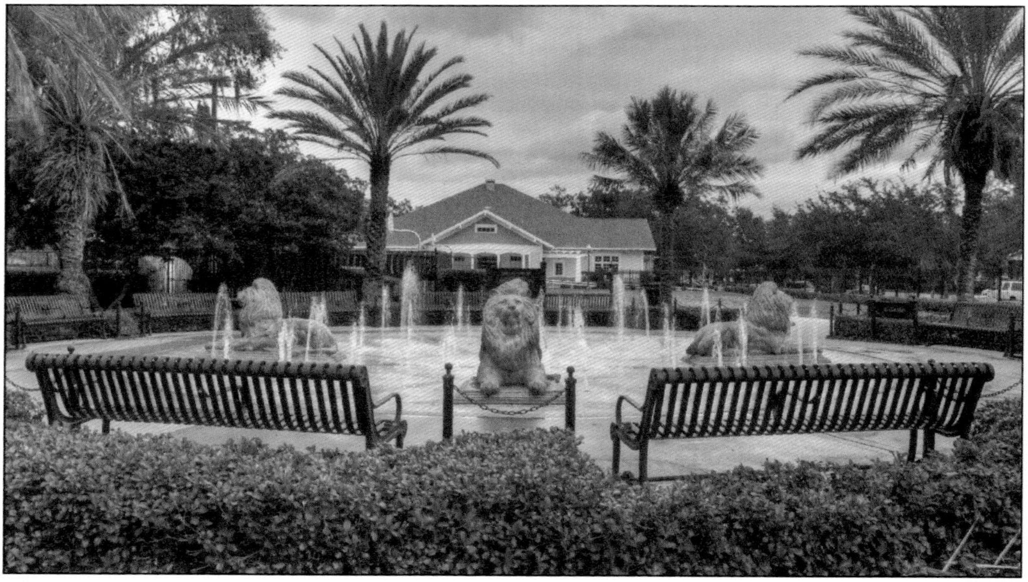

The Kate Jackson Community Center at Anderson Park achieves the vision of Kate Jackson and reflects her commitment to providing children with an attractive and healthy environment that can help them develop into responsible citizens. In the 1990s, the Hyde Park community recognized that the rehabilitation of the area needed to expand beyond individual homes and buildings and a redesign of the park was initiated. (JRSPhotos.com.)

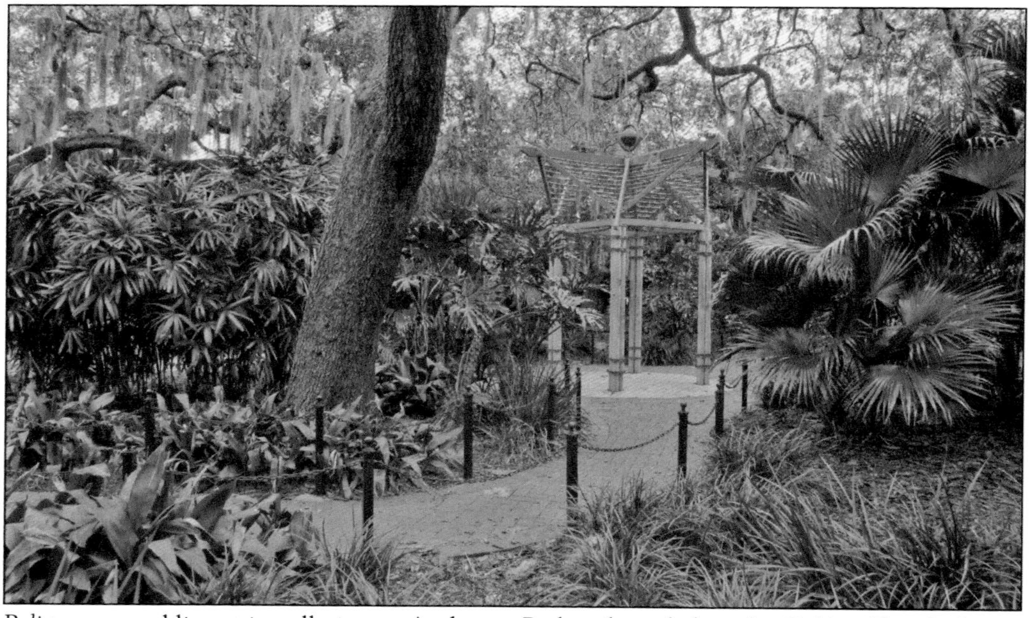

Reliquary, a public art installation at Anderson Park, acknowledges the Gables, Kate Jackson's home that was originally located on the site. The lush landscaping surrounding the sculpture is a nod to Jackson's love of Florida's flora. Reinforcing Jackson's commitment to young people, the sculpture is both serious and playful and allows room for personal interpretation. The project was a collaboration between Lorraine Genovar, Richard Penza Jr., and Wayne Fernandez and was gifted by Norma Gene Lykes. (JRSPhotos.com)

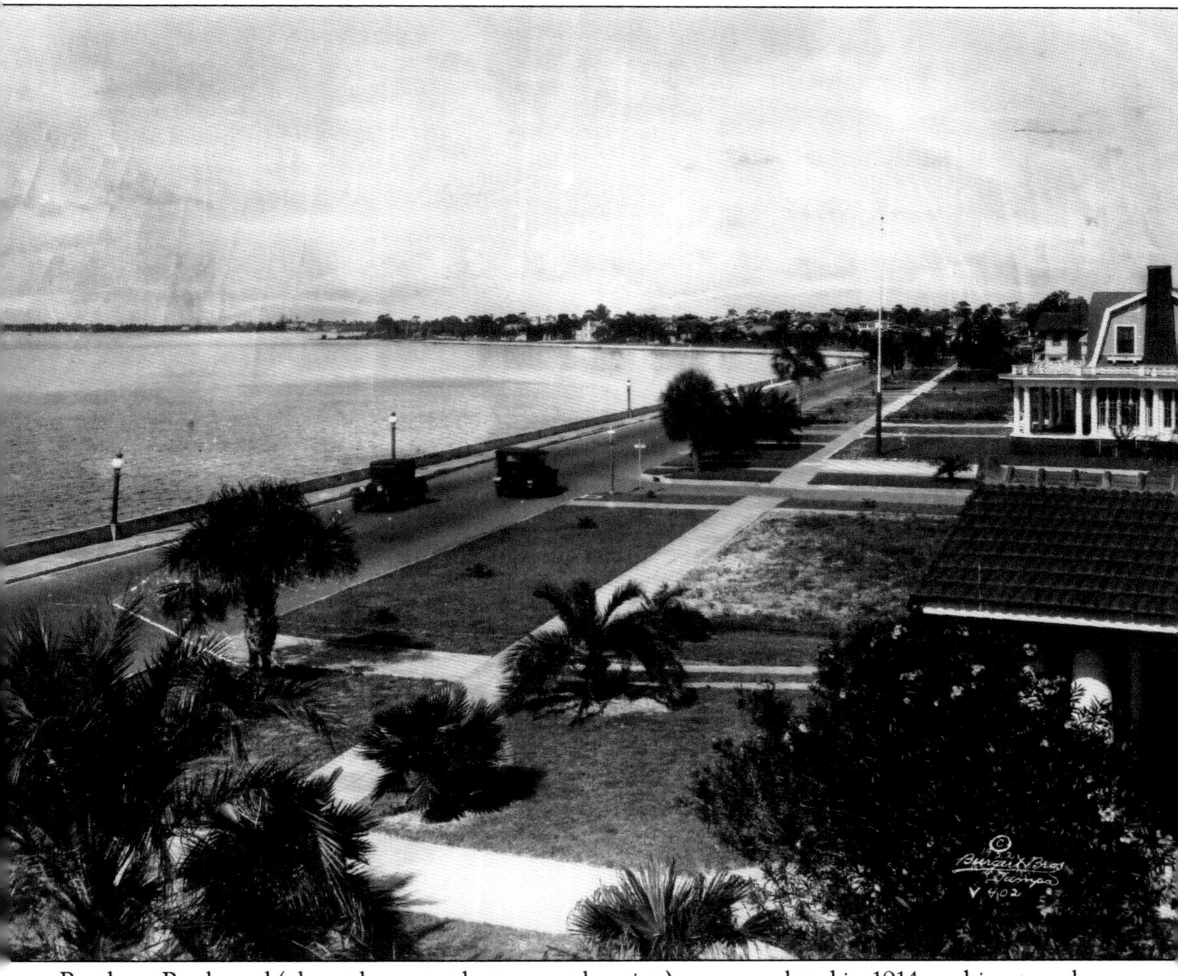

Bayshore Boulevard (along the route that currently exists) was completed in 1914, making travel possible from downtown Tampa, along Hillsborough Bay, to Ballast Point at the southern end of the Interbay Peninsula. The 1920s saw a building boom along Bayshore Boulevard. Many stately homes were built along the boulevard, and a Bayshore residential address was highly regarded. With the exception of a couple of service stations and the Bayshore Royal Hotel, all the buildings along Bayshore were single-family homes—this remains true in the present-day Historic Hyde Park District.

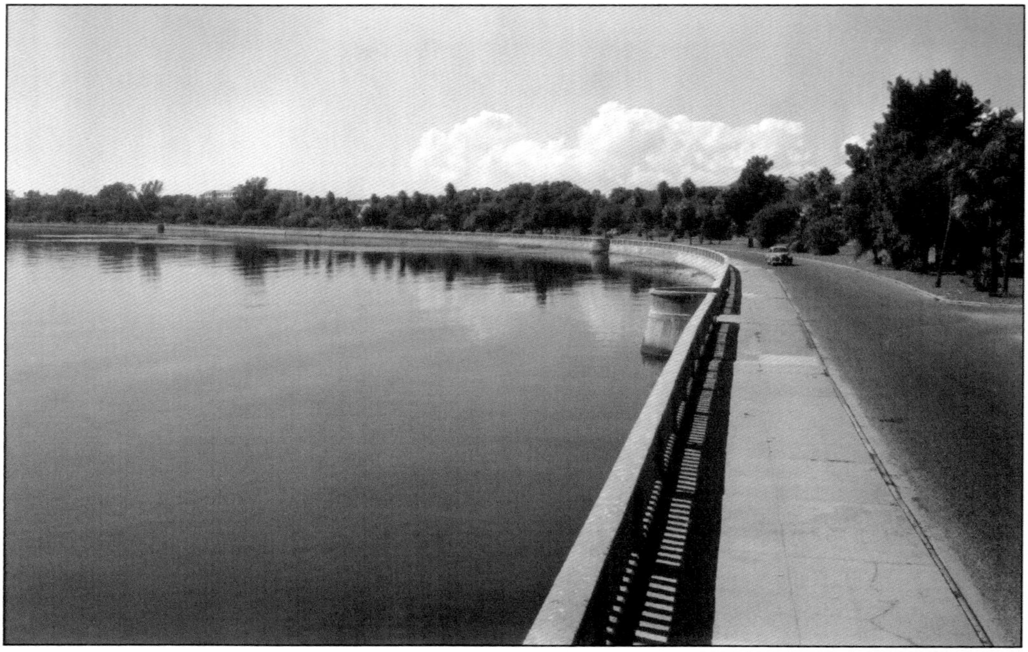

Bayshore Boulevard has provided Hyde Park with a delicate link to the western edge of Hillsborough Bay. Offering space for recreational activities, leisurely passage for pedestrians and bicycles, and a north-south thoroughfare for over 100 years, it also holds the record for being the longest continuous sidewalk in the world. The vision of early developers Alfred Swann and Eugene Holtsinger—to convert a dreary shoreline into an open space that would be a landmark for the entire community to freely enjoy—has been realized. (Below, JRSPhotos.com.)

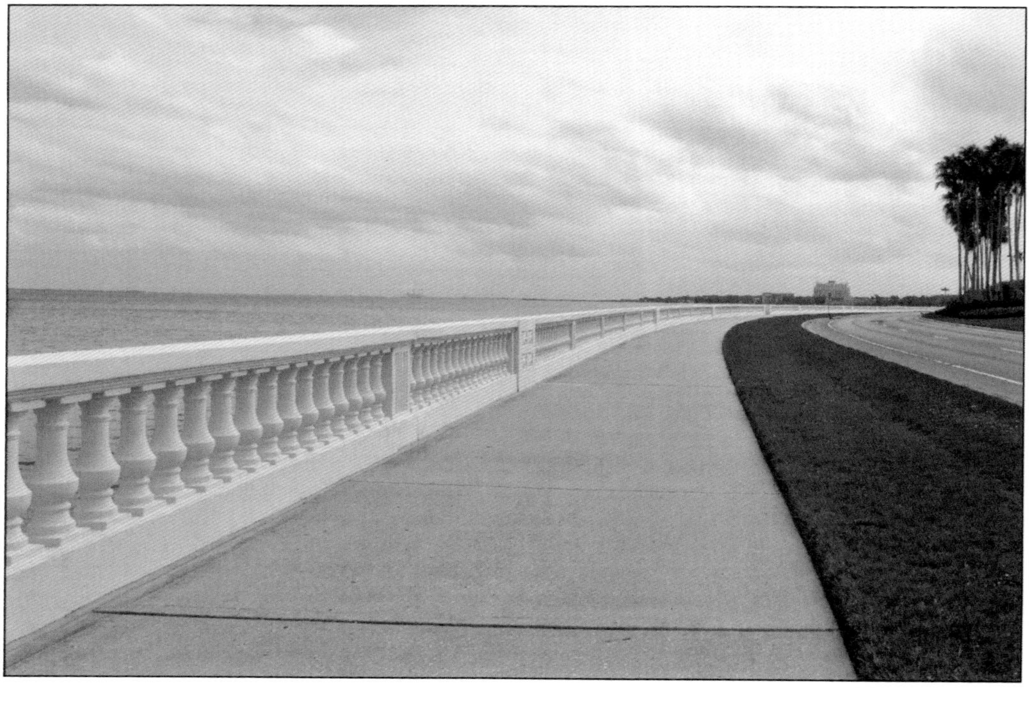

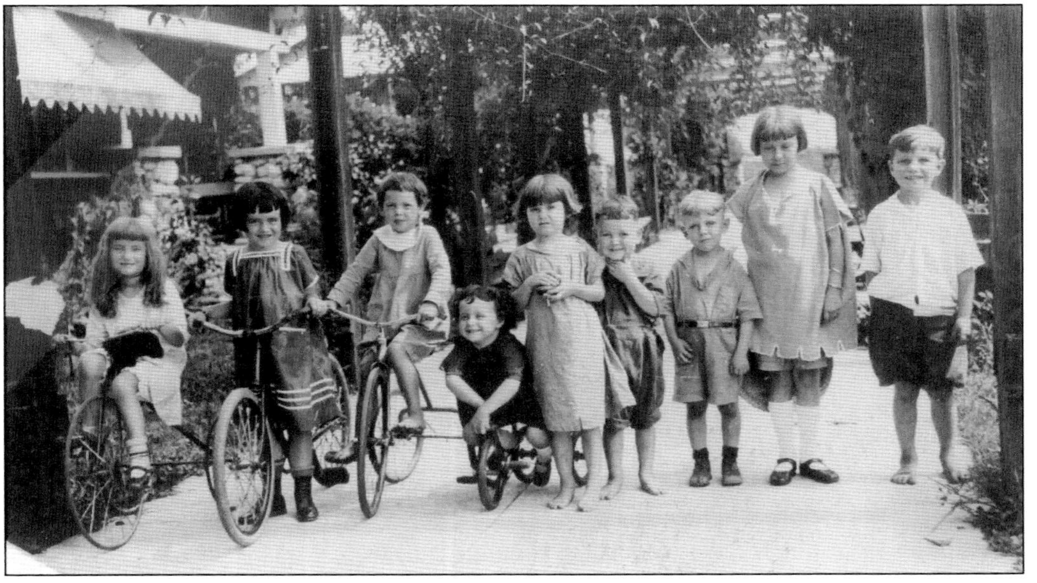

Hyde Park has thrived because of the community's commitment to the idea that the built environment matters and that conscious design can enable people to lead better lives. From the beginning, the relationship to nature and the ability for human interaction has fostered a setting for a wholesome life, upstanding citizenship, and a prosperous country. The children from Bungalow Terrace in the above photograph, taken in 1923, share the same sidewalk and community spirit as the children in the 2009 picture below. The old arbor is long gone, replaced by lush foliage, but the relationship to the environment persists. Henry B. Plant's vision for a magic kingdom by the Hillsborough River continues to evolve and adapt as Hyde Park maintains its mystic spirit. (Above, Tampa Historical Society; below, JRSPhotos.com.)

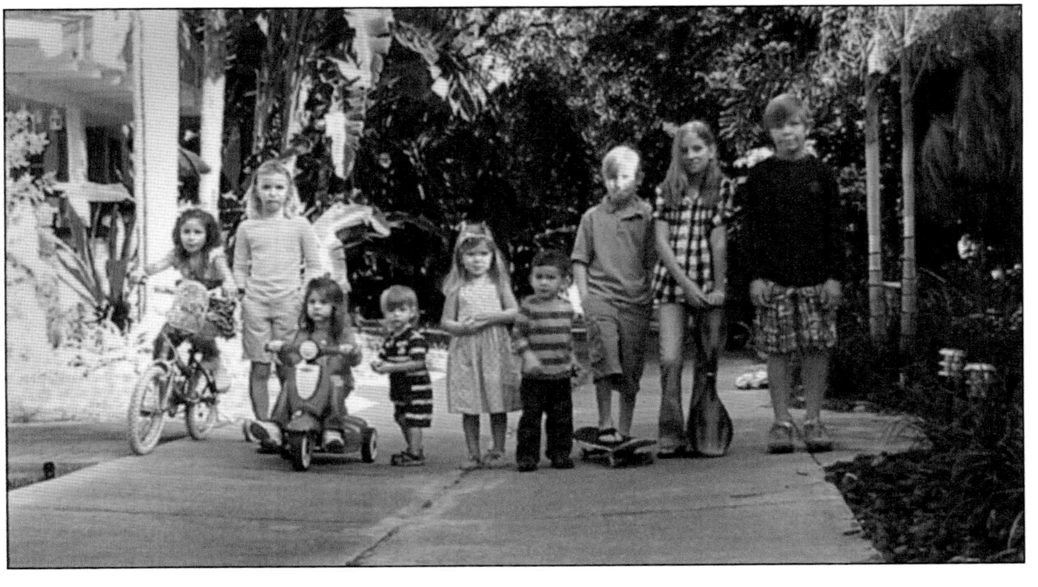

Discover Thousands of Local History Books Featuring Millions of Vintage Images

Arcadia Publishing, the leading local history publisher in the United States, is committed to making history accessible and meaningful through publishing books that celebrate and preserve the heritage of America's people and places.

Find more books like this at
www.arcadiapublishing.com

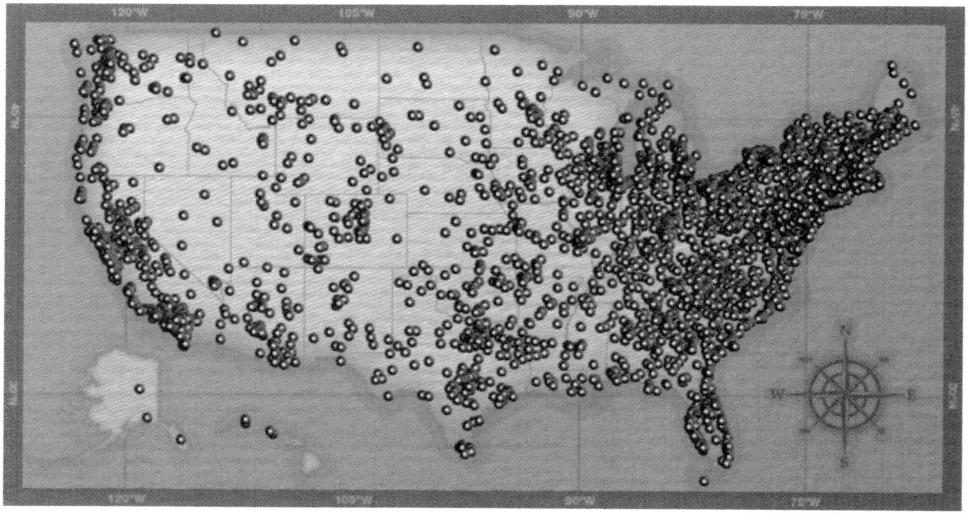

Search for your hometown history, your old stomping grounds, and even your favorite sports team.

Consistent with our mission to preserve history on a local level, this book was printed in South Carolina on American-made paper and manufactured entirely in the United States. Products carrying the accredited Forest Stewardship Council (FSC) label are printed on 100 percent FSC-certified paper.

MADE IN THE USA